DEEDS OF THE SAXONS

MEDIEVAL TEXTS IN TRANSLATION

Widukind of Corvey

DEEDS OF THE SAXONS

Translated with an introduction and notes by Bernard S. Bachrach and David S. Bachrach

THE CATHOLIC UNIVERSITY OF AMERICA PRESS
Washington, D.C.

The paper used in this publication meets the minimum requirements of American National Standards for Information Science—Permanence of Paper for Printed Library Materials, ANSI Z39.48-1984.
∞

Design and typesetting by Kachergis Book Design

Cataloging-in-Publication Data available from the Library of Congress
ISBN 978-0-8132-2693-4

To our friend and colleague
Charles "Chuck" Bowlus, *Victor Lechfeldici*

Contents

Preface

We are dedicating this translation of Widukind's *Deeds of the Saxons* to Charles "Chuck" Bowlus, professor emeritus at the University of Arkansas, Little Rock, who for more than three decades has been the doyen of American specialists in the German-speaking lands of west-central Europe prior to the First Crusade. His numerous publications, headed by two very important monographs, *Franks, Moravians and Magyars: The Struggle for the Middle Danube* and *The Battle of Lechfeld and Its Aftermath, August 955: The End of the Age of Migrations in the Latin West,* are fundamental to a modern understanding of the region. Of particular importance in light of Widukind's *Deeds* is the latter book, since it is one of the major sources for the crucial Battle of the Lechfeld fought on August 10, 955, the study of which has been controversial for more than two centuries. Chuck's treatment of Otto I's victory at the Lechfeld has advanced our knowledge of this key conflict and has overcome vitriolic controversy. Chuck now emerges as *Victor Lechfeldici.*

Simplified Ottonian Dynastic Genealogy

Henry I
(876–936)
King 919
+
1 Hatheburg
(?)
2 Mathilda
(877–968)

(1) Thankmar
(908–38)

(2) Otto I
(912–73)
King 936
+
1 Edith
(910–46)
2 Adelheid
(931–99)

(2) Gerberga
(913–84)
+
1 Gislbert Duke
of Lotharingia
2 King Louis IV
of West Francia
936–54

(2) Hedwig
(915–69)
+
Duke Hugh
of Francia

(2) Henry
(919–55)
+
Judith
of Bavaria

(2) Brun
(925–65)
AB Cologne
Duke of Lotharingia
953–65

Hugh Capet
King of West
Francia
987–96

(2) King Lothair IV
954–86

William
(illegitimate)
AB Mainz
955–68

(1) Liudolf
(930–57)
Duke of Swabia
948–54

(1) Liutgard
(died 953)

(2) Mathilda
(955–99)

(2) Otto II
(955–83)
+
Theophanu
(960–91)

Henry
(951–95)
Duke of
Bavaria
955–78
985–95

Sophie
(975–1039)

Adelheid
(977–1044)

Mathilda
(979–1025)

Otto III
(980–1002)

Henry II
(972–1024)

Simplified Carolingian Dynastic Genealogy

Charlemagne
(742–814)
King 768
Emperor 800

Louis the Pious
(778–840)
King 781
Emperor 814

Lothar I
(795–855)
817 Co-Emperor
840 Emperor

Louis II (825–75)
Lothar II (835–69)
Charles (845–63)

Louis the German
(806–76)
825 King

Louis the Younger (835–82)
Charles III the Fat (839–88)
Karlmann (830–80)+
Liutswind (concubine)

Arnulf of Carinthia
(850–99)
887 East Frankish King
896 Emperor

Louis the Child (893–911)
899 Last Carolingian King
of the East Franks

Charles the Bald
(823–77)
838 King
875 Emperor

Louis II (846–79)

Louis III (863–82)
Karlmann (866–84)
Charles III (879–929)
898 King of West Francia

Louis IV (920–54)
936 King of West Francia
m. Gerberga

Lothar IV (941–86)
King of West Francia 954

Louis V (967–87)
986 Last Carolingian
King in West Francia

Charles (953–93)
977 Duke of Lower Lotharingia

Otto (970–1006)
993 Duke of Lower Lotharingia

Introduction

Widukind and the *Res gestae Saxonicae*

Widukind, a monk at the Saxon monastery of Corvey during the middle third of the tenth century, is known to posterity almost exclusively through his exceptionally important history, *Res gestae Saxonicae.* The only contemporary external reference to Widukind is in a list of monks who entered Corvey during the abbacy of Folcmar (917–42).[1] Here, Widukind is listed as second to last among the fifty monks who entered the monastery under Folcmar, which has led scholars to assign a date of circa 940 to his profession as a monk. As a consequence, Widukind's birth can be assigned somewhere fifteen to twenty years before this to circa 920–25.[2] There is no information about the date of Widukind's death, other than it postdates the completion of his history in 973.

During the late 930s and early 940s the monastery of Corvey was an important royal house that benefited from exceptional patronage and attention. Corvey was one of the first monastaries in the German kingdom, along with Fulda and Hersfeld, to have its privileges and immunities confirmed by the newly enthroned King Otto I in 936.[3] Otto I gave additional privileges to the monastery of Corvey

1. *Catalogus abbatum et nomina fratrum Corbeiensium,* ed. O. Holder-Egger, Monumenta Germaniae Historica (hereafter, MGH) Scriptores (hereafter, SS) 13 (Hanover, 1881), 276.

2. With respect to Widukind's probable date of birth and entry into Corvey we have followed Raymund F. Wood, "The Three Books of the Deeds of the Saxons, by Widukind of Corvey, Translated with Introduction, Notes and Bibliography" (Unpublished Ph.D. dissertation, University of California at Los Angeles, 1949), 40.

3. See *Die Urkunden Konrad I., Heinrich I. und Otto I.* (hereafter, DO), ed. Theodor Sickel (Hanover, 1879–1884), here DO I, no. 3.

in 940, 942, 945, and 946.[4] This pattern of royal favor toward Corvey would continue throughout the remainder of Otto I's reign.[5] It is likely, therefore, that in order to gain admission to such a prominent monastery Widukind came from an important family whose support would be beneficial not only to Corvey, but also to the king. It is also almost certainly the case that Widukind's family was Saxon in light of the author's preoccupation with Saxony, Saxon history, and the instrinsic nobility of the *gens Saxonum,* that is, of the Saxon people.

Although we are limited in what can be said about Widukind's family and origin, the text of the *Res gestae* provides a number of important insights into his education and the breadth of his learning. In addition to the deep familiarity with biblical texts that one might expect to find in an educated monk, Widukind knew and drew upon a wide range of classical authors including Sallust, Suetonius, Tacitus, Livy, Vergil, Lucan, Ovid, Horace, and Juvenal. He also knew and deployed the works of late antique and early medieval writers, including Sulpicius Severus, Jordanes, Bede, Paul the Deacon, the anonymous author of the *Annales* once attributed to Einhard, as well as Einhard himself, and Nithard, who was Charlemagne's grandson. In addition to these largely secular historical works, Widukind was quite familiar with hagiographical texts, such as the *Life of St. Vitus,* the patron saint of Corvey. In fact, this latter text may well have inspired Widukind's own composition of two hagiographical works, now lost, that treated the lives of the saints Thekla and Paul of Thebes.[6]

The *Res gestae Saxonicae,* that is, *The Deeds of the Saxons,* are presented by Widukind in three books, each of which can be read independently of the other two, and each of which may have been completed separately by Widukind over a period of a decade or more. The first section of Book One, comprising chapters 1–15, provides an overview of the history of the Saxons from their arrival by sea in what is today northwestern Germany until their con-

4. See DO I, 27, 48, 73, and 77.

5. See DO I, 153 and 292.

6. See below 1.1.

quest by Charlemagne during the last decades of the eighth century and the first years of the ninth. Chapter 16 provides a transition in which Widukind discusses the end of the Carolingian dynasty (see genealogy) in the east and the establishment of Conrad I (911–18) as king. During the remainder of Book One, comprising chapters 17–41, Widukind provides a political and military narrative of the career of Henry I, first as duke of Saxony (912–19), and subsequently as king of the East Frankish/German realm (919–36). At several points in his narrative, Widukind digresses to discuss relevant political and military affairs among the West Franks, and also provides an interlude in chapters 33–34 in which he discusses at some length the power of a relic of St. Dionysius the Areopagite, and also provides a condensed version of the *Life of St. Vitus,* the patron saint of the monastery of Corvey.

Book Two focuses almost exclusively again on the political and military affairs of the German kingdom, with the majority of attention given to the royal court, and events that took place in Saxony. The book begins with an extended description of Otto I's coronation at Aachen in 936, and concludes with the death of Otto's first wife, the Anglo-Saxon princess Edith, in 946. Widukind devotes considerable attention to the rebellions against Otto's rule that rocked the kingdom in the period 938–39, and highlights the death in battle at Andernach of the king's main opponents Duke Gislebert of Lotharingia and Duke Eberhard of Franconia.

Book Three similarly focuses on political and military affairs, and takes as its perspective the outlook of the royal court. The book begins with Otto I's selection of his son Liudolf as his successor in 946 and the king's coterminous massive invasion of the West Frankish kingdom. Among the most important events described by Widukind are Otto I's victories over the Hungarians and Slavs at the famous battles of the Lechfeld and the Recnitz, both in 955, and his two conquests of the Lombard kingdom in Italy in 951 and 961. The first version of the text (which will be discussed in more detail below) ended at chapter 69 with Otto's final pacification of Italy in 968. However, Widukind extended his text sometime after 973 to take the account all the way through to Otto I's death in 973 and the succession of his son Otto II. Famously, Widukind does not record in Book Three the imperial coronation of Otto I at Rome on February 2, 962, at the hands of Pope John XII (955–64).

Overall, the *Res gestae Saxonicae* is the single most important narrative source for the history of the German kingdom during the tenth century. Although his focus is generally on political and military affairs, Widukind treats an enormous array of topics, including modes of religious expression, architectural developments, the learning of both clergy and laity, religious and court rituals, ecclesiastical organization and politics, diplomacy, and trade. Moreover, Widukind is the only author who provides a continuous narrative for the entire reigns of the first two kings of the Saxon dynasty. In addition, he is one of the handful of authors of his age to provide a synthetic historical account on a single theme in a manner consistent with historiographical tradition of the Carolingian period. For all of these reasons Widukind's testimony is indispensable to modern understanding of tenth-century Germany, and particularly to our understanding of the reigns of Henry I and Otto I.

Widukind as a Historian

In the course of his text, Widukind offers a number of indications of his conception of the role of the historian in setting out events that happened in the past. Beginning early in Book One, Widukind distinguishes clearly between those events about which there can be certainty because of the survival of verifiable information, which are the subject matter of history, and those events about which there can be no certainty, which are the subject matter of tradition or hearsay. In this context, Widukind avers in chapter 2 of Book One that he cannot vouch for the information that has come down to his day about the origins of the Saxon people because, he observes: "I am relying solely on tradition because the passage of so much time has clouded any certainty."[7]

7. See below 1.2.

Widukind accorded considerable authority to information that he obtained from written sources, which generally he found much more reliable than accounts that simply circulated orally. In discussing the early history of the Anglo-Saxons, therefore, Widukind encouraged his audience to seek additional information from written authorities, stating: "If anyone wishes to know more about all of these matters, let him read the history of this people."[8] By contrast, in the C version of his text (more on this below) Widukind rejects information regarding the participation of Archbishop Hatto of Mainz in a plot against Count Adalbert of Babenberg on the grounds that he was not able to confirm the story, and consequently he believed "that it is more likely a fiction taken from common rumors."[9]

In his preference for written testimony over oral reports, Widukind would appear to reject the claim made by Isidore of Seville (c. 560–636) in his exceptionally widely read and appreciated *Etymologies* that the best source of information for writing works of history consists of eyewitness reports.[10] However, Widukind clearly did accept Isidore's argument that history is the presentation of events that actually happened in the past.[11] In his discussion of Otto I's suppression of the rebellion of 938–39, for example, Widukind made clear that he had not been able entirely to untangle the chronology of events. But Widukind emphasized to his audience that whatever errors he had made were not intentional, and that he had worked diligently to ensure that he has presented the material accurately.[12]

However, Widukind's commitment to accuracy did not mean

8. See 1.8.

9. See 1.25.

10. Isidore of Seville, *Etymologiarum sive originum libri xx*, ed. W. M. Lindsay (Oxford, 1911; repr. 1957), 1.40. Concerning the importance of Isidore for medieval writers of history, see D. H. Green, *Medieval Listening and Reading: The Primary Reception of German Literature, 800–1300* (Cambridge, 1994), 237–38; and Leah Shopkow, *History and Community: Norman Historical Writing in the Eleventh and Twelfth Centuries* (Washington, D.C., 1997), 20–21.

11. Isidore, *Etymologiarum*, 1.40.

12. See 2.28.

he felt required to discuss all of the matters that might conceivably relate to the history of the Saxon people, or to the reigns of the first two Saxon kings. In the preface to Book One, Widukind explicitly informs the princess Mathilda, the ostensible audience for the *Res gestae,* that he has chosen to write summarily and selectively. Widukind returned to this theme late in Book Three while summarizing Otto I's achievements during the Italian campaign of 961–62, recalling his own earlier observation that it was beyond his "meager ability" to provide a detailed description of the whole range of the king's triumphs.[13] As a consequence, Widukind's failure to account for a particular event such as Otto I's imperial coronation in 962 likely should be understood as a choice he made rather than the result of a lack of information.

In evaluating Widukind's success in presenting an accurate account of affairs in the German kingdom, and moreover one that follows in proper chronological order, we agree with the conclusion of Raymund Wood, the first translator of Widukind into English, who observed: "Widukind is surprisingly, almost completely, accurate as to the date and circumstances of all the major events of both reigns."[14] In every instance where Widukind's claims can be compared against independently composed texts, whether narrative sources or charters, it is clear that the Saxon monk not only provided an accurate accounting of events, but that he placed the material in the correct chronological order.

In addition, the information developed through the work of archeologists also confirms the fundamental accuracy of Widukind's text, including in instances where the *Res gestae* is the only surviving written source about a particular event. For example, in the context of discussing Otto I's campaign in Bavaria against his son Liudolf in 954, Widukind draws attention to the king's assault on the fortress of Roßtal, located approximately twenty kilometers from the city of Nuremberg.[15] Widukind provides the first reference to this fortress in any surviving text, and consequently

13. See 3.63.

14. Wood, "The Three Books," 50.

15. See 3.34–35.

it is not possible to look in the written record for corroboration that Roßtal was a powerful stronghold. However, the significant excavations undertaken at Roßtal by Peter Ettel make clear that it was a very powerful fortress indeed, dating back to the early ninth century. Moreover, as Ettel's excavations have shown, Widukind also was correct that Otto I's army failed to capture and destroy this fortress despite a determined assault.[16] In this instance, and in many others identified in the notes to this translation, the work of archaeologists, which was not available at the time Wood wrote, confirms the assessment by Wood that Widukind provides a highly reliable account of events over the course of the tenth century.

Widukind's World

In August 843, the three surviving sons of Emperor Louis the Pious (814–40), Charlemagne's heir, ratified the Treaty of Verdun by which the Carolingian empire was divided into three parts of equal value in terms of both human and material resources, but not geographical extent. The eldest son, Lothar I (795–855), received the central segment of lands that had been ruled by his father along with the imperial title and the empire's two capitals at Aachen and Rome. Charles the Bald (823–77), the youngest of Louis the Pious's sons, received West Francia, the region that ultimately would form the basis for the French kingdom. Louis the German (806–76) received the eastern region of the Carolingian empire, which would eventually evolve into the kingdom of Germany.

Following the death of Louis the German in 976, his Carolingian descendants remained rulers of the eastern kingdom until the death of his great-grandson Louis the Child in 911. At this point, the great magnates, including both secular and ecclesiastical leaders, chose Duke Conrad of Franconia as their ruler. Following Conrad's death in 918, his brother Eberhard came to an agreement with Duke Henry of Saxony whereby Henry was acclaimed king

16. Peter Ettel, "Ergebnisse der Ausgrabungen auf der Burg Horsadal, Roßtal bei Nürnberg," in *Frühmittelalterliche Burgenbau in Mittel und Osteuropa*, ed. Joachim Henning and Alexander T. Ruttkay (Bonn, 1998), 127–36.

in 919. Henry I's accession to royal power inaugurated the Saxon dynasty of German kings, which ruled for more than a century. Upon his death in 936, Henry was succeeded by his son Otto I, known as "the Great." Before dying in 973, Otto resuscitated the imperial title (962), which was to be held along with the German kingship by his heirs, Otto II (973–83), Otto III (983–1002), and Henry II (1002–24). The last ruler of the Saxon dynasty died without a male heir and a new ruling house, the Salians, emerged in Germany.

The Economy

The German kingdom ruled by the early Saxon kings, Henry I and Otto I, was built fundamentally upon the economic, administrative, and institutional structures, both central and local, that had been inherited from their Carolingian predecessors. The economy, that is, the production of goods and services, was dominated by agriculture as approximately 90 percent of the population lived in the rural world, and practiced farming or closely related endeavors. These farmers, many of whom were semifree dependents of great secular and ecclesiastical magnates, produced large surpluses, as the soil in much of the German kingdom was of quite high quality, and the growing season was comparatively lengthy due to a pattern of climate warming. In addition, the German kingdom enjoyed the benefits of an expanding system of bipartite estate organization. Under this system, which began to spread in the eastern lands of the Carolingian Empire during the late eighth century, men and women who originally had worked as gang-slaves on their master's lands now were given small plots of land of their own to cultivate. In return, they had to pay rents in cash and kind to their lords, both secular and ecclesiastical, and continue to provide labor on the lands that were retained directly under their lord's personal control, that is, his demesne. The considerable agricultural surpluses that were generated under this new system helped to spur substantial increases in trade and the market economy.

The 10 percent or so of the population that was not involved directly or indirectly in agricultural production was supported, in large part, by commerce and manufacturing. These people lived in the great stone fortress cities that had been constructed during the later Roman Empire, or in newly developing merchant centers, such as Magdeburg, which often also were fortified. It bears emphasis that to date archaeologists have discovered many times more of these fortifications through excavations than are mentioned in surviving written sources of various kinds. Future excavations are likely to increase even further the tally of these fortified sites. Many of these fortified centers of habitation, especially those that served as royal palaces, whether held directly by the king or donated for the use of monks and nuns, were very large complexes of well-constructed stone buildings with amenities such as heated floors and elaborate "plumbing" that employed technology similar to that used by the Romans.[17]

As had been the case under the Carolingians, the great commercial cities of the Rhine corridor between northern Europe and the Mediterranean through Italy were in a growth pattern under the Saxon dynasty. The population of the city of Cologne grew from about 15,000 in circa 800 to about 21,000 in circa 900. The nearby Carolingian capital of Aachen had doubled in size by the year 1000 to 10,000. The walls of the city of Mainz not only were expanded to enclose suburbs, but the population grew from 20,000 in 800 to 30,000 in 1000. The population of Worms reached 20,000 by the end of the first millennium. Ancillary to the direct Rhine route, Trier's population expanded from 15,000 to 20,000 during this period, and Metz had reached 14,000 by the year 900. At the northern terminus of the Rhine corridor, the population of Bruges had

17. See, e.g., Peter Donat, "Berichtigungen und Nachträge: Gebesee," in *Die deutschen Königspfalzen: Repertorium der Pfalzen, Königshöfe und übrigen Aufenthaltsorte der Könige im deutschen Reich des Mittelalters, Vol. 2: Thüringien* (Göttingen, 2000), 684–92, here 686; and Michael Dapper, "Neuinterpretations der Grabungsergebnisse auf der Pfalz Tilleda," in *Deutsche Königspfalzen: Beiträge zu ihrer historischen und archäologischen Erforschung*, Vol. 7: *Zentren herrschaftlicher Repräsentation im Hochmittelalter, Geschichte, Architektur und Zeremoniell*, ed Caspar Ehlers, Jörg Jarnut, and Matthias Wemhoff (Göttingen, 2007), 151–69, here 155.

reached 12,000 by 1000, and Ghent reached 8,000 by the end of the tenth century, which indicates important and growing connections with Scandinavia.[18]

Trade between Italy and the German kingdom made its way both along the Rhine and through the Alps along the Brenner Pass from Verona, which had a population of about 25,000 in 900, to Regensburg, which grew from about 25,000 in 800 to 40,000 in 1000. Trade north and eastward from Regensburg saw Prague reach a population of about 10,000 by circa 1000, with the Thuringian and Saxon cities of Erfurt and Braunschweig reaching the same level at this time.[19] As a corollary to these expanding urban populations, archeological excavations make clear that the German kingdom had a booming rural population as well over the course of the tenth century.[20] The growth of both urban and rural populations is strongly indicative of the rapidly increasing wealth of the German kingdom during the Ottonian century.

Much of the landed wealth of the German kingdom was directly or indirectly under the control of the king through the estates of the royal fisc (i.e., the sum total of lands and incomes of the royal government), and through the holdings of the church, for example, bishoprics, monasteries, and convents, which ultimately were controlled by the king who appointed bishops, abbots, and abbesses. The great secular magnates of the realm, including both those who held royal office as counts or as other types of officials, and those who had not won royal preferment, also possessed considerable landed wealth. However, these secularly held lands could be confiscated by the royal government should the king be displeased by the activities of the magnates.[21]

18. This data is available in Paul Bairoch, Jean Batou, and Pierre Chèvre, *La Population des ville européennes: Banque de données et analyse sommaire des résultats, 800–1850* (Geneva, 1988), 4–69.

19. Ibid.

20. See, e.g., Joachim Henning, "Der slawische Siedlungsraum und die ottonische Expansion östlich der Elbe: Ereignisgeschichte–Archäologie-Dendrochronlogie," *Europa im 10. Jahrhundert: Archäologie einer Aufbruchszeit*, ed. Joachim Henning (Mainz, 2002), 131–46.

21. See the discussion of this process of confiscation by David S. Bachrach, "Ex-

The estates of the royal fisc, tolls on trade, profits of justice, *servitium regis* (the services owed to the king by the church), the profits inherent in the control of the coinage, taxes, and the tributes paid by peoples living beyond the frontiers provided a substantial part of the royal income for Henry I and Otto I, as it had for their Carolingian predecessors. However, unlike the Carolingians, who had access only to the relatively rich silver mines at Melle in northern Aquitaine, the Saxon dynasty, even before the accession of Henry I in 919, obtained immense wealth, by comparison, from the silver mines that had been opened in the Harz mountains over the course of the ninth century. During the tenth century, these vast silver deposits allowed the Ottonian kings to establish scores of mints, and to expand the silver coinage in their kingdom, thereby facilitating commerce.[22]

Expenditures

In addition to building, maintaining, and garrisoning large numbers of fortifications, ranging in scale from wooden palisades built across the open side of plateaus to massive stone fortress cities, Henry I and Otto I invested heavily in the transportation infrastructure of the German kingdom. They saw to it that the road system was improved, the navigability of rivers was maintained, bridges were kept in repair or new ones built, and ports facilities were serviced.[23] Primarily nonmilitary building projects, that is,

---

ercise of Royal Power in Early Medieval Europe: The Case of Otto the Great, 936–973," *Early Medieval Europe* 17 (2009): 389–419.

22. With respect to the enormous wealth generated by the Ottonians through the exploitation of the Harz silver mines, see the collection of essays in *Aspects of Mining and Smelting in the Upper Harz Mounatins (up to the 13th/14th Century) in the Early Times of a Developing European Culture and Economy,* ed. Christiane Segers-Glocke and trans. Harald Witthöft and Claus Wibbelmann (St. Katharinen, 2000).

23. The literature dealing with the infrastructure of the German kingdom during the early Middle Ages is quite large, particularly with regard to archeological studies. See, e.g., the discussion by Thomas Szabo, "Der Übergang von der Antike zum Mittelalter am Beispiel des Straßennetzes," in *Europäische Technik im Mittelalter, 800 bis 1400: Tradition und Innovation, Ein Handbuch,* 4th ed., ed. Uta Lindgren (Berlin, 1996), 25–43.

royal palaces, were the object of immense investment.[24] In addition, the royal government supported the construction of numerous monumental stone cathedral and monastic churches such as those at Ingelheim, Quedlinburg, and most notably Magdeburg.[25] In addition, secular magnates also contributed to the building of churches and the endowing of monastic houses.[26]

To this list of expenditures on the physical infrastructure of the German kingdom can be added the vast resources that were devoted to art, education, and cultural production of all types. These included jewelry, sculpture, frescoes, books, as well as the patronage of scholars and schools. In this context, many thousands of manuscripts were produced in Ottonian writing centers dealing with every aspect of learning from Christian theology to textbooks on the preparation of soldiers for war.[27]

Warfare

Throughout the history of premodern Europe, the greater part of surplus human and material resources was dedicated to mili-

24. The basic starting point for discussions of royal palace complexes in the Ottonian period is now *Die deutsche Königspfalzen: Repertorium der Pfalzen, Königshöfe und übrigen Aufenhaltsorte der Könige im deutschen Reich des Mittelalters,* vol. 14 (Göttingen, 1982–2000).

25. In this context, see Gerhard Leopold, "Archäologische Ausgrabungen an Stätten der ottonischen Herrscher," *Herrschaftsrepräsentation im Ottonischen Sachsen* (1998), 33–76; Ulrich Reuling, "Quedlinburg: Königspfalz-Reichsstift-Markt," in *Deutsche Königspfalzen: Beiträge zu ihrer historischen und archäologischen Erforschung vierter Band: PfalzenReichsgut-Königshöfe,* ed. Lutz Fenske (Göttingen, 1996), 184–247; Holger Grewe, "Die bauliche Entwicklung der Pfalz Ingelheim im Hochmittelalter am Beispiel der Sakralarchitektur," in *Deutsche Königspfalzen: Beiträge zu ihrer historischen und archäologischen Erforschung, vol. 7: Zentren herrschaftlicher Repräsentation im Hochmittelalter, Geschichte, Architektur und Zeremoniell,* ed. Caspar Ehlers, Jörg Jarnut, and Matthias Wemhoff (Göttingen, 2007), 101–20; and Babette Ludowici and Matthias Hardt, "Zwei ottonenzeitliche Kirchen auf dem Magdeburger Domhügel," *Frühmittelalterliche Studien* 38 (2004): 89–99.

26. The basic work on this topic is now Susan Wood, *The Proprietary Church in the Medieval West* (Oxford, 2006).

27. See, e.g., the studies by Hartmut Hoffmann, *Buchkunst und Königtum im ottonischen und frühsalischen Reich,* MGH Schriften 30 (Stuttgart, 1986); and Rosamond McKitterick, "Continuity and Innovation in Tenth-Century Ottonian Culture," in *Intellectual Life in the Middle Ages: Essays Presented to Margaret Gibson,* ed. Lesley Smith and Benedicta Ward

tary matters, that is, war, preparation for war, and war's aftermath. Therefore, it is hardly surprising that since military matters were of central importance to both the king and his subjects, narrative texts, such as Widukind's work, focus attention on the organization of armies both for defensive and offensive purposes.

Like virtually all other governmental operations, the organization of the armed forces that made possible the long-term military success of Henry I and Otto I, as well as that of their successors, was inherited from their Carolingian predecessors.[28] At the most basic level, all able-bodied men, regardless of legal status or wealth, were required to participate in the defense of the local area in which they lived with whatever armament they had available to them. Those members of society, men and women, clerics and laypeople, whose wealth, both landed and moveable, reached a stipulated minimum amount, were required when called upon by the king or his legally designated agents to provide men to serve in royal expeditionary forces. These fighting men, in addition to participating in the local defense alongside their poorer neighbors, could be deployed on campaign for offensive military operations outside the region in which they lived. Those individuals and institutions that possessed multiples of the minimum levels of wealth could be required by the government to provide trained fighting men with appropriate armament for expeditionary service consistent with their total economic assets. Great magnates, both secular and ecclesiastical, who possessed hundreds or even

(London, 1992), 15–24, reprinted with the same pagination in Rosamond McKitterick, *The Frankish Kings and Culture in the Early Middle Ages* (Aldershot, 1995).

28. For what follows regarding the basic structure of the Carolingian military organization, see Étienne Renard, "La Politique Militaire de Charlemagne et la Paysannerie Franque," *Francia* 36 (2009): 1–33; David S. Bachrach, "The Military Organization of Ottonian Germany, c. 900–1018: The Views of Bishop Thietmar of Merseburg," *Journal of Military History* 72 (2008): 1061–88; Eric J. Goldberg, *Struggle for Empire: Kingship and Conflict under Louis the German, 817–876* (Ithaca, N.Y., 2006), 119–31; Bernard S. Bachrach, *Early Carolingian Warfare: Prelude to Empire* (Philadelphia, 2001); and Timothy Reuter, "The Recruitment of Armies in the Early Middle Ages: What Can We Know?" in *Military Aspects of Scandinavian Society in a European Perspective, AD 1000–1300*, ed. A. Norgard Jorgensen and B. L. Clausen (Copenhagen, 1997), 25–31.

thousands of *mansi,* that is, farms, and large quantities of moveable wealth, could, if the king thought it necessary, be required to provide many hundreds of men to serve in the royal army.

The third element in the military organization of the early Saxon dynasty consisted of the large number of household troops who served as well-trained and armed professional soldiers (*milites*) throughout the German kingdom. These men may be contrasted with the ostensibly civilian soldiers of the expeditionary levy who comprised a militia rather than a professional fighting force. A subset of these professional soldiers were mercenaries, who were not permanently attached to the military household of any one magnate, but rather hired on for a specific period of time or a particularly military campaign. The largest of the military households in the German kingdom was that of the king himself. Many of these soldiers were in permanent attendance at the royal court. However, the bulk of the king's military forces generally served as garrison troops in the many scores of royal fortifications, most of which were located along the frontiers.

Education in the German Kingdom

Elite education in the German kingdom, of which Widukind is a prime exemplar, was consistent with the traditions established throughout the Carolingian Empire over the course of the late eighth and ninth centuries in that it focused on learning from books. Children, including some girls, up to the age of fourteen focused on the study of the seven liberal arts in the *trivium* and *quadrivium*.[29] The late antique authors, whose works formed the core of this curriculum, included Cassiodorus, Isidore, Martianus Capella, Donatus, and Victorius of Aquitaine, as well as the *corpus agrimensorum,* which was a late fifth- or early sixth-century compi-

29. For the importance of this kind of "liberal" education in the German kingdom, see Christoph Dette, "Kinder und Jugendliche in der Adelsgesellschaft des frühen Mittelalters," *Archiv für Kulturgeschichte* 76 (1994): 1–34; and Dette, "Schüler im frühen und hohen Mittelalter: Die St. Galler Klosterschule des 9. und 10. Jahrhunderts," *Studien und Mitteilungen zur Geschichte des Benediktinerordens und seiner Zweige* 105 (1994): 7–64.

lation of Roman surveying texts. Charlemagne's legislation, principally in the *Admonitio generalis* and the *Epistola de litteris collendis,* led to the production of vast numbers of textbooks that served both monastic and cathedral schools throughout the Carolingian Empire, including the lands that would evolve into the German kingdom. Over the course of the tenth century, the monastic and cathedral schools of the nascent German kingdom built upon this enormous cultural and educational inheritance through the production of new copies of older texts, and the development of entirely new treatises and genres.[30] It merits attention that the turn of the tenth century did not mark a significant change in the ability of native German speakers to learn and utilize Latin.[31] Men, and some women, who held positions of power and influence were at least bilingual and may well have been polylingual.[32]

The basic education provided by monastic and cathedral schools that focused on grammar and numeracy likely was sufficient for many men, both secular and ecclesiastical, who would go on to hold administrative positions in the Ottonian kingdom. However, in order to do highly specialized work, additional education was required. For men involved in fields such as engineering, architecture, medicine, the law, and warfare, this learning came from specialized handbooks, many of which were late antique in origin.[33]

In addition, the intellectual elite of the Ottonian kingdom grafted new traditions onto old ones so that annotated and updated collections drawn from classical, late antique, and Carolingian sources were used side by side with new handbooks that were drawn from entirely contemporary or near contemporary works.

30. See, e.g., the discussion by McKitterick, "Continuity and Innovation," 15–24.

31. For an overview of this problem, see Rosamond McKitterick, "The Written Word and Oral Communication: Rome's Legacy to the Franks," in *Latin Culture and Medieval Germanic Europe: Germania Latina I,* ed. Richard North and Tette Hofstra (Gröningen, 1992), 89–112, reprinted with the same pagination in Rosamond McKitterick, *The Frankish Kings and Culture in the Early Middle Ages* (Aldershot, 1995).

32. Ibid., 96.

33. A valuable survey of this material is provided by Bernhard Bischoff, "Die Überlieferung der technischen Literature," in *Artigianato et tennica nella societa dell'alto medioevo occidentale, Centro italiano die studi sull'alto medioevo* (Spoleto, 1971), 1.267–97.

Consequently, the Carolingian educational canon was supplemented by a wide variety of new texts including pontificals, handbooks for priests, and musical guides.[34] Similarly, large numbers of legal collections were composed for practical use by Ottonian bishops for specific short-term goals.[35]

The Manuscript Tradition of the *Res gestae*

There are six surviving witnesses to Widukind's text, and these have been divided by scholars into three separate families on the basis of their content.[36] The texts in these three families differ in three important ways. First, the A version of the text, which survives in a single manuscript, ends its discussion of Ottonian affairs in 968 in Book Three, chapter 69. The three surviving texts in the B family and the two surviving texts in the C family bring the account forward to the death of Otto I in 973, adding chapters 70–76 to Book Three. Second, Widukind presents his account regarding the attempted murder of the future King Henry I, while he was still duke of Saxony (912–19), quite differently in the three versions of the text. Version A identifies the culprits in this crime as "some friends" of King Conrad I. Version B places the blame for the murder plot squarely on Archbishop Hatto of Mainz (891–913), who also is blamed for the betrayal and subsequent execution of the Babenberger count Adalbert (c. 854–906). Version C provides a much more circumspect depiction of the murder plot, and notes that there are some people, although not Widukind himself, who held Hatto responsible for the plots against both Count Adalbert and Henry I. Finally, in the course of discussing Otto I's

34. Rosamond McKitterick, "Ottonische Kulture und Bildung," in *Otto der Große. Magdeburg und Europa*, ed. Matthias Puhle (Mainz, 2001), 1.209–24.

35. Rosamond McKitterick, "Bischöfe und die handschriftlichen Überlieferung des Rechts im 10. Jahrhundert," in *Mönchtum-Kirche-Herrschaft, 750–1000. Josef Semmler zum 65. Geburtstag*, ed. Dieter R. Bauer, Rudolf Hiestand, Brigitte Kasten, and Sönke Lorenz (Sigmaringen, 1998), 231–42.

36. The following discussion is based, in large part, on the treatment of the scholarly tradition by Wood, "The Three Books," 68–113, which has not been surpassed in later translations.

invasion of the West Frankish kingdom in 946 in the second chapter of Book Three, the B version of Widukind's text includes a lengthy discussion of the history of the monastery of Corvey and the house's early abbots, which is not included in either the A or the C versions of the text.

Scholars have worked diligently to identify the connection between the three families of texts (A, B, C) and the stages of Widukind's composition of the *Res gestae.* It should be stressed that there are no external sources of information regarding Widukind's process of composition, so that all conclusions about when he wrote and what changes he made are based entirely on clues found within the text itself. The most important of these internal clues is the statement at the end of chapter 69 of Book Three that "here ends book three." On the basis of Widukind's statement here, there is general agreement among scholars that version A of the text was completed circa 967 or 968.[37]

Widukind subsequently took up his quill and added the final seven chapters of Book Three at some point after the death of Otto I in 973. In reconstructing Widukind's method in composing this new version of the text, which forms the basis for both the B and C families of texts, Herman Bloch, who was the first scholar with access to all six of the surviving witnesses to the *Res gestae,* argued that Widukind was not in a position to simply revise the A version of the text. This already had been sent to Princess Mathilda, as the prefaces to each of the three books of the *Res gestae* make clear, and was in the convent library at Quedlinburg in 973.[38] Instead, Bloch argued, Widukind either reworked the entire text from notes, or revised a second copy of the text that had been kept at Widukind's monastery of Corvey. This B version contains

37. For a survey of the earlier scholarship on this point, see Wood, "The Three Books," 86–108. Regarding the later treatment of this dating question, which also holds that the first draft was completed in c. 967–68, see Gerd Althoff, "Widukind von Corvey: Kronzeuge und Herausforderung," *Frühmittelalterliche Studien* 27 (1993): 253–72, here 258–59.

38. Herman Bloch, "Die Sachsengeschichte Widukinds von Korvei," *Neues Archiv* 38 (1913): 97–141.

the extended treatment of Archbishop Hatto's involvement in the murder plot against Henry I, the extended discussion of the abbots of Corvey in the context of Otto I's invasion of West Francia in 946, and the addition of material to cover the period 967–73.[39]

Bloch's suggestions regarding Widukind's drafting of the B version of the *Res gestae* have been sustained by subsequent scholars.[40] The C version of Widukind's text, according to Bloch and subsequent scholars up to the present, represents a second revision of the text, done sometime after 973 by Widukind himself.[41] Crucially, all three of the families of texts of the *Res gestae* have their origins in drafts written by Widukind, and do not represent the addition of material by later authors.[42]

The A version of the text, which represents Widukind's first completed draft of the *Res gestae*, is preserved in an early thirteenth-century manuscript identified by scholars as the Dresden Codex.[43] This text is perhaps based on Widukind's autograph copy that originally was sent to Princess Mathilda and subsequently kept at the convent of Quedlinburg. The B version of the text survives in several versions. A twelfth-century manuscript preserves part of the *Res gestae*, and a sixteenth-century printed edition of Widukind's text preserved a now lost manuscript that was a separate witness to the B version.[44] A third witness to the B version of Widukind's text, first discovered in 1910, survives in a sixteenth-century manuscript, likely copied in 1530 by the Jesuit scholar Konrad Peutinger (died 1532). Peutinger's source text likely was the same lost manuscript on

39. Ibid.

40. Wood, "The Three Books," 104–9; and Helmut Beumann, *Widukind von Korvey: Untersuchungen zur Geschichtsschreibung und Ideengeschichte des 10. Jahrhunderts* (Weimar, 1950), particularly 178–82.

41. See the observations on this point by Wood, "The Three Books," particularly 104–9.

42. The observations on this point by Wood, "The Three Books," 107–8, are confirmed by Beumann, *Widukind von Korvey,* particularly 178.

43. The manuscript tradition is set out very clearly by Wood, "The Three Books," 86–108.

44. Ibid., 95–96.

which the sixteenth-century printed edition of Widukind's work was based. There are two witnesses to the C version of Widukind's *Res gestae.* The first of these is a late eleventh or early twelfth-century manuscript.[45] The second is a thirteenth-century manuscript that was not discovered until 1910.[46]

Printed Editions and Translations

The importance of Widukind's text was recognized from a very early date by publishers, who produced two sixteenth-century editions (1532, 1577), and two seventeenth-century editions (1621, 1688). The first truly scientific edition was undertaken by Georg Waitz in the Monumenta Germaniae Historica (MGH) Scriptores series in 1839. Two subsequent revised editions of Widukind's text were published under the auspices of the MGH by Georg Waitz and Karl A. Kehr in 1866 and 1903, respectively. In 1935, H.-E. Lohmann and Paul Hirsch published a new revised edition of Widukind's text, which took advantage of all six surviving witnesses, for the MGH series Scriptores rerum Germanicarum in usum scholarum, number 60. The Lohmann- Hirsch edition is the basis for the current translation. Because of the enormous popularity of Widukind's work, several further editions have been published, although the basic text has remained unchanged. These include Albert Bauer and Reinhold Rau, *Die Sachsengeschichte des Widukind von Korvei* (Darmstadt, 1971); and Ekkehart Rotter and Bernd Schneidmüller, *Widukind von Corvey: Res gestae Sasonicae, Die Sachsengeschichte* (Leipzig, 1986).

There have been numerous translation of Widukind's text into modern European languages. The earliest of these is Louis Cousin's translation of Widukind into French in 1689.[47] There were at least four translations of Widukind into German during the eighteenth and nineteenth centuries. Paul Hirsch, the editor of the 1935 MGH Widukind text, published his own translation in 1931.[48] Subsequently, both the Bauer-Rau edition and the Rotter-

45. Ibid., 91.
46. Ibid., 94.
47. See Wood, "The Three Books," 114.
48. Ibid., 115–16.

Schneidmüller edition provided Latin and German texts on facing pages. Most recently, Books Two and Three of the *Res gestae* have been translated into French as part of a project directed by Cédric Giraud and Benoît-Michel Tock to translate tenth and eleventh-century Latin works from the German kingdom.[49] The text also benefited from a detailed commentary and translation into English by Raymund F. Wood, who undertook this project for his dissertation at the University of California at Los Angeles, where he received his doctorate in 1949.

The Reception of Widukind's Text

As the considerable attention given to Widukind by editors and translators indicates, Widukind's *Res gestae* was recognized from a very early date to be of considerable importance for modern understanding of the early medieval German kingdom. Such a view is consistent with the reception of Widukind's works by his immediate contemporaries. Bishop Thietmar of Merseburg (died 1018) relied very heavily on Widukind's text for the composition of his own *Chronicon,* which indicates that a copy of the *Res gestae* was located at the cathedral library of Merseburg during the early eleventh century. Frutolf, who served as prior of the monastery of St. Michael at Bamberg in the early twelfth century, also drew extensively on the *Res gestae* in the composition of his *Chronicon universale.* Similarly, the anonymous author of the early thirteenth-century *Chronica universalis Mettensis* drew heavily on Widukind, which suggests the availability of a copy of the *Res gestae* at Metz. Indeed, the presence of this text at Metz is confirmed by the use of Widukind's *Res gestae* by Sigebert of Gembloux, who served as the schoolmaster at the monastery of St. Vincent at Metz for two decades during the mid-eleventh century (1050–70). The anonymous author of a mid-twelfth-century text, who is usually denoted as the *Annalista Saxo,* also made direct use of a manuscript of the *Res gestae.*[50]

49. Cédric Giraud and Benoît-Michel Tock, *Rois, reines et évеques: L'Allemagne aux Xe et XIe siècles: Recueil de textes traduits* (Turnhout, 2009).

50. Wood, "The Three Books," 67–69, provides a detailed discussion of the evidence for the use by various authors of Widukind's work.

Despite the considerable popularity of Widukind's text among both medieval authors of historical works and early modern editors and publishers, early scholarly opinion dealing with the historicity of Widukind's text largely was negative. Rudolf Köpke, the first scholar to undertake a systematic examination of the historical value of the *Res gestae*, concluded that it was largely a tissue of hearsay and fabrications.[51] Köpke was followed by Wilhelm Gundlach, who in 1899 made the famous claim that Widukind was a "trickster in a monk's habit."[52] Early in the next century, Karl Hainer characterized Widukind as an epic poet who had no interest in writing history.[53] Robert Holtzmann, in his revised edition of Wilhelm Wattenbach's volume of source criticism, took an even harsher view of the historical value of the *Res gestae* and concluded in 1938 that Widukind was a naïve monk who uncritically wrote down what he heard without leaving the monastery of Corvey.[54] Holtzmann added further that Widukind did not have access to written sources of information and was therefore entirely dependent on hearsay, which meant that he included numerous fables in his work.[55]

The process of rehabilitating the reputation of Widukind's work began with two historical analyses written a year apart in 1949 and 1950. The first of these was Wood's translation and commentary on Widukind's text. He made the case, as noted above, that wherever it is possible to check the accuracy of Widukind's text against surviving written sources, it becomes clear that the *Res gestae* provides an accurate account of affairs.[56] Much more influential, however, has been the work of Helmut Beumann, who beginning in

51. Rudolf Köpke, *Widukind von Korvei* (Berlin, 1867).

52. Wilhelm Gundlach, "Spielmann in der Kutte," in *Heldenlieder der deutschen Kaiserzeit* (Graz, 1896), 1.112.

53. Carl Hainer, "Das epische Element bei den Geschichtsschreibern des früheren Mittelalters" (Ph.D. dissertation, Gießen, 1914). On the nature of Hainer's views, see Beumann, *Widukind von Korvey*, 51–65.

54. Wilhelm Wattenbach and Robert Holtzmann, *Deutschlands Geschichtsquellen im Mittelalter: Deutsche Kaiserzeit* (Berlin, 1938), 27–28.

55. Ibid., 28.

56. Wood, "The Three Books," 50.

1950, made the convincing case that Widukind is to be taken seriously as a trustworthy source of information about tenth-century Saxony and the German kingdom.[57]

Beumann stressed that Widukind not only had available a large number of models of history writing from his study at Corvey, but that the monk adhered to a rigorous historical method when he wrote.[58] Beumann also took pains to demonstrate that, contrary to the argument made by Holtzmann, Widukind had access to considerable information from a wide variety of sources. Beumann emphasizes, for example, Widukind's close connection to leading figures of the Ottonian dynasty and his ability to obtain significant information from them.[59] Even more crucially, Beumann also argued that rather than simply relying on rumor or anecdotes from acquaintances at his monastery to write his history, Widukind also had access to written documents, including those produced by the royal government and by the papacy.[60]

Largely as a result of Beumann's efforts, the *Res gestae* now generally is considered by scholars to provide a considerable corpus of accurate information about affairs in Saxony and the broader German kingdom, from both his own day and from earlier periods as well. In this vein, the leading contemporary specialist in Ottonian history, Gerd Althoff, stresses that the quality of the information provided by Widukind must be assessed in the context of the intended audience for the work.[61] Pursuing this theme, Althoff emphasizes that Widukind was commissioned by a leading member of the Ottonian royal family, Archbishop William of Mainz, the

57. See, e.g., Helmut Beumann, "Die Historiographie des Mittelalters als Quelle für die Ideengeschichte des Königtums," *Historische Zeitschrift* 180 (1955): 449–88; Beumann, "Historiographische Konzeption und politische Ziele Widukinds von Corvey," *La storiografia altomedievale: Settimane di studio del centro italiano di studi sull'alto medioevo* 17 (1970): 857–94; and Beumann, "Imperator Romanorum, rex gentium. Zu Widukind III 76," in *Tradition als historische Kraft: Interdisziplinäre Forschungen zur Geschichte des früheren Mittelalter,* ed. Norbert Kamp and Joachim Wollasch (Berlin, 1982), 214–30.

58. Beumann, *Widukind von Korvey,* 53–60.

59. Beumann, "Historiographische Konzeption," 885 ff.

60. Beumann, "*Imperator Romanorum*," 217 and 221.

61. This is the gravimen of Althoff, "Widukind von Corvey: Kronzeuge und Herausforderung," 253–72.

queen-mother Mathilda, or Otto I himself, to write the *Res gestae* as a didactic tool for the young Princess Mathilda, the abbess of Quedlinburg, in order to prepare her for a major role in the government of the kingdom.[62] As a consequence, according to Althoff, the information provided by Widukind had to be a trustworthy representation of reality. In response to critics of Widukind's text, Althoff has observed, "In Widukind's work, we have presentations of this century [the tenth century] which were written down in the context of a very serious work. It would require considerable intellectual arrogance for anachronists to belittle this work as unserious."[63]

The intellectual historian Karl Morrison independently came to the conclusion that Widukind's *Res gestae* had the very important real-world purpose of preparing the princess and abbess Mathilda for her responsibilities as a member of the ruling dynasty.[64] In this context, Morrison stresses that Mathilda, despite her youth, did exercise considerable political power from 968, when she was the sole member of the Ottonian family north of the Alps, until her death in 999.[65] In an effort to prepare her, and her entourage, for this role, Widukind, according to Morrison, was commissioned to write a text that not only would provide the princess and her advisers with considerable valuable information, but would require them to participate in their own education by filling in the gaps in the narrative that Widukind purposely left there.[66] Thus, rather than composing a *bricolage,* as some of his modern critics had claimed, Widukind, in Morrison's view, had a high opinion of the knowledge of his audience about both historical matters and current affairs, and expected them to consider what he had left out of the text and to discuss these matters.[67]

62. Althoff, "Widukind von Corvey: Kronzeuge und Herausforderung," 262–72.

63. Ibid., 272.

64. Karl F. Morrison, "Widukind's Mirror for a Princess: An Exercise in Self-Knowledge," in *Forchungen zur Reichs-, Papst- und Landesgeschichte. Peter Herde zum 65. Geburtstag von Freunden, Schülern und Kollegen dargebracht,* 2 vols., ed. Karl Borchardt and Enno Bünz (Stutgart, 1998), 2.49–71.

65. Ibid., 50.

66. Ibid., 53.

67. Ibid., 67–68, and passim.

The only significant modern critique of the historical value of the information presented by Widukind in the *Res gestae* is Johannes Fried's effort to return to the model presented by Holtzmann, discussed above, of Widukind as an untrustworthy recorder of oral information.[68] Fried argues, as part of a broad-gauged attack on the historical value of all early medieval narrative sources, that written texts based on the transmission of information through oral means simply cannot be trusted. However, Fried conspicuously does not address in his studies the specific arguments made by Beumann that Widukind had access to written sources of information. In addition, Fried does not answer the argument of Althoff and Morrison that Widukind's patrons not only thought that the monk could provide accurate information to Mathilda, but commissioned him to do so. For Widukind to have provided inaccurate information to Mathilda might have caused significant difficulties for the young abbess's advisers in their efforts to help her govern the German kingdom. The failure to provide accurate information, available from other people, would also have undermined the reputation of Widukind, who, as noted above, benefited from royal patronage for his work. Moreover, Fried does not distinguish in his studies between the information that is central to the author's *parti pris,* and the information that provides the context in which the central narrative is told. Thus, if Widukind can be shown to have provided a version of a particular event that was desired by his patrons, it is specifically here that one would expect to find that the information not directly related to the arc of the author's narrative is accurate. Finally, Fried does not take into account the vast corpus of information derived from archaeological investigations that have confirmed information provided by Widukind in the *Res gestae.* For all of these reasons,

68. See, in this context, Johannes Fried, "Die Kunst der Aktualisierung in der oralen Gesellschaft: Die Königserhebung Heinrichs I: als Exempel," *Geschichte in Wissenschaft und Unterricht* 44 (1993): 493–503; Fried, "Die Königserhebung Heinrichs I: Erinnerung, Mündlichkeit und Traditionsbildung im 10. Jahrhundert," in *Mittelalterforschung nach der Wende 1989,* ed. Michael Borgolte (Munich, 1995), 267–318; Fried, "Erinnerung und Vergessen. Die Gegenwart stiftet die Einheit der Vergangenheit," *Historische Zeitschrift* 273 (2001): 561–93; and Fried, *Die Schleier der Erinnerung: Grundzüge einer historischen Memorik* (Munich, 2004).

Fried's efforts to marginalize the historical value of the information provided by Widukind in the *Res gestae* have not gained the acceptance of specialists in Ottonian history and historiography.[69]

Principles of Translation

We have undertaken throughout our work to provide a translation that is based on the principle of *sensum pro sensu* rather than *verbum pro verbo.* Although most of Widukind's text is written in a straightforward manner, the basic differences between Latin and English syntax often require the addition of pronouns and proper names to make sense of subject, direct object, and indirect object. We have tried to keep such additions to a minimum, and to provide notes where the identities of individuals are not clear from the context of a particular passage in the text.

Personal and place-names pose difficulties in every translation. Our principle has been to use the form of personal names that is most familiar to modern Anglophone readers. For example, we have translated Heinricus as Henry rather than as Heinrich. In those cases where there is no generally recognized English version of a name, we have used the form that will be most familiar to an Anglophone audience.

Finally, Widukind's style is marked by a certain classicizing tendency. In part, this practice derives from Widukind's borrowing from classical models. However, in our view, it is also the case that Widukind's decision to use classical terms to denote current affairs, such as *milites,* reflects his view that the structures of royal power in his day corresponded quite closely with the institutions that he read about in classical texts. Consequently, we have chosen to translate the text in such a manner as to make clear Widukind's views in this regard. Most prominently, we have chosen to translate *res publica* as state and *miles* as soldier.

69. See, e.g., the survey of this question by Johannes Laudage, "Widukind von Corvey und die Deutsche Geschichtswissenschaft," in *Von Fakten und Fiktionen: Mittelalterliche Geschichtsdarstellungen und ihre kritische Aufarbeitung,* ed. Johannes Laudage (Cologne, 2003), 193–224, especially 209–24; and Markus Brömel, "Widukind von Corvey: Kronzeuge und Herausforderung," in *Auf den Spuren der Ottonen III* (Halle, 2002), 17–25, here 18.

THREE BOOKS OF

Deeds of the Saxons

BOOK ONE

Here begins the preface to the first book for Lady Mathilda, the daughter of the Emperor.

To Lady Mathilda, in her blossoming maidenhood,[1] illustrious for her imperial majesty and her singular wisdom, I Widukind of Corvey, the least of the servants of Stephen and Vitus,[2] martyrs of Christ, completely at your service, offer true greetings in the name of our Savior. Although the unique glory of your father's power exalts you, and your highly renowned wisdom graces you, our humility presumes upon the ever-present clemency of your scepter,[3] because our devotion, even though it is not worthy, has been received by your grace. For in reading the deeds of your exceptionally powerful father and most glorious grandfather, which have been committed to memory by our labor, you have what is necessary to transform the best and most glorious into something even better and even more glorious.[4] We confess that we were not able to in-

1. Mathilda (955–99) was the daughter of Otto I and his second wife, Adelheid. At the time of the composition of Widukind's text, in 967, Mathilda was twelve or thirteen years old and was being prepared for her role as regent in the absence of both her father and her brother, Otto II, in Italy.

2. These are the patron saints of the monastery of Corvey.

3. This is a reference to Mathilda's impending service as regent, during the absence of her father Otto I (936–73) and her brother Otto II (973–83) in Italy.

4. The subject of *optima* and *gloriosissima* is a feminine singular. Consequently, Widukind might be suggesting that the object of this work was to provide Mathilda with a means of improving herself. However, in his subsequent presentation of Henry I and Otto I, Mathilda's grandfather and father, Widukind regularly stresses the ways in which their deeds improved and strengthened the *res publica.* Consequently, we see Widukind's decision to leave unnamed the direct object of *efficiaris* as a conscious

clude all of their deeds.[5] Rather, we have written summarily and selectively[6] so that the language will be clear and not seem pedantic to the readers.[7] But first, I have taken care to write a little bit about the origin and status of the people whom Henry ruled initially as lord of their affairs,[8] so that in reading these things, you can delight your soul, relieve your cares, and have time for beautiful leisure.[9] Therefore, may your splendor read this book, and be mindful of the piety and devotion with which we wrote it. Farewell.

---

act of ambiguity, with the implication that Mathilda would be in a position to improve both herself and the *res publica* by reading his text.

5. Widukind is emphasizing here that he has omitted information about both Henry I and Otto I. This has two important implications. First, he is seeking to avoid potential criticism for omitting information to which others may have access. Second, in the context of understanding Widukind as a historian, he is making clear that his text is not all-inclusive, but rather that he is approaching his work selectively.

6. Sallust, *Catilinae,* 4.

7. Widukind is conflating two issues here, namely content and presentation. Over the course of the *Res gestae,* Widukind regularly condenses or summarizes events, and chooses to omit matters that are recorded, sometimes at length, in other contemporary historical works. In addition, most of Widukind's text also is written in simple, straightforward prose. Ironically, it is precisely in the preface to each book, including this one, that Widukind demonstrates his rhetorical skills, and potentially runs the risk of having his language be judged excessive, i.e., *fastidiosus.*

8. Widukind uses the unusual circumlocution *rerum dominus* in place of king. This usage recalls Suetonius's *Vita* of Octavian, chs. 40 and 155, where the term is used to denote the Roman people as rulers of the world.

9. The implication seems to be that by reading Widukind's text Mathilda will save sufficient time in learning her duties that she will have an opportunity to enjoy leisure time as well. The reference here to *otium* draws the attention of the reader to Cicero's *Dream of Scipio,* which appears in the sixth book of his *De re publica.* The *Dream* was widely popularized during the early Middle Ages by Macrobius in his *Comentarii in Somnium Scipionis,* 2nd ed., ed. J. Willis (Leipzig, 1970). Cicero's text, which deals in great detail with the importance of leisure to the Roman senatorial class, was adopted by clerical writers as an important model for the way in which monks should live. For the influence of the *Dream* and Macrobius's commentary during the Middle Ages, see *Commentary on the Dream of Scipio by Macrobius,* trans. William Harris Stahl (New York, 1952), 39–55.

1. That the author wrote little books other than this one.

After the first of our works, in which I portrayed the triumphs of the soldiers of the highest emperor, no one ought to wonder that I wished to commit to writing the deeds of our princes.[10] In that earlier work, I fulfilled, insofar as I was able, the obligations due to my profession.[11] Now, I do not shrink from exerting myself in the same manner, to the extent that I can, on behalf of my family and my people.

2. Regarding the origin of the Saxon people.

First, I will present a little bit of information about the origin and status of the people.[12] In this section, I am relying solely on tradition because the passage of so much time has clouded any certainty.[13] There is a great deal of disagreement about this matter. Some think that the Saxons had their origins among the Danes and Northmen.[14] Others believe, as I heard someone saying when I was a youth, the Saxons descended from the Greeks.[15] They say the Saxons were survivors of the Macedonian army that followed Alexander the Great, and was dispersed all over the world following his premature death.[16] There is no doubt this is an old and no-

10. Widukind's other works are now lost. The comparison here between the *summus imperator* and *principes nostri* indicates that Widukind's earlier texts dealt with God, and that the *milites* in question were martyrs and saints. These earlier works included a poetic *passio* of the sainted virgin Thekla, and a poetic *vita* of Paul of Thebes. See the discussion in Wilhelm Wattenbach and Robert Holtzmann, *Deutschlands Geschichtsquellen im Mittlelalter: Die Zeit der Sachsen und Salier, Das Zeitalter des ottonischen Staates (900–1050)*, rev., ed. Franz-Josef Schmale (Cologne, 1967), 26.

11. This is Widukind's profession as a monk at the monastery of Corvey.

12. Widukind is referring here to the Saxon *gens*, and particularly to their rise from the status as a client people to a ruling people.

13. Widukind is drawing a distinction here between tradition and history, and noting that there are different criteria for each.

14. Widukind might be referring here to Rabanus Maurus, *De invention linguarum*, PL 112, col. 1581; and Ermoldus, *In honorem Hludovici imperatoris*, 4.18.

15. This passage makes clear that Widukind sees oral testimony as comprising one source of information for traditions.

16. Widukind's knowledge of Alexander the Great and the Macedonians likely

ble people. This is proven by the fact that they are mentioned in a speech by Agrippa to the Jews in Josephus, and are commented on by the poet Lucan.[17]

3. That they set out in ships for a place called Hadeln.

We know for certain that the Saxons came to this region by ship. They first arrived at a place that is still called Hadeln up to the present day.[18]

4. That the Thuringians were very angry about their arrival.

The inhabitants, who have been identified as the Thuringians, were very angry about the arrival of the Saxons, and attacked them. The Saxons fiercely resisted the Thuringians and captured a port. After they had fought for some time, and many had died, both

came from Curtius Rufus, *Historia Alexandri,* at least one copy of which was produced at Lorsch during the first half of the tenth century. See M. Winterbottom, "Curtius Rufus," *Texts and Transmission: A Survey of the Latin Classics,* ed. L. D. Reynolds and P. K. Marshall (Oxford, 1983), 35–36; and Bernhard Bischoff, *Manuscripts and Libraries in the Age of Charlemagne,* trans. and ed. Michael Gorman (Cambridge, 1994), 150. There is no extant evidence of a manuscript of Curtius Rufus at Corvey during the tenth century. However, Widukind's reference to Alexander may point to the possession by the monastery of this text at one time.

17. The Saxons are not mentioned in either the Greek text of Josephus, *Bellum Judaicum,* 2.16, nor in Hegesippus's Latin reworking of the Josephus text, *De Excidio Urbis Hierosolymitanae* PL 15, 2062–310. Widukind may have been thinking of Hegesippus, *De Excidio,* 5.15, where Josephus is presented addressing his fellow Jews saying, "tremit Saxonia inaccessa paludibus—validissimum genus hominum perhibetur et praestans ceteris," i.e.,"he trembles at Saxony, inaccessible because of swamps, he names them the most powerful people of all mankind, standing above the rest." A number of manuscripts of Lucan, *Pharsalia,* 1.423, mention *Saxones* in place of *Suessones.* See the discussion in *Res gestae,* ed. Bauer and Rau, 22n2.

18. Hadeln is located on the left bank of the lower Elbe. Widukind likely obtained this information from the *Translatio Sancti Alexandri,* which is available in the edition by Bruno Krusch, "Die Übertragung des Heiligen Alexander von Rom nach Wildeshausen durch den Enkel Widukinds 851: Die älteste niedersächsische Geschichtsdenkmal," *Nachrichten von der Gesellschaft der Wissenschaften zu Göttingen, philosophische-historische Klasse* 2, no. 13 (1933): 405–36. The section pertaining to the origins of Saxony, including the first landing of the Saxons at Hadeln, is reproduced in *Res gestae,* ed. Bauer and Rau, 12.

sides were prepared to discuss peace and to enter into an agreement.[19] They made a treaty with the following clauses, namely that the Saxons would have the freedom to buy and sell. However, they would not take up farming, and would refrain from killing or robbing the Thuringians. This treaty remained inviolate for a long while. However, since the Saxons lacked any money, or anything that they might buy or sell, they judged that the peace agreement was useless to them.[20]

5. How a youth obtained land with gold.

It happened during that time that a certain youth disembarked from the ships loaded with a great deal of gold, including a golden necklace and golden armlets. One of the Thuringians, whom the youth encountered along his path, said to him: "What do you want with such a huge amount of gold hanging around your emaciated neck?"[21] The youth answered: "I am looking for a buyer. I carry this gold for no other reason. For if I am starving, how can I enjoy this gold?" So the Thuringian asked him about the quality of the gold, and how much it cost.[22] The Saxon responded saying, "I have not set a price. Whatever you give me, I will accept with thanks." Then the Thuringian, laughing at the youth, said, "What if I fill your pouch with this dust?" For at that particular spot, the ground was quite turned up. Without any delay, the Saxon opened up his pouch and received the earth, and then handed over the gold to the Thuringian. Both returned happily to their own people.

The Thuringians praised their fellow Thuringian to the heav-

19. The reference to a merchant treaty suggests Widukind's familiarity with this institution from contemporary practice.

20. It is noteworthy that Widukind sees money, *pecunia,* as essential to commerce.

21. Juvenal, *Satires,* 14.146.

22. The expression *quantitas et qualitas* used here by Widukind recalls a letter sent by Archbishop Hincmar of Rheims to King Charles the Bald of West Francia in 868 regarding the service owed by the holder of a *beneficium* to a church, and hence to the king. Hincmar described this obligation "secundum quantitatem et qualitatem beneficii." See *Ad Carolum Calvum regem pro Ecclesiae libertatum defensione,* PL 125, col. 1050.

ens[23] for having deceived the Saxon by means of such an impressive fraud.[24] They considered him the most fortunate among all mortals for having gained such a huge quantity of gold for such a small price. Certain of this victory, they celebrated as if in triumph over the Saxons themselves.[25] In the meantime, the Saxon stripped of his gold but loaded with a great deal of earth, approached the ships. His friends ran up to him, wondering what he had done. Some of his friends began to laugh at him. Others began to reprove him. They all thought that he was crazy. But then he demanded silence and said, "Follow me, oh best of Saxons, and you will see how my madness benefits you." Then, although doubtful, they followed him as if he were their leader. He took up the earth and spread it as thinly as possible over the nearby fields, and then secured these places with fortified encampments.[26]

6. *The Thuringians accuse the Saxons of violating the treaty.*

However, when the Thuringians saw the Saxon fortified camp, its existence seemed intolerable to them.[27] They sent messengers to complain about the Saxons violating the treaty and breaking the peace. The Saxons responded that they had kept the treaty unbroken up to the present. They wished to keep in peace the land that they had purchased with their own gold, but they would certainly defend it by force of arms. When they heard this, the Thuringians cursed the Saxon gold, which earlier they had proclaimed as a

23. The passage here is modeled on Sallust, *Catilinae,* 48.

24. The phrase *nobilis fraus* is indicative of a cultural attitude that doing something in the best possible way is worthy of being called noble, even if the deed is nefarious. This attitude recalls the Greek concept of *arete,* which subsequently was inherited by the Romans.

25. These terms recall the vocabulary for Roman military success. See the detailed discussion of Roman and early medieval ceremonies for military victory by Michael McCormick, *Eternal Victory: Triumphal Rulership in Late Antiquity, Byzantium and the Early Medieval West* (Cambridge, 1990).

26. This account parallels the story of Dido as the Phoenicians settled in the future site of Carthage. See Vergil, *Aeneid,* 4.365–68. The language here, particularly *castrorum,* is consistent with Roman military terminology.

27. Widukind uses the term *castra* rather than *castrum* here. The former is a marching camp, while the latter is a fortification.

source of joy, and also cursed the one whom shortly before they had proclaimed as lucky, calling him the author of their destruction and of the destruction of their region.

Then, burning with anger and blind with lust for battle,[28] the Thuringians attacked the Saxon encampment, but without any order or plan. The Saxons, who were prepared, received the enemy onslaught and cut them down. As this battle turned out well for the Saxons, by the law of war, they obtained all of the territory that was located nearby. For a long time there was conflict between the two peoples.

Eventually, the Thuringians came to believe that the Saxons were stronger than they, and sent messengers to ask that both sides meet unarmed at a specified place and time so that they could again discuss peace. The Saxons responded that they would agree to this request. In those days, however, the Saxons used very large knives, which the Angles still use today, keeping the custom of the ancient people.[29] Equipped with these knives, the Saxons departed under arms[30] from their camp and met the Thuringians at the specified place. When the Saxons saw that the enemy was unarmed, and that all of the leaders of the Thuringians were there, they decided that the time had come to gain the entire region. So they pulled out their knives, and rushed unexpectedly at the unarmed men. The Saxons killed all of them so that not even one survived,[31] and from this point on used their dominant position to terrorize the neighboring peoples.

7. Why they are called Saxons.

There were some who held that this name was given to them because of this deed.[32] In our language, these knives are called a

28. The phrase *caeco marte* is taken from Vergil, *Aeneid,* 2.335.

29. Widukind is again conflating Angles and Saxons, claiming here that the former used the traditional Saxon knives.

30. The word *sagum* refers to a mantle put on by the Romans when they went on campaign, hence the phrase *in sagis esse,* "meant to be under arms."

31. Exodus 14.28.

32. That is, the Saxon attack against the Thuringians.

"sahs." Thus, they are called Saxons because they killed such a multitude with their knives.[33]

8. The name of the Saxons became celebrated, and they were called by the Britons to provide help.

While these events were going on in Saxony, which now had become the name of this region, Britain was being attacked by neighboring nations. Britain long before had been established among the provinces by the ruler Vespasian,[34] and had lived happily for a long time as a client of the Romans. But now Britain appeared to be deprived of Roman help. For following the murder of Emperor Martialis by his soldiers,[35] the Roman people were worn down by external wars and did not have sufficient strength to provide aid to their friends. Therefore, for the protection of the region, the Romans constructed a huge defensive work stretching from sea to sea where it seemed that the enemy would attack.[36] They then departed the region.

But for a fierce enemy that was ready for war, it was not at all difficult to destroy this defensive work, when faced by a soft people who were hesitant to go into battle. Therefore, as the fame of the deeds of the Saxons spread, the Britons sent a suppliant legation to ask for their aid. The representatives said: "O greatest Saxons, the miserable Britons, worn down by the repeated attacks of their enemies, and utterly crushed, having learned of your magnifi-

33. The claim that the Saxons derived their name from their knives was also made by Nennius, *Historia Brittonum,* ch. 46, MGH Auctores antiquissimi 13, ed. Theodor Mommsen (Berlin, 1888).

34. Widukind chooses here to denote Vespasian (69–79 A.D.) as *princeps* rather than as *imperator,* a term that he later uses to denote Otto I.

35. There was no Emperor Martialis. Paul the Deacon, *Historia Romana,* 14.19, does discuss Emperor Marcianus (450–57), who was murdered. It is possible that Widukind miscopied the name when reading Paul the Deacon's text.

36. This would appear to be the Antonine Wall in northern England, which is mentioned in several works that likely were available to Widukind, including Aurelius Victor, *Liber de Caesaribus,* ch. 20; Eutropius, *Breviarium ab urbe condita,* 8.19; Orosius, *Historiarum adversus paganos libri septem,* 7.17; Gildas, *De excidio Britanniae,* 15; and Bede, *Historia ecclesiastica,* 1.5.

cent victories, sent us to you to beg that you do not withhold your aid from them. They ordered that a wide and spacious land, filled with a great abundance of all things, be given over to your authority. Up until now, we have lived freely as a client and under the protection of the Romans. After the Romans, we do not know anyone better than you. Therefore, we seek refuge beneath the wings of your military strength.[37] We will be superior to our enemies with your strength and with your arms. We will freely accept whatever kind of service that you require."

The fathers briefly responded with this statement:[38] "You should know that the Saxons are the fast friends of the Britons, and will always stand by them in times of need, and for their advantage." The messengers happily returned to their fatherland, and brought even greater joy to their comrades with this hoped-for news. Then the promised army was deployed to Britain, and was happily received by friends.[39] In a short time, the army freed the region of thieves and returned the fatherland to its inhabitants.[40] Nor did this require much work. Those who heard reports of the Saxons were overwhelmed, struck down by fear. They were routed while the Saxons were still far away.

The peoples opposed to the Britons were the Scots and the Picts.[41] While they were fighting against these peoples, the Saxons received everything that they required from the Britons.[42] They remained in this region for some time and made good use of their feigned friendship with the Britons. The commanders of the army saw that the land was broad and fertile. They also understood both that the inhabitants lacked an interest in fighting, and that

37. The use of the word *ala* (wing) is a double entendre. The term *ala* generally denotes, in a military context, a unit of cavalry. However, the image of being protected under a wing also has a powerful resonance.

38. Widukind uses the term fathers, i.e., *patres,* to denote the Saxon leadership.

39. *Amici* (friends) is being used here in the Roman diplomatic sense of an inferior ally.

40. Book of Baruch 6.56.

41. These are the Irish and the inhabitants of southern Scotland.

42. Regarding the "hospitality" offered to the Saxons by the Britons, see the sixth-century Romano-Briton Gildas, *De excidio et conquestu Britanniae,* ch. 23.

the greater part of the Saxons did not have secure homes.[43] Therefore, the commanders sent messages to recall the larger army.[44] The Saxons then made peace with the Scots and Picts, and in conjunction with them, made war on the Britons, and drove them from the region.[45] The Saxons then divided the lands under their own authority. And because this island is situated in a certain angle of the sea, the people there are called Anglo-Saxons even into our own time.[46]

If anyone wishes to know more about all of these matters, let him read the history of this people[47] where he will find how and under which leaders all of this took place. They will also learn how the Saxons came to the name of Christianity through the most holy man of that time, namely Pope Gregory.[48] We now return to the path of the history on which we began.

9. *Thiadrich was chosen as king, and summoned the Saxons to aid him against Irminfrid.*

After this, Hugh, king of the Franks, died.[49] He did not leave

43. Sallust, *Catilinae,* 6. It is worth noting that at the time the Saxons invaded Britain, their homeland was subject to substantial flooding due to climate change resulting in the so-called Second Dunkirk Transgression.

44. The implication here is that a large army initially came to Britain, but most of the men subsequently went home. Once the commanders realized that potential for settlement, the original forces were recalled.

45. The defeat of the British at the hands of these multiple invasions is described in detail by Gildas, *De excidio et conquestu Britanniae.*

46. In reality, the name is a formed by the conjunction of Angles, one of the Germanic peoples to migrate to Britain, with Saxons. Widukind certainly knew that the Angles had settled in England from reading the account in Bede, *Historia ecclesiastica,* 2.1, where Pope Gregory the Great is reported to have said that slaves being sold in the market in Rome were appropriately called Angles because they had the faces of angels. The use of this bit of geographical lore conveniently permitted Widukind to omit any reference to other immigrants into England who might steal some of the glory of conquest from the Saxons.

47. Bede's *Historia ecclesiastica.*

48. Pope Gregory the Great (590–604).

49. Traditionally, scholars have identified this Hugh with Clovis I (481–511). See the discussion in *Widukindi monachi Corbeieinsis Rerum gestarum Saxonicarum libri tres,* ed. Paul Hirsch and H.-E. Lohmann, MGH scriptores editi separati 60 (Hanover, 1935), 10n8; *Res gestae,* ed. Bauer and Rau, 28–29n10a. However, this makes little sense given

any heirs other than a single daughter named Amalberga, who married Irminfrid, the king of the Thuringians. The Frankish people had been treated humanely and mildly by their lord. So, in order to repay him with a demonstration of their esteem, they anointed as their king a son named Thiadrich, whom Hugh had with a concubine.[50] When Thiadrich had been designated as king, he took care to send a legation to Irminfrid to discuss peace and friendship. The legate said: "The greatest and most powerful of mortals, my lord Thiadrich, sent me to you expressing the hope that you are healthy, and will flourish for a long time in your large and great empire. Thiadrich says that he does not wish to be your lord, but rather your friend, not your emperor but rather your kinsman. He wishes to keep inviolate his obligations of kinship to you to the end. He asks only that you not create discord where there is now concord[51] among the Frankish people, since they now follow him, as the one whom they established as king for themselves."

As was appropriate for his royal dignity, Irminfrid responded politely to the legate that he was pleased with the decisions of the Frankish people, and had no desire to create dissension out of their agreement. Rather, he desired peace above all. However, with regard to the business of the kingdom,[52] Irminfrid wished to defer his answer until he was in the presence of his friends. Then treating the legate honorably, Irminfrid had him remain for some time.

However, when the queen heard that the legation from her brother had come and had spoken with the king about business of the kingdom, she advised Iring[53] that together they ought to persuade her husband that the kingdom should come to her by hered-

---

that it was well known to all readers of Gregory of Tours that Clovis had four surviving sons, and that his daughter Clothilde (died 531) married the Visigothic king Amalric. Instead, Widukind may have been referring here to Amalasintha, the daughter of Theoderic the Great (493–526).

50. Gregory of Tours, *Historiae*, 2.28, describes Theuderich, Clovis's first son, as illegitimate.

51. Ovid, *Metamorphoses*, 1.433.

52. The reference here is to Thiadrich's accession. This passage recalls 2 Maccabees 10.11.

53. Iring was a close confidant of both the king and the queen.

itary right since she was the daughter of a king and daughter of a queen.[54] Thiadrich should be Irminfrid's slave, having been born to a concubine. It would be indecent for Irminfrid ever to give his hand to his own slave.[55] Iring himself was a bold man, physically strong, possessing a sharp intellect,[56] offering keen counsel, tenacious in carrying out his duties, and with the capacity to persuade others of what he wished. It was with these qualities that Iring had won over Irminfrid's heart.[57]

After summoning his magnates and close friends, Irminfrid set out in their presence the words of the legate.[58] They all agreed that Irminfrid should make the decision for peace[59] and concord because he could not withstand an attack by the Franks, especially when he was being pressed from the other side by the arms of an even more bitter enemy.[60] But Iring, satisfying the desires of the wanton woman,[61] persuaded Irminfrid that he ought not give in to the Franks. He had a more just claim to the royal succession. Moreover, the size of his empire, his military forces, arms, and other wartime necessities were equal to those of Thiadrich.[62]

54. The argument is that Amalberga was the legitimate daughter of Hugh, and so the right of succession should pass through her rather than through her illegitimate brother. This argument was much more likely to be compelling to Widukind's audience in the tenth century than it was in the early sixth century.

55. To give his hand was a mark of equality or even submission.

56. Widukind appears to have drawn here on Vergil, *Aeneid,* 9.592; and Sallust, *Jugurtha,* 7.

57. Widukind's detailed discussion of Iring's physical and mental capacities provide an interesting "mirror" for royal advisers in a manner analogous to the popular mirror of princes genre.

58. This passage provides a useful insight into the composition of a royal council.

59. The phrase *quae pacis sunt* is borrowed from Luke 14.32.

60. The reference here seems to be to the Saxons. The council is advising Irminfrid to refrain from engaging in a war on two fronts. This advice was readily available to readers of Widukind's day through the observations of Gregory of Tours. With regard to the military lessons provided by Gregory of Tours, see Bernard S. Bachrach, "Gregory of Tours as a Military Historian," in *The World of Gregory of Tours,* ed. Kathleen Mitchell and Ian Wood (Leiden, 2002), 351–63.

61. This is Amalberga.

62. This list foreshadows the list of advantages enjoyed by King Conrad I and his brother Eberhard, which were insufficient to overcome their lack of good fortune. See below 1.26.

In accord with these sentiments, Irminfrid responded to the legate that he did not deny his friendship and kinship with Thiadrich, but that he could not help marveling that he was able to claim power before he gained his freedom. Born a slave, how did Thiadrich seek to claim lordship over him? Thiadrich could not give his hand to his own slave.[63]

The legate was very upset about this, and said: "I would prefer to hand over my head to you rather than hear words of this kind from you, knowing how much Frankish and Thuringian blood will be shed." After he said this, the legate returned to Thiadrich, and did not hide what he had heard. Thiadrich replied, hiding his rage under a serene visage,[64] "It is fitting for us to hurry to serve Irminfrid so that having been deprived of our liberty, we might at least keep our useless life."[65]

As Thiadrich approached the frontier of the Thuringians with a large army, he found his brother-in-law with an equally powerful force waiting for him at a place called Runibergun.[66] The battle hung in the balance for a full day, and then a second.[67] On the third day, Irminfrid was defeated and fled from Thiadrich. Irminfrid retreated with his remaining forces to a fortress called Scheidungen,[68] which was located on a river called the Unstrut.

63. The implication is that Thiadrich, as a slave, could not free his own slaves by manumitting them, i.e., sending them off with his hand.

64. See Gregory of Tours, *Historiae,* 2.27.

65. This passage demonstrates that sarcasm was part of Widukind's rhetorical palette.

66. The battle of Runibergun took place in 531. The location of the battle is unknown, but scholars have suggested several possibilities including Ronnenberg southwest of Hanover; Ronneberge near Nebra on the Unstrut river some fifteen kilometers from Burgscheidungen; and Ruhnsburg on the western side of the hilly range in northern Thuringia called the Hainleite. See the discussion in *Res gestae,* ed. Bauer and Rau, 31n17. This battle is discussed in detail by Gregory of Tours, *Historiae,* 3.7. Also see the later discussion of the battle in *Annales Quedlinburgenses,* ed. G. H. Pertz, MGH Scriptores 3 (Hanover, 1849), 32.

67. The phrase *pugnatum est ancipiti* is borrowed from Caesar, *Commentarii de bello Gallico,* 1.26.

68. This is Burgscheidungen, located along the Unstrut river in the modern German state of Saxony-Anhalt.

Thiadrich summoned the senior officers and troop commanders of his army, and asked for their views regarding whether they should pursue Irminfrid, or return to their fatherland. Among those whom Thiadrich consulted was Waldrich. He said, "I think that in order to bury our dead, and care for the wounded, and to mobilize a larger army, we ought to return to the fatherland. For having lost so many thousands of your men, I do not think that we have sufficient forces remaining at present to pursue this fight. If the innumerable barbarian nations rise up against us, what forces will you use to conquer them, after so many of our men have been wounded?"

However, Thiadrich also had a very clever slave whose advice he frequently had tested and found sound. As a consequence, Thiadrich had developed a certain intimacy with him.[69] After being asked to give his view, this man said: "It is always the most desirable course to persevere when engaged in honorable matters. This is the path that our ancestors followed, rarely or never giving up on a task once they had begun. Nor do I believe that our own labors match theirs. They overcame the enormous armies of other peoples with their much smaller forces.[70] Now that the land is in our power, will our departure offer the defeated a chance for victory? I would love to return to my fatherland and see my closest friends, if I believed that our enemy would waste this time. Perhaps our wounded need this respite. Leave the care of the fortified camps to

69. This kind of *familiaritas* is discussed by Cicero, *De oficiis*, 1.17.55.

70. Widukind here is utilizing the well-known topos of minimizing the numbers of the "home side" and providing an exaggerated size for the enemy. For this well-known tendency among both ancient and medieval authors, see Hans Delbrück, *Geschichte der Kriegskunst im Rahmen der politischen Geschichte*, 6 vols. (Berlin, 1900–1936), the first three volumes of which were translated into English by Walter J. Renfroe as *History of the Art of War: Within the Framework of Political History* (Westport, Conn., 1975–82). For the discussion of the tendencies of chroniclers regarding the depiction of the number of men on the "home side" as small, see *Volume II: The Barbarian Invasions* (1980, rep. 1990, Westport, Conn.), 227; and Delbrück, *Numbers in History* (London, 1913), 11–12, and 14. For an overview of the entire issue of numbers in early medieval narrative sources, see the discussion by Bernard S. Bachrach, "Early Medieval Military Demography: Some Observations on the Methods of Hans Delbrück," *The Circle of War*, ed. Donald Kagay and L. J. Andrew Villalon (Woodbridge, 1999), 3–20.

the wounded. I reckon that for those with a vigorous attitude, this is their greatest desire.

Of course, our army has been greatly diminished by the deaths of so many men. Have all of the enemy escaped death? No, only a few remain! Their leader, himself, has hidden himself away like some little beast in its den, surrounded by the walls of a fortress. He does not dare even to take a peek at the sky out of fear of us. But he does not lack money with which to employ the barbarian nations.[71] Nor does he lack military forces, although these are now worn out. However, they will be restored completely in our absence. It is not fitting for the victorious to give over the site of their victory to the defeated. Do we have sufficient garrisons to man every fortress?[72] We will lose all of these strongholds in the time it takes us to depart and return."

After the slave had spoken, Thiadrich and all those eager for the glory of victory decided to remain in camp and sent word to the Saxons, who had now been the bitter enemies of the Thuringians for a long time, and asked if they would provide aid. Thiadrich offered that if the Saxons defeated Irminfrid, and captured his fortress, he would hand over the land to them as their eternal possession. Without delay, the Saxons dispatched nine commanders, each with one thousand fighting men. The commanders all came into Thiadrich's camp, each accompanied by one hundred fighting men, leaving the remaining forces outside. The commanders greeted Thiadrich with words of peace,[73] and he cheerfully received them. After they all had shaken hands, Thiadrich gave an extensive report to the Saxons.[74]

71. This passage suggests the use of cash grants for diplomatic purposes, which was quite similar to Byzantine diplomatic practice of Widukind's day, rather than the employment of individuals or even small groups of men as mercenaries.

72. Widukind's observation here is consistent with the military policies of Kings Henry I and Otto I that required the establishment of garrisons to man the scores of fortresses that were constructed to maintain control in the lands conquered by these two rulers east of the Saale and Elbe rivers.

73. 1 Maccabees 7.10.

74. Vergil, *Aeneid,* 1.520 and 11.248.

They said, "The Saxon people, who sent us to you, are devoted to you and ready to follow your commands. We are prepared for whatever you order. We are prepared to defeat your enemies or, if this is what fortune demands, we are prepared to die for you. You should know that the Saxons wish for nothing other than to be victorious or to die. We cannot make any greater offering to our allies than to spurn death for them.[75] It is our deepest desire that you learn this through your own experience."

After the Saxons had spoken in this way, the Franks were amazed at the enormous size and fierce spirit of these men. They also wondered at their unfamiliar manner of dress, their arms, their hair flowing over their shoulders, and, above all, at the great constancy of their spirit. For they were dressed in military cloaks, and were equipped with long spears and stood leaning on small shields, with large knives across their backs.[76]

There were some who said that the Franks did not need so many friends of this type. For the Saxons were an indomitable race of men, and if they inhabited the lands now being discussed, it seemed likely that it would be they who someday destroyed the Frankish empire.[77] But Thiadrich was concerned for his own needs, and putting his trust in these men, he ordered them to prepare to assault the fortress. Leaving the presence of the king, the Saxons set up their fortified camp on the south side of the fortress in meadows adjacent to the river. At first light the next day, they took up their arms, attacked the outer works of the fortress, and burned them.[78] After they had captured and burned the outer works, the Saxons formed a phalanx opposite the eastern gate of

75. Widukind's use of the term *amici* here permits the inference that he is inverting a tenth-century model of Saxon superiority over the Franks by casting the former as the junior partner in the alliance.

76. Literally, at their kidneys, *ad renes.*

77. This is a foreshadowing of events during the early tenth century.

78. Widukind is contrasting the outer fortification of the *oppidum* with the main fortification of the *urbs.* In Widukind's day, the common style of fortification included a main fortress (*Hauptburg*), and an outer bailey (*Vorburg*) that enclosed a settlement, workshops, and other support staff for a garrison.

the main fortress. The men inside the walls, as they saw the phalanx being formed and realized that they were in extreme danger, boldly burst out of the gates and rushed against their adversaries in a blind rage. After both sides had hurled their spears, they began to fight with swords.[79]

A vicious battle ensued. Many died on both sides. The Thuringians were fighting for their fatherland, their wives and children, and finally for their own lives. The Saxons were fighting for glory and to gain land. There was a huge clamor from men encouraging each other, from the breaking of arms, and the groans of the dying. The entire day passed in this spectacle. Finally, when the dead lay everywhere, and cries were rising all over, and neither side had given any ground, the late hour finally brought the battle to an end.[80] Many of the Thuringians were killed on this day, and many were wounded. The Saxon dead numbered six thousand.

10. *Iring incites Thiadrich against the Saxons.*

Therefore, Iring, accompanied by a suppliant legation, was dispatched by Irminfrid along with all of his treasure to have discussions with Thiadrich about peace and a voluntary submission. When Iring arrived, he said, "He who was once your kinsman, and is now your slave, sent his treasure to you so that even if you do not show him mercy, at least you will have some compassion for your sister, and for your nephews who now find themselves in exceptionally difficult circumstances." Iring wept while he was speaking. Then, one of the commanders, whom Iring had corrupted with gold,[81] added that it was appropriate to a king's clemency that he not spurn such a request, and that he not forget what they had in common. Rather, it would be more useful to accept as a loyal supporter a man whom he had defeated and was now contrite, and who would never be able to rebel against Thiadrich, than it would be to rely on this indomitable race of men,[82] which en-

79. Sallust, *Catilinae,* 60.

80. Sallust, *Jugurtha,* 60.

81. These are the magnates of the Franks.

82. These are the Saxons.

dured through every difficulty, and from whom the Frankish empire could expect nothing but danger. In the just completed war, Thiadrich had been able to see how hard and unbeatable the Saxons really were. It would be better to make use of the Thuringians and together drive the Saxons from his lands.

Against his will Thiadrich was moved by these words. He promised that the next day he would receive his brother-in-law, and withdraw from his alliance with the Saxons. When Iring heard this, he threw himself at the feet of the king, and praised this demonstration of imperial mercy. And having sent the desired message to his lord,[83] Iring made him happy and the entire fortress more secure. However, Iring remained in the camp in order to keep anything adverse from happening that night.[84]

In the meantime, since the fortress had been made more secure by the promise of peace, a man left the stronghold with his hawk looking for prey along the banks of the aforementioned river.[85] After he had sent his bird aloft, one of the Saxons caught it on the opposite shore. When asked to return it, the Saxon refused. Then the first man said, "If you give it me, I will share a secret that will be useful to you and your companions." The Saxon responded, "Tell me, and you will have what you seek." Then the first man said, "The kings have made a peace agreement, and if you are found in camp tomorrow, you certainly will be captured or killed." Then the Saxon asked, "Are you serious, or playing some sort of game?" The first man answered, "The second hour tomorrow,[86] will prove that you must act and that I do not jest. Take counsel with your people, and seek safety in flight." The Saxon immediately let go the hawk, and told his comrades what he had heard. They were very upset about this, and unsure of what they should do.

83. Iring's lord is Irminfried.

84. Iring remained in the Frankish camp in order to ensure that Thiadrich did not renege on his agreement.

85. This is the Unstrut river.

86. The attack was to come at 8:00 in the morning.

11. Hathagath rouses the Saxons to fight.

At that time, there was an older man among the veteran soldiers in camp who, despite his age, was still vigorous.[87] By virtue of his achievements, this man named Hathagath, was called father of the fathers. He grabbed up a banner, which they held sacred, bearing an image of a lion and a dragon above whom was flying an eagle.[88] It was intended to show the intensity of their bravery, prudence, and other virtues. Making clear his resolve through his upright posture, Hathagath declared: "Up until now, I have lived among the best Saxons, and age has brought me to this, the penultimate stage of life. I have never seen my Saxons flee. How can I now be forced to do what I never learned? I know how to fight. But I do not know how to flee, nor do I wish to. If the fates do not permit me to live longer, at least they grant what is sweetest to me, namely to die with my friends. The examples of the strength of our fathers are to be found in the bodies of our friends that lie around us. They preferred to die rather than to be conquered. It is better to set free your indefatigable spirits than to give way before your enemies. But what need do I have to belabor you with exhortations to spurn death? Behold, we shall go forth carefree to a slaughter, not to a battle. Because of the promised peace, and our heavy losses, our adversaries suspect nothing. Worn out as they are by today's battle, they are not afraid, and have not posted the customary watches and guard. We will attack them by surprise, while they are buried in sleep. The task is quite small. Follow me as your leader, and I will offer up my hoary head to you if things do not turn out as I say."

Aroused by his excellent speech, the Saxons spent the remain-

87. See Vergil, *Aeneid,* 6.304, where Charon, although ancient, is still vigorous.

88. Widukind may be drawing here on the tradition of the Roman dragon (*draco*) banner, which was in use by the third century. This type of banner became so common that by the sixth century one of the common terms in the Eastern Roman Empire for a standard bearer was a *drakonarios.* See John the Lydian, *De Magistratibus: On the Magistracies of the Roman Constitutions,* trans. Thomas Francis Carney (Lawrence, Kan., 1971), 1.46.

der of the day eating and resting. Then at the first vigil of night,[89] when people customarily are in the deepest sleep, the signal was given, and the Saxons took up their arms. With their leader preceding them, they rushed over the walls, finding them empty of guards or a watch, and entered the fortress with a great shout. Their adversaries were roused by the noise. Some sought safety in flight. Some wandered like drunkards through the streets and along the walls of the fortress. Some ran to the Saxons thinking that they were their fellow citizens. The Saxons killed all of the adults, and kept the youths as booty.[90] The night was full of shouts, and death, and theft. No place in the entire fortress was quiet until the reddish dawn broke and declared a bloodless victory.[91] Finally, with the capture of the king, namely Irminfrid, the victory was complete. However, when he was sent for, it was found that Irminfrid along with his wife, sons, and a small entourage, had escaped.

12. *After they captured the city, the Saxons lay down their eagle.*

When morning came, the Saxons placed an eagle before the eastern gate,[92] and constructed an altar of victory following the error of their fathers.[93] They worshipped their divinities in their own manner. In worshipping one of them, called Mars, they imitate Hercules with an image of columns.[94] They worship this deity in the place of the sun, whom the Greeks called Apollo. From this, it seems likely that those, who think that the Saxons had their

89. This is the midnight monastic office.

90. Sallust, *Jugurtha,* 54 and 91. Widukind uses similar imagery when discussing the treatment of prisoners following the capture of fortifications by Henry I and Otto I. See below 1.35 and 3.52.

91. Sallust, *Catilinae,* 61. This bloodless victory was of the sun over the night, which stood in contrast to the exceptionally bloody victory of the Saxons over the Thuringians.

92. The eagle was the symbol of the Roman legion, a fact with which Widukind was very familiar through his reading of Roman historical works.

93. Widukind is commenting here on the paganism of the Saxons before their forced conversion to Christianity under Charlemagne.

94. The reference here is to the Columns of Hercules.

origin among the Greeks, have a point because the one whom we call Mars, is called Hirmin or Hermis in Greek.[95] We use that word[96] up to the present day both to praise and to condemn, although we do not know what it really means.

They spent three days celebrating their victory, dividing up the booty from the enemy, celebrating funeral rites on behalf of the dead, and praising their leader to the heavens. They acclaimed him for having a divine spirit and heavenly strength since it was through his constancy that he brought them to achieve this victory.[97] All of this was completed, according to the memory of our ancestors, on the first of October.[98] These days of error have been transformed through the decrees of religious men into fasts, prayers, and offerings by all of those who became Christians before us.

13. *Thiadrich gave the land to the Saxons, and Irminfrid was killed.*

When all of this was completed, the Saxons returned to Thiadrich in the camp. He received them with considerable praise and granted this land to them as an eternal possession. They were named the comrades and friends of the Franks. They first settled in the fortress whose walls they had spared from the fire so that they could use them for their own.[99]

But I do not wish to leave out what happened to the kings, because it is a remarkable account. Iring was sent to Thiadrich on the same day that the city was captured.[100] The night of the attack, he had remained in camp as a guest of Thiadrich. When Thiadrich heard that Irminfrid had escaped, he acted to bring him back by trickery, and to have him killed by Iring at the point when it appeared that Irminfrid was to receive very generous gifts from Thiadrich and to be honored with great power in his kingdom.

95. Widukind is incorrect here. The Greek god Hermes is to be identified with the Roman god Mercury, not Mars.

96. That is, Hermes.

97. The reference here is to Hathagath.

98. These events took place in 531.

99. This is the fortress at Burgscheidungen.

100. See below 1.16.

Thiadrich himself would stand aside from Irminfrid's murder as if he had nothing to do with it.

At first, Iring was unwilling to accept this task. However, finally corrupted by false promises, he gave in, and said that he was prepared to do Thiadrich's will. Irminfrid was recalled, and threw himself at the feet of Thiadrich.[101] Iring, who was standing nearby with his sword drawn as if a royal bodyguard, killed his prostrate lord. The king immediately turned to him and said, "You have made yourself hateful to all men by this deed, by the killing of your lord. You have an open path to leave us. We do not wish to have any part or share in your evil." Iring responded, "It is right that I have become hateful to all men because I have submitted to your deceptions. Before I depart, I will purge this evil that I have done by avenging my lord."

And, since he was standing with his sword still drawn, Iring cut down Thiadrich and placed the body of his lord over Thiadrich's corpse so that in death Irminfrid might at least conquer the man who had defeated him in life. Then, making a path with his sword, Iring departed. The reader will have to decide whether this account is to be believed.[102] We cannot help but wonder, however, that this story has been so widely preserved that we use Iring's name, up to the present day, to denote the Milky Way.[103]

14. How the Saxons divided the land, and that they live as three peoples and by three laws.

After the Saxons gained the land, they remained in complete peace, enjoying their partnership and friendship with the Franks.

101. The description of Iring throwing himself at the feet of Thiadrich likely recalled to Widukind's audience the contemporary ceremony of *supplicatio.* For a detailed discussion of this ceremony in the contemporary West, see Geoffrey Koziol, *Begging Pardon and Favor: Ritual and Political Order in Early Medieval France* (Ithaca, 1992).

102. Widukind appears to draw upon Sallust, *Jugurtha,* 17, to find a convenient way of distancing himself from the unlikely account that he has presented.

103. The implication here is that men of Widukind's day called the Milky Way, i.e., our galaxy, "Iring's way." See the discussion of Iring and the Milky Way in Frutolf, *Chronicon Universale,* ed. G. H. Pertz, MGH SS 6 (Hanover, 1844), 178.

They distributed part of their lands to friends, who had provided them with aid, and also to freedmen.[104] They imposed tribute on the remainder of the peoples whom they had defeated.

It is for the following reason that the Saxon people, aside from those in slavery, is divided into three parts according to their descent and to their law. Leadership over the entire people was entrusted to three leading men, each of whom was content with the power of mobilizing the army from within specified boundaries. We call these the armies of the eastern peoples,[105] the Engern,[106] and the Westphalians, because of the places where the people lived and because of what they called themselves. If a general war broke out,[107] a man was chosen by lot to take a leading role in conducting the war,[108] and the Saxons were all supposed to obey him. However, once the war was over, each of the Saxons lived content with his own power with equal rights under his own law.[109] It is not my purpose to explain the variety of our laws in this book, since a thorough description of the Saxon law can be found in many other works.[110] The Swabians settled the region across the Bode,[111] which they invaded at the time when the Saxons, along with the Lombards, invaded Italy, as their history recounts.[112] It is

104. Rudolf of Fulda, *Translatio s. Alexandri,* ed. G. H. Pertz, MGH SS 2 (Hanover, 1829), 675, records that the Saxons, who were weakened by war, gave up the eastern portions of their lands to be held by others.

105. These are the Ostphalians.

106. This is the region of Engern located in a portion of the modern German states of Lower Saxony and Westphalia.

107. Exodus 1.10.

108. Sallust, *Jugurtha,* 20.

109. See Bede, *Historia ecclesiastica,* 5.10, who comments on the acephalous nature of Saxon political organization.

110. Widukind may be referring here to the *lex Saxonum* that was promulgated by Charlemagne. See *Leges Saxonum und Lex Thuringorum,* ed. Claudius Freiherr von Schwerin, Fontes Iuris Germanci Antiqui in usum Scholarum separatim editi (Hanover, 1918).

111. The Bode is a left tributary of the Saale river, which rises in the Harz mountains. Widukind's suggestion that the Swabians had settled here likely was influenced by the fact that this region of Saxony was known to contemporaries as Schwabengau, i.e., the district of the Swabians.

112. The Lombard invasion of Italy began in 568. See Paul the Deacon, *Historia Langobardorum,* 2.6.

for this reason that the Swabians use different laws than the Saxons. Ultimately, the Saxons experienced varying degrees of Frankish trustworthiness. But it is not necessary for us to discuss this, since much can be found in writing about their deeds. The Saxons remained bound to their ancestral error until the time of Charlemagne.[113]

15. *How Charlemagne converted them to Christianity.*

Not only was Charlemagne the most powerful of kings, his power was equaled by his wisdom. As there was no man in his age who was wiser than he, Charlemagne decided that it was not proper to permit a neighboring and noble people to be bound by vain error. He used every means to bring them to the correct path.[114] He forced them to this, sometimes with seductive enticements, and sometimes with war. Finally, in the thirtieth year of his imperial rule—for he had been transformed from a king into an emperor—he finally obtained the end for which he had not ceased to struggle over these many years.[115] As a consequence, those who had been the companions and friends of the Franks now were their brothers. As we see today, it was as if they had been transformed into one people through their Christian faith.

16. *Regarding Louis, Brun, Otto, and King Conrad.*

The last of the Carolingians who ruled the East Franks was Louis,[116] the son of Arnulf, who was the son of the brother of Charles, the great-grandfather of King Lothar.[117] Louis did not

113. Widukind is observing here that the Saxons remained pagans.

114. The correct path is the Christian faith.

115. Charlemagne (768–814) first campaigned in Saxony in 772, and the last Saxon uprising against Frankish rule took place in 804. Charlemagne was crowned emperor in 800.

116. The title of this chapter refers to King Louis the Child (899–911), Duke Brun of Saxony (866–80), Duke Otto I of Saxony (880–912), and King Conrad I of East Francia (911–18).

117. Widukind makes an error here. Arnulf of Carinthia, king of East Francia (887–99), was the illegitimate son of Carloman (died 880), who was eldest son of

live for many years after marrying Liutgard, the sister of Brun and the great duke Otto.[118] Their father was Liudolf, who traveled to Rome and brought back relics of blessed Pope Innocent.[119] It is from this background that Brun, while he administered the entire duchy of Saxony, led an army against the Danes. Overwhelmed by a sudden flood before he reached the place where the battle was to take place, Brun perished along with the entire army.[120] He left the duchy to his brother, who was inferior to him in age, but who was superior to him in every virtue.[121] King Louis did not have a son. So all of the Franks and Saxons sought to give the royal crown to Otto.[122] He declined the offer as if the burden of rule was too heavy for him. By Otto's counsel, Conrad, formerly duke of the Franks, was anointed as king. However, Otto always and everywhere acted as the one who actually wielded power.[123]

King Louis the German (840–877). Arnulf's uncle was Charles III (died 888), the youngest son of Louis the German. Charles III ruled the entire Frankish Empire for three years (884–87), before being deposed by Arnulf in the eastern kingdom in 887. The great grandfather of King Lothar IV of West Francia (954–86) was King Charles the Bald (840–77), the son of Louis the Pious (814–40), and the grandson of Charlemagne.

118. Liutgard, the daughter of Duke Liudolf of Saxony (c. 850–66), married Louis the Younger (died 882) in 869. This Louis was the second son of King Louis the German.

119. Pope Innocent I (401–17). This translation of relics is recorded by Agius, *Vita Hathumodae,* MGH SS 4, 168.

120. The deaths of Duke Brun, numerous magnates, and an entire Saxon army are recorded in the *Annales Fuldenses, an. 880*. It is clear that Widukind is not drawing on the book of Exodus here since Brun and the Saxons are not being compared to Pharaoh and the Egyptians.

121. Notice here Widukind's deft use of chiasmus.

122. This is Duke Otto of Saxony, the father of King Henry I.

123. Widukind may be alluding here to the letter of Pippin III, while still mayor of the palace, in which he asked Pope Zachary (741–52) if it were proper that the Merovingian king Childeric III (752–54) had the title of king but that he, Pippin, held all of the power. In response, Pope Zachary averred that it would be proper to depose Childeric and for Pippin to assume the royal title.

17. Regarding King Henry.

Otto had a son who was needed by the whole world.[124] The greatest and best of kings, Henry was the first who ruled independently in Saxony. Henry adorned his life with every kind of virtue from his earliest years. From day to day, he grew stronger through his exceptional prudence,[125] and the glory of all of his accomplishments. From his youth, Henry devoted every bit of his strength to bringing glory to his people, and to strengthening peace. When the father saw the wisdom of the youth, and his exceptional judgment, he dispatched Henry with a Saxon levy and the ducal military household against the Daleminzi, whom he himself had fought for many years.[126] The Daleminzi were not able to withstand Henry's attack, and summoned against him the Avars, whom we now call the Hungarians, a people that is exceptionally brutal in war.[127]

18. Regarding the Hungarians, who are also called Avars.

The Avars, as some people believe, are the remainder of the Huns. The Huns derive from the Goths. However, the Goths, as Jordanes tells us, came from an island called Sulza.[128] They are called Goths

124. Henry I became duke of Saxony in 912 and king in 919.

125. Luke 2.52.

126. In a manner consistent with other contemporary authors, such as Flodoard, Widukind distinguishes between men who were mobilized to serve as part-time soldiers or militia on the basis of military obligations dating back to the Merovingian period (and also adopted by the Anglo-Saxons in England) and men who were professional soldiers. When discussing the Saxons, Widukind uses the term *exercitus* to denote the militia men levied for expeditionary military service, and some variation of *milites* to denote the duke's own professional military household. The Daleminzi were a Slavic people living in the region between the middle Saale and the middle Elbe. They were part of the broad confederation of tribes known to contemporaries as the Sorbs.

127. *Annales Corbeienses,* MGH SS 3, 4, records an attack by the Hungarians into Saxony in 906, i.e., six years before Henry became duke in 912. Widukind's description of the Hungarians appears to have borrowed from Vergil, *Aeneid,* 1.14.

128. Jordanes, *De origine actibusque Getarum,* ed. Theodor Mommsen, MGH Auctores antiquissimi 5 (Berlin, 1882), ch. 3, calls the island Scandzia.

because their leader's name was Gotha. Some women with the army were brought before Gotha and accused of working with poisons. They were investigated and found guilty. However, since there were a large number of them, Gotha held back the punishment they deserved, and instead banished them from the army. The exiled women sought out a nearby forest. Since it was bounded by the sea and by the Moetian swamps,[129] there did not appear any way for them to leave. Some of the women were pregnant when they arrived, and some of them now had their babies. These offspring then had more and more children until the people became very large. They lived like wild animals, uncivilized and indomitable, and became exceptionally keen hunters.[130]

After many centuries of living there, they were completely unaware of any other part of the world. But it happened that they found a doe while hunting and pursued it until, following its lead, they crossed through the Moetian swamps on a route that heretofore had remained impassible to any man.[131] Once through, they saw cities and fortifications, and a previously unknown race of men. They then returned along the same path and told their comrades what they had seen. A great many of them then set out, driven by curiosity, to test what they had heard. When the people of the nearby cities and strongholds saw this unknown multitude, whose clothing and appearance seemed horrible, they thought that they were demons and fled. At first, the newcomers were stupefied, amazed at the appearance of these new things, and abstained from murder and rapine. However, since no one resisted them they were overcome by human desire. They murdered a great many people and, from that point on, did not spare anything. After they had taken a huge quantity of booty, they returned to their settlements. But seeing how ev-

129. Roman Moesia was located along the south bank of the Danube river and includes modern Macedonia, southern Serbia, and northern Bulgaria.

130. Widukind may have read about the Amazon-like ancestors of the Avars from Jordanes, *De origine actibusque Getarum*, ch. 44; or from reading Vergil, *Aeneid*, 1.491.

131. This topos of the doe leading the army safely across a barrier may have been borrowed from Gregory of Tours, *Historiae*, 2.37, where a deer leads Clovis's army across a ford before the battle of Vouillé against the Visigoths.

erything had fallen to them, they returned with their wives, children, and all of their farming equipment. They devastated all the peoples who lived nearby, and finally began to settle in Pannonia.[132]

19. The Hungarians were confined by Charlemagne, but were set free by Arnulf.

The Hungarians were defeated by Charlemagne, driven across the Danube river, enclosed within a huge wall, and prohibited from raiding other peoples in their customary manner.[133] However, during the reign of Arnulf,[134] this work was undone, and a path was opened up for them to renew their killing since the emperor angered Zwentibold, the king of the Moravians.[135] The great slaughter and tremendous injuries inflicted by the Hungarians on the Frankish empire are attested by the cities and regions that remain desolate up to the present day. We judge it useful to provide information about this people so that your highness will understand the kind of people against whom your grandfather and father fought, and from what kind of enemies almost all of Europe has been liberated by strength of your grandfather's and father's wisdom and under their banners.[136]

20. How the Hungarians devastated Saxony.

The Hungarian army, mentioned above, was guided by the Slavs and inflicted great slaughter in Saxony.[137] After taking huge quanti-

132. This erstwhile Roman province is located in the western half of modern Hungary.

133. In this case, Widukind actually is talking about the Avars. The discussion here relates to Charlemagne's campaigns against the Avars in 790–92. Regarding Charlemagne's supposed enclosure of the Avars/Hungarians, also see Liutprand of Cremona, *Liudprandi Cremonensis Opera Omnia: Antapodosis, Homelia Paschalis, Historia Ottonis, Relatio de Legatione Constantinopolitana,* ed. P. Chiesa (Turnholt, 1998), here *Antapodosis,* 1.5; and in English, *The Complete Works of Liudprand of Cremona,* ed. and trans. Paolo Squatriti (Washington, D. C., 2007).

134. King Arnulf of East Francia (887–99).

135. Zwentibold or Svatopluk I (871–94).

136. The phrase *armorum insignia* may refer to the symbols on the shields or armor of the Ottonian troops, most likely images of the cross, or to battle standards.

137. This raid likely refers to a major Hungarian attack that was undertaken in

ties of booty, they returned to Daleminzia and met another Hungarian army there. The second Hungarian army threatened to make war on the allies of the first army because they refused to provide help to them,[138] while leading the first army to such great plunder. So it happened that Saxony was laid waste a second time by the Hungarians. The first army awaited the second in Daleminzia, and by their presence caused such a dearth of food that the Daleminzi were forced that year to leave their own homes and serve other nations to obtain sustenance.

21. Henry became duke of Saxony.

When the father of the fatherland and great duke Otto died,[139] he left to his illustrious and magnificent son Henry ducal power in all of Saxony. Otto had two other sons, named Thankmar and Liudolf, but they had died before their father. However, King Conrad had often experienced the strength of the new duke, and feared to grant him all of his father's power. Because of this, Conrad incurred the indignation of the entire Saxon army.[140] Conrad deceptively said many things in praise of the glory of the great duke Otto, and promised that he would give even greater reward to Henry, and would honor him with an even greater office. However, the Saxons did not listen to these insincere offers, and persuaded their duke that if Conrad did not wish to honor Henry willingly with his father's office, Henry would be able to have what he wished against the king's will. For his part, the king realized that the Sax-

908. See Adalbert of Magdeburg, *Reginonis abbatis Prumiensis Chronicon cum continuatione Treverensi*, ed. F. Kurze, MGH Scriptores rerum germanicarum in usum scholarum (hereafter, SRG) 50 (Hanover, 1890), *an.* 908; and in English translation, *History and Politics in Late Carolingian and Ottonian Europe: The Chronicle of Regino of Prüm and Adalbert of Magdeburg*, ed. and trans. Simon MacLean (Manchester, 2009).

138. The Daleminzi apparently refused to help some of the Hungarians, although they had already helped other Hungarian raiders.

139. Duke Otto of Saxony died in 912.

140. The term "army" (*exercitus*) is to be understood as all Saxon men of arms-bearing age, who were required, on the basis of their wealth, to serve in the expeditionary levy. The implication here is that the right to participate politically was limited to those who bore arms.

ons now regarded him in even more suspect manner than was their custom, and knew that he would not be able to defeat the duke in a publicly sanctioned war because the latter was supported by a powerful military household and an exceptionally large military levy.[141] So Conrad took action to have Henry killed by some kind of trick.

22. *Regarding Henry, Bishop Hatto, and Count Adalbert.*

VERSION B

The most appropriate man for this task, as it is said, was the bishop of the see of Mainz, named Hatto.[142] He was born into a socially obscure family, but had a sharp intelligence. However, it was difficult to determine whether his advice led to better or worse ends. This can be seen from one of his deeds. For there was struggle between Conrad, the father of King Conrad, and Adalbert,[143] Henry's nephew from his sister.[144] The first killed was Adalbert's brother.[145] Then, Conrad was killed by Adalbert in revenge for the death of his brother.[146] None of the kings were able to calm this

141. Widukind is distinguishing here between the *milites* and the *exercitus.* The term *bellum publicum,* or publicly sanctioned war, would appear to draw on the terminology utilized in contemporary penitential literature that distinguished between just and unjust conflict. See the discussion of penances imposed on fighting men by David S. Bachrach, *Religion and the Conduct of War, c. 300–c. 1215* (Woodbridge, 2003).

142. Archbishop Hatto I of Mainz (891–913).

143. This is the so-called Babenberger feud, a struggle for power in eastern Franconia between the Conradine family and the Franconian branch of the Babenberger family. On one side were the three brothers Adalbert (c. 854–906), Adalhard (died 903), and Henry (died 902), the sons of Henry of Babenberg (died 886) and the nephews of Poppo (died 906) who held high office in Thuringia during the reign of Charles III. On the other side were four brothers, Conrad the Elder (died 906), Eberhard (died 902), Gerhard (died 910), and Rudolf I (died 908), the sons of Count Udo of Lahngau (died 879), who provided crucial support to Arnulf of Carinthia in his coup d'état against Charles III in 887. See the discussion by Regino, *Chronicon, an.* 902.

144. Hadwig, the wife of Duke Otto of Saxony, was the sister of the Babenberger brothers Adalbert, Adalhard, and Henry.

145. Adalbert's brother Henry fell in battle against the Conradines in 903. The third brother Adalhard was captured and then beheaded in revenge for the death of the Conradine Eberhard in the same battle.

146. Conrad the Elder was killed on February 27, 906 at the battle of Fritzlar. See Regino of Prüm, *Chronicon, an.* 906.

enormous struggle between such powerful men.[147] Therefore, the highest priest was sent to resolve this very great discord.[148] He entered Adalbert's fortress, and promised under oath that he would make peace between Adalbert and the king, and then bring Adalbert safely back to his own property.[149] Adalbert accepted this agreement, and asked that Hatto deign to have something to eat as a demonstration of his grace and friendship.[150] But Hatto refused, and immediately departed the stronghold.

After he had passed through the outer fortress,[151] with his entire entourage, Hatto is reported to have shouted, "Alas, one often desires what one has already refused when offered. I am wearied by the length of this journey, and the lateness of the hour. We cannot spend the whole day traveling while fasting." Adalbert happily bowed to the archbishop's knees and asked him to return to the fortress to have something to eat. The bishop returned with Adalbert, and considered himself freed from the bond of his oath since he had brought him back safe to his own property. After this, Adalbert was presented to the king by the bishop, and was sentenced to death.[152]

What is more vile than this act of treachery? But it is true that by cutting off this one head, the heads of many other people were saved. And what is better than advice that resolves conflict and

147. Louis the Child (899–911) was the only king during the period of this conflict, and his main supporters were the Conradines and their allies, including Archbishop Hatto of Mainz.

148. Archbishop Hatto of Mainz.

149. This sequence of events took place in 906 during King Louis's siege of Adalbert's fortress at Obertheres, near the modern city of Haßfurt in the northern Bavarian district of Unterfranken. See the discussion of these events by Liudprand, *Antapodosis*, 2.6.

150. Sharing a meal was a common means of demonstrating publicly that the participants had made peace. See the discussion by Gerd Althoff, "Der frieden-bündnis- und gemeinschaftstiftende Charakter des Mahles im früheren Mittelalter," in *Essen und Trinken in Mittelalter und Neuzeit*, ed. Irmgard Bitsch, Trude Ehlert, and Xenja von Ertzdorff (Sigmaringen, 1997), 13–25.

151. Widukind is contrasting here the *oppidum* or outer fortress (*Vorburg*) with the *urbs* or main fortification (*Hauptburg*).

152. King Louis ordered Adalbert to be executed in 906.

brings peace? And so, with this same fickleness,[153] Hatto approached the man who was granted to us as our own through the mercy of the Highest,[154] and had a golden torque made for him, and invited him to a meal, so that Hatto might honor him with generous gifts. In the meantime, the bishop went to the goldsmith to see the work, and is reported to have groaned when he saw the torque. The smith asked Hatto why he had groaned. He responded that this torque would be stained by the blood of a great man, and one dear to him, namely Henry.

The smith kept silent about what he had heard. But when the work was completed and delivered, the smith asked for and received permission to go on a journey. The smith then went to the duke, who was traveling on the business just mentioned,[155] and told him what he had heard. Henry, who was very angry, summoned the bishop's messenger, who had come some time earlier to issue an invitation, and said: "Go, tell Hatto that Henry does not have a harder neck than Adalbert, and that we think it is better for us to remain at home and consider how we might serve him, than to burden him excessively with our enormous entourage."[156]

Henry immediately seized all of the lands in Saxony and Thuringia that belonged to Hatto. Henry then overwhelmed with frequent attacks Burchard and Bardo, one of whom was the brother-in-law of the king.[157] Henry subsequently divided up their lands

153. All of chapter 22 up to this point is missing from the C version of Widukind's text. In place of this section, C has: "At this time, the bishop in the see of Mainz was named Hatto. He offered sharp counsel, and was very clever. Through his customary mercurial behavior, he led many people to their deaths. Then, wishing to please King Conrad and the Frankish people at the same time, in his customary manner," followed by the B version of the text for the remainder of the chapter.

154. The reference here is to King Henry, whom Widukind claims was granted to the Saxons by God.

155. Henry was traveling to visit Archbishop Hatto at Mainz.

156. Version C adds the following sentence here: "It is said that Adalbert once received security from this bishop, and was deceived by him. But because we cannot confirm this, and have not been able to corroborate the story, we think that it is more likely a fiction taken from common rumors."

157. Burchard and Bardo were the sons of Duke Burchard of Thuringia and the

and possessions among his own soldiers. Hatto, when he saw that his clever plans had come to nothing, died a few days later overcome by sadness and illness. There are those who say that Hatto was struck by lightning from the sky, and weakened by this blow, died three days later.

VERSION A

Some of the king's friends devised plots against Henry. These plots were exposed, however, by a smith who was making a golden torque to be used in this deception. One of the plotters came to the goldsmith to see the work being done and, after he had examined it, is reported to have let out a deep groan. When the smith asked about the reason for such a groan, he received this response, namely that in a short time this torque would be stained by the blood of that best of men, Henry. The smith, acting as if he took no notice of what was said, kept his silence. However, when the work was completed, he asked for and received permission to go on a journey. He met the duke at a place called Kassel,[158] and asked Henry in secret why he had come. Henry answered that he had been invited to a feast where he would be honored, and that he wished to go to this event. The goldsmith then straightaway told Henry what he had heard, and kept the duke from completing his journey.

Henry summoned the messenger, who had just arrived to issue the invitation, and ordered him to give thanks to his lords for this well-intended invitation, but noted that he could not come at present to visit them because of some unexpected attacks by the barbarians.[159] Otherwise, however, he would remain their servant without any hesitation. Henry then marched east after mobilizing

Sorbian March (892–908). It is not known which of them was King Conrad's brother-in-law. Henry I's attacks against them were intended to secure his position as the dominant figure in Thuringia, a role earlier filled by his father, Otto, from 908 to 912.

158. Kassel is located on the Fulda river in the northern part of the modern German state of Hessen.

159. The reference here likely is to Slavs.

his forces and occupied all the lands located throughout Saxony and Thuringia that belonged to Hatto, who was bishop of Mainz at that time. He then overwhelmed Burchard and Bardo, one of whom was the brother-in-law of the king, with so many raids that they gave up their lands. Henry then distributed all of their possessions among his soldiers. Hatto, seeing that all of his plots had come to nothing, and that the Saxons were flourishing, was overcome equally by great sadness and disease, and died a few days later. He was a man of great wisdom, and during the reign of Louis the Child, he kept a sharp eye on the empire of the Franks.[160] He resolved many conflicts in the kingdom, and he adorned the cathedral at Mainz with a noble construction.[161]

23. *Regarding King Conrad and his brother Eberhard.*

The king then sent his brother[162] with an army into Saxony to devastate the duchy. As he approached the fortress of Eresburg,[163] Eberhard is reported to have spoken quite arrogantly because he had no greater worry than that the Saxons would not dare to show themselves outside their walls, and, consequently, deprive him of the chance to fight them. No sooner had he spoken,[164] than behold, the Saxons attacked him a mile from the fortress. After the battle had begun, so many Franks were killed that the bards asked where was there a hell big enough to hold such a great number of dead? Thus, the king's brother, Eberhard, was freed from his fear that the Saxons would not show themselves, for he saw them standing before him. Shamefully driven off by the Saxons, Eberhard then fled.

160. The implication is that Duke Henry was busy collecting intelligence about affairs in the Frankish kingdom.

161. Archbishop Hatto consecrated the Cathedral of St. John at Mainz in 911. This cathedral was replaced by Archbishop Willigs (975–1011) with a new structure dedicated to St. Martin.

162. Duke Eberhard of Franconia (918–39).

163. This fortress was located in Obermarsberg, a neighborhood in the modern city of Marsberg in the German state of North-Rhine-Westphalia. The fortress was constructed on a promontory above the Diemel river, a left tributary of the Weser. *Annales Corbeienses, an.* 915, records a "bellum in Heresburg."

164. See Daniel 4.28 for the likely source of this idiom.

24. Conrad besieges Henry.

When the king learned of his brother's defeat, he mobilized the entire military strength of the Franks and set forth to seek Henry. Then, when Conrad discovered that Henry was defending the fortress called Grone, the king attempted to besiege him there.[165] Conrad dispatched a messenger to discuss Henry's voluntary surrender. Conrad promised that he would be Henry's friend and would not treat him as though he were an enemy. Then Thietmar, coming from the east, met this messenger.[166] Thietmar was a man singularly experienced in the study of war,[167] having a wide variety of talents, and offering very good counsel. Moreover, he surpassed most men with his inborn shrewdness. Thietmar approached the king's messengers and asked where his army ought to set up camp. Henry, who had been persuaded to surrender to the Franks, now took heart hearing about the army, because he believed that it was there. But Thietmar was spinning a tall tale. He had come with just five men. But when the duke asked how many legions he had brought with him,[168] Thietmar responded that he could marshal almost thirty legions.[169] The messengers, who had been fooled by this display,

165. Grone was a fortified royal palace complex dating to the Carolingian period. The main part of the fortress consisted of a rectangular stone fortification measuring 110 meters by 120 meters. The bailey (*Vorburg*) at Grone was protected by a rectangular earth and timber wall measuring 150 meters by 100 meters. See Thomas Zotz, "Die Goslarer Pfalz im Umfeld der königlichen Herrschaftssistze in Sachsen. Topographie, Architektur und historische Bedeutung," in "Deutsche Königspfalzen: Beiträge zu ihrer historischen und archäologischen Erforschung vierter Band: Pfalzen—Reichsgut-Königshöfe," ed. Lutz Fenske (Göttingen, 1996), 248–87, here 259.

166. This is likely Count Thietmar of the *pagus* of Nordthüringen.

167. Widukind would appear to have borrowed the phrase *disciplinae militaris peritissimus* from Caesar, *Comentarii de bello Gallico,* 1.21, where the Roman general described P. Considius as a man who was held to be a man *rei militaris peritissimus* in the armies of both Sulla and Crassus. This phrase was to have an active *Nachleben* taken up by a number of classical authors, including Lucius Ampelius, who used Caesar's description of P. Considius to describe King Pyrrus, whom he identified as "Omnium Graecorum sapientissimus et militaris disciplinae peritissimus fuit." See Lucius Ampelius, *Liber Memorialis,* ed. Eduard von Woelfflin (Leipzig, 1873), ch. 28.

168. Widukind's standard term for a military unit commanded by a senior military officer is a *legio.*

169. The Latin here is *legiones.*

returned to the king. In this manner, Thietmar conquered with his wit those whom Duke Henry himself could not conquer by arms. Before first light, the Franks abandoned their encampment, and each one returned to his own home.[170]

25. King Conrad's conversation before his death.

The king then marched into Bavaria and fought against Arnulf.[171] It was there, as they say, that Conrad was wounded and returned to his fatherland. When he realized that he was dying and, just as importantly, that he had lost his earlier good fortune, Conrad summoned his brother, who had come to visit him, and addressed him in this manner: "I know my brother," he said, "that I am not able to hold on to this life much longer. God, who ordains such things, has ordered it, and I am overcome by a serious illness. Therefore, consider this matter that affects you the most, reflect on what is required by the entire kingdom of the Franks, and accept the advice of your brother. We have the ability to mobilize and lead professional soldiers and the levy. We have fortresses, and arms, and the royal insignia. We have everything that is required of kings[172] other than good luck and a suitable temperament. Good fortune along with the most noble of qualifications has passed to Henry. So the height of public power in the state has passed, in turn, to the Saxons. Take up these insignia, the holy lance, the golden buckles with their cloak, the sword of the ancient kings, and crown, and go to Henry. Make peace with him so that you can have a perpetual compact with him.[173] Why should the Frankish people, along with you, die at his hands? For truly, he will be king and emperor of many peoples."[174]

170. This is a full demobilization of the expeditionary levy and military households of magnates loyal to the king.

171. Duke Arnulf of Bavaria (907–37). King Conrad I's struggle against Duke Arnulf is recorded in *Annales Alamannici, an.* 918, MGH SS 1, 56; *Annales Iuvavenses maximi, an.* 917, MGH SS 30.2, 742; and Adalbert of Magdeburg, *Continuatio, an.* 917.

172. Sallus, *Jugurtha,* 33.72.

173. Widukind uses the term *foederatus* for the Franks, which makes clear that they now held a subordinate position to the Saxons.

174. Widukind is employing here the model of an emperor as one who rules over several peoples.

After Conrad had spoken, his brother responded, weeping, that he would agree. After this, the king died.[175] Conrad was a brave and powerful man, effective both in managing the kingdom and in prosecuting war.[176] He was generous and cheerful, and outstanding in all of the virtues. He was buried in his city of Weilburg to the tears and mourning of all of the Franks.[177]

26. *Eberhard establishes Henry as king.*

As the king had ordered, Eberhard went to Henry, and placed himself and the entire royal treasury at his disposal. Eberhard made peace and earned Henry's friendship, which he maintained on friendly and faithful terms until the end of Henry's life. Then, when all of the leaders and magnates of the army of the Franks[178] had gathered in a place called Fritzlar, Eberhard designated Henry as king before the entire Frankish and Saxon people.[179] However, when the highest priest, who at this time was Heriger,[180] offered Henry unction along with the crown, Henry did not spurn the offer, but also did not accept it. He said, "It is enough for me that I am called and designated as king in front of my magnates by God's will and your favor. Unction and a crown are for those who

175. King Conrad died on December 23, 918.

176. The phrase *domi militiaque* recalls Livy, *Ab urbe condita,* 6.41, where the author discusses taking the auguries before doing anything in war or peace, at home or in the field ("bello ac pace domi militiaeque"). This phrase also was used frequently by Sallust, *Catilinae,* 5, 6, 9, 53.

177. Weilburg is located in the valley of the Lahn river near the confluence of the Lahn with its left tributary, the Weil, which gives the city its name. See the discussion of this fortification by Reinhard Friedrich, "Ottonenzeitliche Befestigungen im Rheinland und im Rhein-Main-Gebiet," *Europa im 10. Jahrhundert: Archäologie einer Aufbruchszeit,* ed. Joachim Henning (Mainz, 2002), 351–63, here 360.

178. The assembly took place in mid-May 919. Widukind is distinguishing here between those who hold offices (i.e., *principes*) and those who were powerful because of the wealth and prestige of their families (i.e., *maiores natu*). This same distinction is drawn by Emperor Arnulf of Carinthia in a circular letter issued to all of the officeholders and magnates in Saxony. See *Die Urkunden Arnolfs,* ed. Paul Kehr. MGH Diplomata regum Germaniae ex stirpe Karolinorum 3 (Berlin, 1940), nr. 155.

179. Fritzlar is located on the north bank of the Eder river near the Franconian frontier with Saxony.

180. Archbishop Heriger of Mainz (913–27).

are better than we are. We judge that we are not worthy of such an honor." This speech was well received by the entire crowd.[181] Raising their right arms toward heaven, they crowded around greeting the new king with a great shout.

27. After he became king, Henry quickly restored the disordered kingdom.

After Henry had become king in this manner, he marched with his whole force to fight against Burchard, the duke of Swabia.[182] Burchard, although a fearsome warrior, realized, because he was also a very prudent man, that he would not be able to withstand an attack by the king. So he submitted himself, as well as all of his fortresses and his people to Henry.

After this success, Henry marched to Bavaria where Arnulf ruled as duke. Henry found Arnulf defending the city, which is called Regensburg, and besieged him there.[183] When Arnulf realized that he could not resist the king, he opened the gates and went out to meet the king. He submitted himself and his entire duchy to Henry.[184] Arnulf was received honorably by Henry and named a friend of the king.[185]

From this point on, the king continually gained strength and prospered.[186] As he grew ever more powerful, he gained in both prestige and reputation. After he had restored, pacified, and uni-

181. Acts 6.5.

182. Duke Burchard II of Swabia (917–26).

183. Widukind is telescoping events here. Although Henry may have invaded Bavaria in 919, shortly after the surrender of Burchard, the final settlement with Duke Arnulf did not come until 921. For an invasion in 919, see *Annales Iuvavenses maximi, an.* 920 (= 919). For the second campaign in 921, see Liudprand, *Antapodosis,* 2.21; and *Fragmentum de Arnulfo duce Bavariae,* MG SS 17, 570.

184. Widukind uses the traditional Carolingian political term *regnum* to denote Bavaria.

185. Widukind uses the term *amicus* in the Roman sense of a subordinate ally. Gerd Althoff, in *Amicitia und pacta: Bündnis, Einung, Politik und Gebetsgedenken im beginnenden 10. Jahrhundert* (Hanover, 1992) postulates, using this example among several, that Henry I developed a new style of rule based on a novel concept of friendship. This argument is largely unconvincing, as demonstrated in the detailed analysis of the question by Susanne Kaeding, Britta Kümmerlen, and Kerstin Seidel, "Heinrich I.—ein 'Freundschaftskönig,'" *Concilium medii aevi* 3 (2000): 265–326.

186. 1 Samuel 2.26.

fied the kingdom, which had been troubled on all sides by both civil and external wars, Henry marched against Gaul and the kingdom of Lothar.[187]

28. Regarding Louis and his sons.

Lothar was the son of Emperor Louis,[188] the son of Charlemagne.[189] Lothar's brothers were Charles and Louis.[190] Charles received the regions of Aquitaine and Gascony whose frontiers were marked in the west by the Spanish city of Barcelona, in the north by the English Channel, in the south by the Alpine summits, and on the east by the Meuse river. The region between the Meuse and the Rhine was granted as a kingdom to Lothar. Louis's kingdom extended from the Rhine to the frontiers of Illyricum and Pannonia,[191] and from the Eider river to the frontier with the Danes.[192] These brothers fought a famous battle at Fontenoy before this division of the kingdom took place.[193] However, once the division took place, it remained inviolable, until all of these kingdoms came by right of inheritance to Charles,[194] the great-grandfather of Lothar, as we mentioned above.[195]

29. Regarding Charles, Odo, and their successors.

One of the east Franks, a man named Odo, who was brave and wise, came to Charles and offered a plan to defeat the Danes, who had disturbed Charles's kingdom for many years.[196] And so it happened that on one day, as many as one hundred thousand of the

187. These are the West Frankish kingdom and Lotharingia.

188. Emperor Louis the Pious (814–40).

189. Lothar I (840–55).

190. Charles the Bald (840–77) and Louis the German (840–76).

191. These areas correspond roughly with modern Albania and western Hungary.

192. The division of the Carolingian Empire was the result of the Treaty of Verdun in 843.

193. The battle of Fontenoy took place on June 25, 841.

194. Emperor Charles III was the last Carolingian to rule the united empire.

195. Widukind incorrectly identified Charles III as the great-grandfather of Lothar IV above in 1.16.

196. King Charles III the Simple of West Francia (898–923; died 929) and King Odo or Eudes of West Francia (888–98).

Danes were killed.[197] Because of this success, Odo gained renown and distinction, and was considered second only to the king, not least because Odo was content to have just a single servant in his entourage when he visited Charles.[198]

However, as Charles was dying, he ordered Odo to be mindful of the favor that he had shown him, and to have pity on Charles's son if one should be born to him. For Charles did not yet have a son at this time, but the queen was pregnant. When a son was born after the death of the father, Odo named him king, and gave him his father's name.[199] But Emperor Arnulf, who had expelled the elder Charles from Germany, gained control over the entire kingdom following the latter's death.[200] Odo obtained the crown, scepter, and other royal regalia from Arnulf, and received the power of command by the grace of his lord, Emperor Arnulf.[201] It is for this reason that even up to the present there is conflict between the Carolingians and Odo's descendants, and also conflict between the Carolingian kings and the east Franks regarding the kingdom of Lothar.[202]

197. While just a duke, Odo gained his reputation as a military leader during the Viking siege of Paris in 886.

198. Widukind may have been thinking here of Sulpicius Severus, *Vita Martini*, 2, where the saint is described as being content to have just a single *servus* as his companion. For an English translation of this text, see *The Life of Saint Martin of Tours*, trans. F. R. Hoare, in *Soldiers of Christ: Saints and Saints' Lives from Late Antiquity and the Early Middle Ages*, ed. Thomas F. X. Noble and Thomas Head (London, 1995), 31–74.

199. Widukind has confused matters here. Charles III was born half a year after the death of his father, Louis II the Stammerer (877–79). However, Louis II was succeeded by his two older sons, Louis III (died 882) and Carloman II (died 884). Emperor Charles III then ruled the entire Carolingian Empire in the period 884–87, before being deposed by Arnulf of Carinthia. The West Franks then chose Odo as their king, who ruled from 888 to 898.

200. Arnulf certainly exercised power as the hegemonic figure in the kingdoms of the erstwhile Carolingian Empire. However, he was never ruler in West Francia.

201. Widukind's use of the phrase *imperium obtinere* has clear classical connotations, indicating that only Arnulf, as emperor, had the authority to delegate the power of command, i.e., *imperium*.

202. This is the struggle between the Carolingians and the Ottonians to control Lotharingia.

30. How Henry obtained the kingdom of the Lotharingians.

It was for this reason that King Henry marched against Charles,[203] and frequently defeated his army, as fortune aided this brave man.[204] For Hugh,[205] whose father Robert,[206] the son of Odo, had been killed by Charles's army, sent a message to Charles, captured him by trickery, and kept him in official custody until the end of his life.[207] When King Henry learned of Charles's fate, he was saddened and marveled at the variability of fate that is the common lot of man, because Charles was no less distinguished by his piety than by his strength in arms.

Henry decided that it would be preferable to avoid combat and hoped, instead, to overcome the Lotharingians through diplomacy. For they were a mercurial people much given to intrigue, prompt to go to war, and inclined toward novelty. At that time there was a man among the Lotharingians named Christian who, seeing that the king always succeeded, sought some way to gain the king's grace.[208] So, pretending that he was ill, Christian summoned Gislebert, who had become ruler of the region as the suc-

203. King Charles III of West Francia and Lotharingia, often denoted by scholars as Charles the Simple, not to be confused with his older contemporary Charles III the Fat.

204. For another perspective regarding King Henry's conquest of Lotharingia, see *Les Annales de Flodoard*, ed. Ph. Lauer (Paris, 1905), *an.* 920–23. For an English translation of this text, see *The Annals of Flodoard of Rheims, 916–919*, trans. and ed. Steven Fanning and Bernard S. Bachrach (Peterborough, 2004). Widukind's language here echoes Livy, *Ab urbe condita*, 34.37; and Terrence, *Phormio*, 1.4.25.

205. Widukind is here confusing Hugh the Great (898–956) with Count Heribert II of Vermandois (died 943).

206. Count Robert, the brother of King Odo, rebelled against Charles III in 923, and was killed at the battle of Soissons on June 15 of that year. Robert's son was Hugh the Great, the father of Hugh Capet, the first king of the Capetian dynasty from 987 to 996.

207. Count Heribert II captured King Charles III in August 923, and kept him in custody until the latter's death on October 7, 929. Widukind is drawing here on an image in Acts 5.18.

208. Christian appears as a count in surviving documents between 919 and 928. See the discussion by Robert Parisot, *Le royaume de Lorraine sous les Carolingiens, 843–923* (Paris, 1899), 626n2.

cessor to his father,[209] captured him by trickery, and sent him under guard to King Henry. As this Gislebert was born into a noble lineage and an ancient family, the king happily received him, and judged that through Gislebert he had gained the entire duchy of Lotharingia. But then seeing that the youth was very industrious, and was distinguished by his lineage, power, and wealth, Henry began to treat him well. Finally, Henry betrothed his daughter Gerberga to Gislebert and thus joining Gislebert to himself through marriage as well as through friendship, Henry assigned all of Lotharingia to him.

31. Regarding the sons of King Henry and Queen Mathilda and her line of descent.

The distinguished, most noble, and singularly wise queen, named Mathilda, bore him several sons.[210] The firstborn, the love of the world, was named Otto. The second was marked with his father's name, the brave and industrious man, Henry.[211] The third born was named Brun, whom we see holding the office of the highest priest and of a great duke.[212] Let no one say that Brun bears some guilt for this, since we read that Samuel, the saint, and many others were both priests and judges.[213] Mathilda also bore another daughter who married Duke Hugh.[214]

209. Gislebert (died 939) was the son of Count Reginar I (died 915), who had held the dominant position in lower Lotharingia during the reign of Louis the Child, and then prepared the way for Charles III to gain control of the duchy in 911. Gislebert became duke of Lotharingia in 928, and married Henry I's daughter Gerberga (914–85) about this same time.

210. Henry I's second wife Mathilda died in 968, about the time that Widukind was completing his first version of the *Res gestae.*

211. Henry (919–55) was duke of Bavaria from 948 until his death.

212. Brun (925–65) became archbishop of Cologne in July 953 and duke of Lotharingia from September 953 until his death.

213. There was some contemporary concern about Brun serving as both archbishop and duke. Brun's biographer Ruotger, *Vita Brunonis,* ed. Walter Berschin and Angelika Häse (Heidelberg, 1993), worked diligently throughout his text to excuse this apparent conflict.

214. This is Hadwig (910–65), who married Hugh the Great in 937. She is named in a royal charter issued by Henry I on May 9, 935. See DH I, nr. 37.

The lady queen was the daughter of Thiadrich, whose brothers were Widukind, Immed, and Reginbern. Reginberg was the one who fought against those Danes, who had been devastating Saxony for a long time, and defeated them, freeing his fatherland from their attacks up to the present day.[215] These brothers were descended from the great leader Widukind, who waged war against Charlemagne for almost thirty years.[216]

32. Regarding the Hungarians and their captive, and that because of him peace was concluded for nine years.

When the civil wars finally ended, the Hungarians again raided all of Saxony, burning cities and strongholds, and carrying out such a great slaughter everywhere that they threatened to destroy the region entirely.[217] The king was defending a fortress called Werla,[218] because he did not yet trust his still untrained military forces, who were unaccustomed to open battle, to engage such a savage enemy.[219] The Hungarians carried out such a slaughter during those days and burned so many monasteries that we judge it better to remain silent rather than to repeat our calamities. However, it happened that one of the leaders of the Hungarians was captured and carried bound to the king. The Hungarians prized

215. The date for this battle cannot be ascertained from the surviving sources.

216. The Saxon wars as a whole lasted for thirty years. However, Widukind participated for only a decade.

217. This raid took place in 924.

218. Werla, now Werlaburgdorf, is located in the Wolfenbüttel district of the German state of Lower Saxony. Under Henry I and Otto I this site boasted a very large palace complex dating back to the Carolingian period. It was protected by three sets of fortifications enclosing some eighteen hectares. See the discussion by Hermann Schroller, "Die Ausgrabung der Pfalz Werla und ihre Probleme," *Deutsche Königspfalzen: Beiträge zu ihrer historischen und archäologischen Erforschung*, vol. 2 (Göttingen, 1965), 140–49; and Adolf Gauer, "Das Palatium der Pfalz Werla. Archäologischer Befund und schriftliche Überlieferung," in *Deutsche Königspfalzen: Beiträge zur ihrer historischen und archäeologischen Erforschung*, vol. 3 (Göttingen, 1979), 263–77.

219. Widukind is describing here the military forces available to Henry at Werla in 924, not the entirety of the king's military forces. See Bernard S. Bachrach and David S. Bachrach, "Saxon Military Revolution, 912–973? Myth and Reality," *Early Medieval Europe* 15 (2007): 186–222.

him greatly, and offered up an immense weight in gold and silver for his return. The king, spurning their gold, demanded peace instead. When he finally had this, Henry returned the captive with other gifts, and peace was then established for the next nine years.

33. Regarding the hand of Dionysius the martyr.

When the king crossed the Rhine to spread his rule over the Lotharingians, a messenger came to him from Charles and, after greeting him with humble words, said: "My lord Charles, once possessing royal power, and now deprived of it, sent me to tell you that nothing would be sweeter to him or bring him more joy, now that he is surrounded by enemies, than to hear something about the glory of your magnificent success, and to be consoled by reports of your strength. And he sent this to you as a symbol of his faith and sincerity." The messenger then withdrew from his pouch the hand of the precious martyr Dionysius, contained in gold and gems.[220] He then said, "Take this token of our perpetual compact and mutual love. He wished to share with you this part of the sole solace of those Franks who inhabit Gaul now that the distinguished martyr Vitus has deserted us, to our loss, and has gone to Saxony for your perpetual peace.[221] For since his body was taken from us, we have experienced ceaseless civil and external wars. Indeed, in the same year both the Danes and the Northmen invaded our region." The king receiving this divine gift with every possible thanks, prostrated himself before the holy relics, and kissing them, venerated them with the greatest reverence.

34. Regarding Saint Vitus the martyr.

The famous martyr, about whom Charles's messenger spoke, was born to a noble but pagan family in the province of Lycia.[222]

220. This is St. Dionysius the Areopagite whose feast day is October 9.

221. The relics of St. Vitus were transferred to the monastery of Corvey in 836. See the discussion in the *Annales Corbeienses, an.* 836.

222. This chapter is a condensed version of the *Passio Sancti Viti,* first written around 600. The full text is published in *Acta Sanctorum* 20, no. 2 (June 15): 1021–23.

His father brought him before Valerian, the governor of the province, who forced him to make an offering before images of their gods. In the meantime, however, the governor lost the use of his hand, which was then restored to health through Vitus's prayers. The arms of the executioners also grew withered, but they were restored by the merits of this martyr. When the father saw that Vitus laughed at torture, he brought him home and locked him in a small room filled with every type of delicacy.[223] It was here that Hylas, this was the name of the father, went blind when he saw some secret rites. Thus overcome, the father renounced idols, and acknowledged Christ.

However, once he had regained his sight through his son Vitus's merits, Hylas denied Christ and sought to kill his son. Warned and led by an angel, Modestus, his now aged teacher, gathered up the boy, sailed across the sea, and arrived at the Sele river.[224] There they rested under a tree busying themselves with prayers as eagles brought them their daily nourishment. The boy preached Christ to the people who visited them, and converted many of them, leading them to undergo baptism. After this, he set off for Rome, having been summoned by the caesar Diocletian.[225] After the emperor's son had been freed from a demon by Vitus's prayers, Vitus was supposed to make an offering of incense to the gods. Because Vitus responded harshly to the emperor, he was thrown to the beasts, but was not harmed by them. Vitus was then thrown into a burning furnace, but he left unharmed as an angel calmed the flames. He was then cast into prison bound with enormous iron chains, but he was visited there by the Lord and by a crowd of angels. Finally, he was pressed into a torture device known as a *catasta,* along with Modestus and a certain noblewoman named Crescen-

---

Lycia is located in modern Turkey. The manuscript of the *Passio* used by Widukind evidently mistakenly identified Lycia rather than Sicily as the birthplace of Vitus.

223. The father apparently was hoping to overwhelm Vitus's efforts to live a simple life.

224. This river flows through Campania in southwestern Italy from its headwaters in Monti Picentini.

225. In the tetrarchy system, Diocletian was an *augustus* rather than a *caesar.*

tia. When all of their tortured bones had been broken, they were consoled by Christ. For the torturers were struck by bolts from heaven, and were terrified by a great burst of thunder, and fled from Vitus. Suddenly Vitus found himself in the place where earlier he had preached, because an angel of the Lord had brought him there. Then, after they had said their final prayers, they gave their souls up to heaven.

A certain noblewoman named Florentina buried their bodies in that same place, which is called Marianus. I am recounting to your highness Vitus's final prayer so that you will understand how you might burn with love for him, and that by the ardor of this love, you might earn his eternal patronage. "Lord Jesus Christ," he said, "living son of God, perfect the desire of their hearts, and free them from every impediment of this age, and lead them to your glory. Do this for all those who glorify you for my sake, and who wish to gain glory from the passion of my martyrdom." After he spoke, there came a divine promise that everything he requested would be granted.

After a long time had passed, a certain man named Fulrad[226] came to Rome. After reading the deeds of this precious martyr, Fulrad found the location of his tomb. Going there, Fulrad took the sacred relics, and bore them to the district of Paris.[227] During the reign of Emperor Louis, the relics were transferred to Saxony.[228] As Charles's messenger admitted, because of this act, the power of the Franks began to diminish and the power of the Saxons began to grow and increase until the Saxons undertook their present very great burden.[229] For, as we seen in the case of your father, the love and head of the whole world, Germany, Italy, and Gaul, indeed almost all of Europe, are not sufficient to bear the majesty of his power. Therefore, praise such a great patron at whose appearance Saxony was brought from servitude to freedom, from tributary to

226. Abbot Fulrad of St. Denis (750–84).

227. The monastery of St. Denis was constructed several miles north of Paris.

228. The relics of St. Vitus were brought to Widukind's monastery of Corvey in 836.

229. Livy, *Ab urbe condita, praefatio,* 4.

the mistress of many peoples.[230] Such a mighty friend of the highest God does not require our thanks, but we servants require his grace. In order that you might have him as your intercessor with the Heavenly Emperor, we wish to have you as an advocate with terrestrial kings, that is, your father and your brother.

35. How King Henry used his nine years of peace.

During the nine years of peace that King Henry had with the Hungarians, he demonstrated such care in protecting the fatherland and in defeating the barbarian nations that it is beyond my capacity to describe his achievements, although they should not be passed over in silence. First, he selected every ninth man from among the *agrarii milites*[231] to live in fortifications. Each ninth man would build dwellings for the other eight, and would receive and store a third part of all of the grain. The other eight would sow and reap grain, and would gather up a ninth and would set this aside on their own properties. Henry desired that all law courts, assemblies, and festivals should be held in the fortifications. They were to train in these fortifications day and night so that they would learn in times of peace what to do when they faced the enemy. Aside from these strongholds, there were very few fortifications, and even these had poor walls.

After Henry had accustomed his subjects to this legal obligation and discipline, he immediately attacked the Slavs who are called the Hevelli.[232] First, Henry wore them down with numer-

230. This passage reverses Lamentations 1.1, where Israel, once great among the nations, has become like a widow; once a queen, now a slave.

231. This term has been the focus of enormous scholarly controversy. For an overview of this scholarship, see Edward J. Schoenfeld, "Anglo-Saxon 'Burhs' and Continental 'Burgen': Early Medieval Fortifications in Constitutional Perspective," *Haskins Society Journal* 6 (1994): 49–66. In our view, Widukind is describing here men who had obligations to serve in the local levy for the defense of their home regions. Henry's reform was intended to improve local defenses against Hungarian attacks, and particularly to train local militiamen to be able to operate both in defense of strongholds and in the field in conjunction with better trained and armed professional fighting men.

232. The Hevelli were part of the large Weleti confederation of Slavic peoples

ous battles. Then he established his encampment on the ice during the coldest part of the winter. Finally, through hunger, iron, and cold, he captured the fortress called Brandenburg.[233] Then, having captured the entire region along with this fortress, Henry turned his banners against Daleminzia where his father long before had placed him in command of an army. There, he besieged a fortress called Gana, and finally captured it after twenty days.[234] Henry distributed the booty from the fortress among his soldiers. All of the adults were killed, while the youths and maidens were led off as slaves. After this, Henry marched to Prague, the fortress of the Bohemians, with his entire army. He received the surrender of the king of the Bohemians.[235] Certain miraculous stories are told about this king, but we think that it is better to remain silent about them because we have no proof that they happened.[236] He was the brother of Boleslav who remained loyal and helpful to the emperor as long as he lived.[237] So Henry made the Bohemians tributaries and returned to Saxony.

36. Regarding the Redarii and how they were defeated.

And so, after the following neighboring peoples were made tributaries by King Henry, namely the Obodrites, Wilzi, Hevelli, Daleminzi, Bohemians, and Redarii, and peace had been estab-

---

who lived in the region between the lower Elbe and the Oder. This passage seems to draw upon images in Caesar, *De bello Gallico,* 4.1.

233. Cicero, *In Pisonem,* 40.

234. The location of this fortress is still the subject of some scholarly debate. Many scholars, however, agree that it is likely to be identified with the large tenth-century fortress that is situated between Hof and Stauchitz on the Jahna river some eleven kilometers southwest of the modern Elbe river town of Riesa.

235. This was Duke Wenceslaus of Bohemia (921 to 929 or 935). The *Annales Pragenses,* ed. G. H. Pertz, MGH SS 3 (Hanover, 1849), 119, gives a date of 929 for the death of Wenceslaus. However, Gumpold, *Vita Vencezlavi Ducis,* ch. 19, ed. Georg Watiz (Hanover, 1841), 220, gives a date of September 28, 935.

236. These are miracles stories about Wenceslaus.

237. Duke Boleslav I of Bohemia (929 or 935 to 972). Widukind anachronistically is styling Henry I as emperor rather than as king in recognition of his major triumph over three separate Slavic peoples.

lished, the Redarii rebelled.[238] They mobilized a huge force and attacked a stronghold called Walsleben, which they captured, killing everyone living there, comprising a great multitude.[239] All of the barbarian nations were inspired by this act, and dared to rebel as well.

In order to repress the ferocity of the barbarians, the expeditionary levy as well as a force of professional soldiers were dispatched under the command of Bernhard, who already held authority over the province of the Redarii. Thietmar also was dispatched to join the legate as a colleague.[240] They were ordered to besiege the stronghold called Lenzen.[241]

On the fifth day of the siege,[242] which was a Friday, scouts announced that an army of barbarians was not far off, and that the barbarians had decided to launch an attack on the Saxon encampment that night. After this had been confirmed by many others, the people believed the report, since it was corroborated. When the people had gathered around the tents of the legate,[243] he issued orders, following the advice that had been given to him that very hour by his colleague.[244] The men were to remain prepared through the night in order to prevent a barbarian assault on their camp.

When the large group of defenders had been ordered to stand down, emotions in camp were very mixed. Some were melancholy and others were happy. Some dreaded the battle and others were

238. The Redarii were members of the Weleti confederation and lived along the shores of the Baltic sea east to the Oder river. The Obodrites comprised a large confederation of Slavic peoples living between the lower Elbe and the Baltic sea. Wilzi is an alternate name for the entire Weleti confederation.

239. Walsleben, a Saxon fortification, is located in the modern district of Stendal in the German state of Saxony-Anhalt, approximately twenty-two kilometers west-southwest of the confluence of the Havel and Elbe rivers.

240. This is likely the same Count Thietmar who saved Henry during the siege of Eresburg, noted above in 1.23.

241. Lenzen is located on the east bank of the Elbe, approximately eighty-five kilometers northwest of Walsleben.

242. The fifth day of the siege took place on September 3, 929.

243. The legate (i.e., *legatus*) is Bernhard.

244. The colleague (i.e., *collega*) is Count Thietmar.

looking forward to it. The fighting men moved between hope and fear according to the nature of their personalities.[245] In the meantime, the day went by, and the night was much darker than usual because of a huge rainstorm. Thus, by God's will, the evil plan of the barbarians was thwarted.[246]

As had been ordered, the Saxons remained armed throughout the night. Then, at first light, after the signal had been given, they all received the sacrament.[247] Then each man promised under oath, first to the commanders, and then to each other, that they would do their duty in the present battle. After the sun rose, for fine clear weather had returned after the rain storm, they raised their banners and marched out of camp.[248]

The legate,[249] who was in the first rank, launched an attack against the barbarians. But he was not able to overcome the innumerable enemy with his small force. When he returned to the army, he reported that the barbarians did not have many mounted men. However, because of their enormous number of men on foot, and because the rain the previous night had created such an obstacle, the enemy could not be drawn to engage in battle against his own mounted troops.

As the sun blazed down on the wet clothing of the barbarians, and made steam rise up to the sky, the people of God gained hope and faith as the brightness and serenity of His countenance shined around them.[250] Then the signal was given, and the legate urged on the legions that charged with a great shout against the enemy. When it became clear that the great number of the enemy would not allow the Saxons to drive through them, they struck them on the left and right with their weapons. Whenever the Saxons were

245. Vergil, *Aeneid*, 1.218.

246. The Slavs could not launch their planned night attack because of the heavy downpour.

247. The men all received the eucharist after the celebration of mass.

248. *Annales Corbeienses, an.* 929, also notes the large scale of the battle at Lenzen and the fact that it began just after sunrise.

249. This is Bernhard.

250. Luke 2.9.

able to separate some of the Slavs from their fellows, they killed them all.

As the battle intensified, with many dead on each side, and the barbarians still managing to maintain their formation, the legate ordered his colleague to provide support to the legions.[251] So Thietmar dispatched a commander with fifty heavily armed mounted troops against the enemy's flank and disrupted their entire formation. From this point on, the enemy faced only flight and death. When they had been slaughtered through the fields, some of the survivors attempted to flee to the fortress. But the colleague prevented them from doing this, so they entered a nearby lake. So it happened that of this enormous multitude, almost all were killed by the sword or drowned in the lake. None of the foot soldiers survived, and just a few of the enemy mounted troops. The battle ended with the defeat of all of their adversaries.

There was a huge burst of joy following the victory. Everyone praised the commanders, and each of the soldiers praised his fellows. Even the cowards enjoyed some praise, as often happens when there is such good fortune.[252] The next day, they marched to the aforementioned fortress. The defenders lay down their arms and asked only for their lives. They received this. The unarmed men were ordered to depart the city. However, the slaves, and all of the money along with the wives, children, and goods of the king of the barbarians were carried into captivity. On our side, two men named Liuthar died,[253] along with many other noblemen. The legate, his colleague, and other commanders returned to Saxony as victors. They were received honorably by the king and given all due praise since with God's favor and mercy their small forces

251. Widukind uses the term *legiones* here to indicate the units of foot soldiers who were already committed to the battle.

252. Sallust, *Jugurtha*, 53.

253. These were the counts of Walbeck and Stade, the great-grandfathers of Bishop Thietmar of Merseburg. See Thietmar of Merseburg, *Chronik*, ed. and trans. Werner Trillmich, 8th ed. (Darmstadt, 2002), 1.10. Also see *Annales Corbeienses, an.* 929. For an English translation of this text, see *Ottonian Germany: The Chronicon of Thietmar of Merseburg*, ed. and trans. David A. Warner (Manchester, 2001).

had gained a magnificent victory. The next day, all of the captives, as they had promised, were beheaded.[254]

37. Regarding the marriage of the king's son.

The joy over the recent victory added to the royal marriage that was being celebrated with great magnificence at this time. For the king gave the daughter of King Edmund, who also was the sister of Adalstan, to his son Otto as a wife.[255] She bore Otto a son named Liudolf,[256] a great man who deservedly was dear to all the people. She also bore him a daughter named Liutgard, who married Duke Conrad of the Franks.[257]

38. The king's speech and how he defeated the Hungarians in an open battle.

Now that the king had a military force that was proven in mounted combat, he decided to fight against the ancient foe, namely the Hungarians. So he summoned the entire people and addressed them with the following oration: "Once your empire was disrupted on every side by countless dangers, but now it is free. You, yourselves, know this well having labored under the grinding weight of civil conflicts and foreign wars. And now, through the grace of the Highest Divinity, by our own labor, and by your strength, there is peace and unity. The barbarians have been defeated and subjected in service to us. There is just one thing remaining for us to do. We must also join together against our common enemy, the Avars.[258] I have plundered you, your sons, and your daughters, to fill their treasuries.[259] And now I am forced to plunder the churches and the ser-

254. This is the first reference to the beheading of captives, and it is not clear whether it refers to the slaves and royal family taken at Lenzen, to the captives taken in the battle, or to both.

255. This was Edith, the daughter of King Edward of Wessex (901–24) and sister of Kings Aethelstan (924–40) and Edmund (940–46).

256. Liudolf (930–57).

257. Liutgard married Conrad the Red in 947 and died in 953. Conrad the Red (922–55) was duke of Lotharingia from 945 until being deposed for rebellion against King Otto I in 953. However, his family's base of power was in Franconia.

258. Widukind is again using Avars as a synonym for Hungarians.

259. The reference here is to the treasuries of the Hungarians.

vants of those churches, leaving us naked and with no money. Consider among yourselves what should be done about this, and choose. Should I take the treasures that were consecrated to the divine office, and hand them over to purchase our redemption from the enemies of God?"

At this, the people raised their voices to heaven saying that they wished above all to be redeemed by the living and true God because He was faithful and just in all of His paths, and holy in all of His works.[260] Promising to the king their full effort against this most vicious of peoples, they raised their right hands into the air and affirmed this pact. After he had made this agreement with the entire people, the king dismissed the assembled multitude.

After these events, the Hungarian legates came to the king to receive their customary gifts. But they departed from him to return to their own land empty-handed. When they heard this, the Avars did not delay. They hurried to enter Saxony with a large hostile force. They took the route through Daleminzia and sought help from their old friends. But the Daleminzi, knowing that the Hungarians were hurrying to Saxony, and that the Saxons were ready to fight them, gave a very fat dog to the Hungarians as their gift. The Hungarians did not have time to avenge this insult as they were hurrying on to a different fight. For quite a while the Daleminzi pursued their "friends" while mocking them.

When the Hungarians crossed the Thuringian frontier with their surprise attack, they raided throughout the land. They then divided their forces, with some heading west, and others seeking to enter Saxony from the east and the south. But the Saxons together with the Thuringians gathered to fight them. They killed the leaders of the Hungarians, and scattered the survivors of this western army[261] throughout the whole region. Some were overwhelmed by hunger, others were destroyed by the cold, still others were killed or captured. As was fitting for such men, they died miserably.

The army that had remained in the east learned that a sister of

260. Psalm 144.17.

261. The reference here is to the Hungarian column that had advanced west.

the king lived in a nearby stronghold, and had a great deal of gold and silver.[262] She had married Wido the Thuringian because she had been born to a concubine.[263] So they began to attack this fortress with such a large force that they would have captured it if the night had not impeded their vision. But that very night, the Hungarians learned of the defeat of their comrades, and that the king was coming against them with a powerful army. For the king had established his camp near a place called Riade.[264] Overcome by fear, the Hungarians abandoned their camp and, in their customary manner, gathered together their scattered forces with fire and giant smoke signals.

The next day, the king brought up his army and exhorted the men to commit their hopes to divine mercy, and not to doubt that divine aid would be there for them as it had been in all their other battles. The Hungarians were the common enemy of all of them, and they should focus their thoughts on protecting their fatherland and their families. They would soon see that the enemy would flee if they stood firmly in battle. The soldiers were emboldened by this rousing oration. Then the men in the first rank, then in the second, and then in the last saw the emperor and an angel flying before him.[265] For the large banner was marked with the angel's name and image. They took great comfort and resolve from this.

The king feared, correctly as it turned out, that once the enemy

262. The site of this fortification has not been identified, although Jechaburg in the modern city of Sondershausen about fifty kilometers north of Erfurt has been suggested as a possible location. See *Res gestae,* ed. Bauer and Rau, 76n102.

263. Widukind is explaining why King Henry's unnamed sister was married to someone who was not of the highest nobility.

264. The location of Riade remains a point of controversy. One suggestion is Kalbsrieth which is located on the Helme river shortly before it empties into the Unstrut. See *Res gestae,* ed. Bauer and Rau, 76n103. However, in his description of these events, Liudprand of Cremona places the battle of Riade about eighty kilometers further east, in the vicinity of Merseburg, on the east bank of the Saale river. See Liudprand, *Antapodosis,* 2.25–31.

265. The image has been identified by scholars as the Archangel Michael. See *Res gestae,* ed. Bauer and Rau, 77n104.

saw his heavily armed soldiers, they would immediately flee. So he deployed a unit of lightly armed Thuringians along with a small number of heavily armed soldiers so that the enemy would pursue the former, and thus be led to the main force of the army. This was done, but the Hungarians still fled when they caught sight of the heavily armed main force. They fled for eight miles but very few of them were killed or captured.[266] However, their camp was captured and all of the captives were set free.

39. How the victor returned, and some observations about his manner of life.

The king returned as a victor and, as was appropriate, he gave thanks in every possible way to honor God for the victory that was granted to him by the divine will over these enemies. He gave over for the support of the church those payments that he was accustomed to give to the enemy, and he ordered that gifts be made to the poor. He was then hailed as father of the fatherland, lord of the world, and emperor. Reports of his power and strength spread far and wide to all the peoples and kings. The rulers of other kingdoms came to him and sought his favor, desiring the proven friendship of such a great man. Among them was Heribert,[267] the brother-in-law of Hugh,[268] because Raoul,[269] who had been made king against every custom and law,[270] had attacked him. Heribert asked Henry to protect him from his own lord. The king was a man who did not deny the requests of his friends. Therefore, the king set out for Gaul and spoke with the king.[271] Then, having completed this business, Henry returned to Saxony.

Since it was Henry's duty to exalt his own people, there were

266. *Annales Corbieneses, an.* 933, by contrast, claims that Henry destroyed the Hungarian army.

267. Count Heribert II of Vermandois.

268. Hugh the Great.

269. King Raoul of West Francia (923–36) was the son-in-law of King Robert I, and brother-in-law of Hugh the Great.

270. Sallust, *Catilinae,* 15.

271. The two kings are Henry I and Raoul.

few if any illustrious men in all of Saxony whom he did not honor with an exceptional gift or office or some other kind of governmental position.[272] Henry was characterized by outstanding prudence and wisdom. He had, in addition, a powerful body that completed the adornment of his royal dignity. He was so much superior to everyone else in military exercises and games that he terrified them. He was so skillful in the hunt that one time he killed more than forty wild beasts. And although he was friendly enough at feasts, he did nothing that diminished his royal stature. Indeed, he imparted such favor and fear to his soldiers, in equal proportion, that even when Henry was being sportive, they did not believe that they could permit themselves to show the same kind of playfulness.

40. *How he defeated the Danes.*

After he had defeated all of the neighboring peoples, Henry attacked and defeated the Danes with his army because they had launched naval raids against the Frisians.[273] After he forced the Danes to pay tribute, Henry had their king, named Knuba, receive baptism.[274] Then, after finally defeating all of the neighboring peoples, Henry decided to go to Rome. However, he was forced to put off this journey when overcome by illness.

41. *How he grew very ill, died, and was buried.*

When Henry realized that he was now very ill, he summoned the entire people and designated his son Otto as king. He dis-

272. Widukind uses the general term *officium* which is then contrasted with the much more specific *quaestura.* However, Widukind then qualifies what was in the Roman imperial sense a specific office relating to the management of fiscal affairs with the indefinite pronoun *aliqua,* i.e., some kind of quaestorship.

273. *Annales Corbeienses, an.* 934, records Henry I's defeat of the Danes.

274. This king appears to have been a Swede who ruled the region around the important trading center of Hedeby (German Haithabu) in the southern part of the Jutland peninsula. See the discussion of these events by Niels Lund, "The Baptism of Harald Bluetooth," in *The Viking Age: Ireland and the West,* ed. John Sheehan and Donnchadh O Corráin (Dublin, 2010), 234–39.

tributed goods and treasures to his other sons. However, he established Otto, who was the eldest and best, as ruler over his brothers and all of the Franks.[275] When his final testament was completed properly, and all of his affairs had been settled, Henry died as lord of the world and greatest of the kings of Europe, second to none in the strength of his spirit and body. He left a son who was greater than himself. He left to his son a great and wide empire that had not been left to him by his own father, but rather had been gained through his own efforts, and which had been granted to him by God alone. He lived for sixty years and reigned for sixteen.[276] To the grief and tears of many peoples, his body was carried by his sons to the city called Quedlinburg, and was buried in the basilica of St. Peter before the altar.

Here ends book one.

275. Otto was not the eldest of Henry I's sons. Thankmar was the eldest, but his mother had been set aside by Henry so that he could marry Mathilda.

276. Henry actually ruled for seventeen years, coming to power in May 919 and dying in July 936.

BOOK TWO

Here begins the second book of the deeds of the Saxons.

To Lady Mathilda, the daughter of the emperor, here begins the preface of book two.

May this enormous labor, which I have begun, or rather have reworked since the greater part of it has already been completed, be supported by your grace.[1] For you are recognized correctly as the mistress of all of Europe, although the power of your father has now extended to Africa and Asia. For I hope that whatever should be found in this work that is less desirable shall be removed through the glorious mildness of your clemency, so that this work shall remain dedicated with the same devotion with which it was begun.

Here ends the preface.

Here begins book two.

1. Regarding the assembly of the people at the palace of Aachen, the election of a new king, and his anointing.

After the death of the father of the fatherland, Henry, the greatest and best of kings, the entire Frankish and Saxon people chose as their ruler Otto, his son, who long before had been designated as king by his father.[2] Announcing the location of the universal elec-

1. This passage may be understood to reflect Widukind's method of composition, namely that he completed the greater part of the text and then submitted it for approval to the royal court.

2. The coronation took place on August 7, 936.

tion,[3] they ordered that it be held at the palace at Aachen.[4] This place is nearby Jülich, which was named after its founder Julius Caesar.[5] When Otto arrived there, the dukes and leading counts,[6] and a large number of other military officers, who had gathered in the courtyard of the basilica that is associated with Charlemagne, placed their new leader on a throne that had been constructed within that same basilica. They offered him their hands, swore loyalty to him, promised their support against all his enemies, and thus made him king according to their custom.

While the dukes and other high officials were doing this, the highest priest[7] along with clerics of every rank and the entire people undertook a procession within the basilica in honor of the new king. As the king was walking, the highest priest met him, and touched the king's right hand with his own left hand. The high priest was bearing his staff in his right hand, and was dressed in his alb, and further adorned with his stole, and chasuble. He walked to the middle of the sanctuary and stood still. The high priest then turned to the people who were standing all around—for circular ambulatories had been constructed both above and below in this basilica—so that he could be seen by the entire people,[8] and said: "Behold, I bring before you Otto, the elect of God, who long ago was designated by Henry, the ruler of the world, and who now

3. Widukind uses the expression *universalis electio* to denote the coronation of Otto, with the implication that despite his earlier reference to the *populus Francorum atque Saxonum,* the new ruler was to be king of all of East Francia/Germany.

4. The subject of "ordered" is not specified by Widukind, although it seems likely to us to refer to Henry I and Otto I.

5. Widukind clearly wished here to avoid referring to Charlemagne, with whom Aachen was most closely associated. It is likely that the coronation some months earlier of Louis IV (936–54) as king of West Francia at nearby Laon played into Widukind's decision. As the son of King Charles III the Simple and the direct descendant of Charlemagne, Louis IV certainly had a greater claim to possess Aachen than did Otto I. See the discussion by Herbert Zielinski, "Zur Aachener Königserhebung von 936," *Deutsches Archiv für Erforschung des Mittelalters* 28 (1972): 210–20, here 219.

6. Widukind uses the term *praefectus* here as a synonym for count.

7. Archbishop Hildebert of Mainz (927–37).

8. Widukind's observations here accord with the physical layout of the church at Aachen.

has been made king by all of the leaders. If this election pleases you, show it by raising your right arms to heaven."

In response, the entire people raised their arms to heaven and cried out with a great shout for the new leader to have good fortune. Then the bishop walked behind the altar, on which the royal insignia had been placed, along with the king, who was wearing a tight tunic in the Frankish style.[9] These insignia were a sword with a belt, a cloak with clasps, a staff with a scepter, and the crown.

At this time, the highest priest was a man named Hildebert, a Frank by birth, a monk by profession, raised and educated at the monastery of Fulda, who came to this office by merit. First raised up as the abbot of Fulda, he then gained the summit of the highest see, the bishopric of Mainz. He was a man of marvelous sanctity, possessing a spiritual wisdom that went beyond mortal bounds, and was quite illustrious in scholarly pursuits. Among his other gifts of grace, he is reported to have received the gift of prophesy.

There was a conflict about which bishop should consecrate the king, namely between the prelates of Trier and Cologne,[10] with the first claiming the right because his was an older see founded by St. Peter the Apostle, and the latter because the place of consecration was in his diocese, so that both believed that the honor of the consecration belonged to them.[11] But both gave up their claims in the face of Hildebert's universally recognized superiority.

Hildebert then went to the altar, picked up the sword and belt, turned to the king, and said: "Take this sword with which you shall defeat all of the enemies of Christ, barbarians, and evil Christians. All of the power of the entire empire of the Franks has been granted to you by divine authority so that there will be true peace for all Christians." Then taking up the cloak with clasps, Hilde-

9. Einhard, *Vita Karoli Magni*, ch. 23, observed that Charlemagne always wore the traditional dress of the Franks, except for two occasions while at Rome, when he dressed in Roman garb at the request of the popes Hadrian I (772–95) and Leo III (795–816).

10. Archbishop Robert of Trier (931–56), the brother of Otto I's mother, Mathilda, and Archbishop Wigfried of Cologne (924–53).

11. Aachen is located in the diocese of Cologne.

bert placed it on Otto saying, "You are reminded by these horns pointing toward the ground[12] of the zealous faith with which you should burn, and of the peace that you should maintain up to the end of your life." Then Hildebert picked up the scepter and staff and said: "You are warned by these symbols that it is your responsibility to restrain your subjects with paternal discipline. You should offer a hand of mercy first to the servants of God, to widows, and to orphans. The oil of compassion should never be missing from your head so that you will be crowned both in the present and in the future with the eternal prize."

Otto then was anointed with holy oil, and crowned with the golden diadem by Bishops Hildebert and Wigfried.[13] When the entire legal consecration was complete, Otto was led by the bishops to the throne to which he ascended by a winding stair. The throne was placed between two exceptionally beautiful columns constructed of marble from where Otto could see everyone and could, himself, be seen by all who were in attendance.

2. *Regarding the king's duties and his princes.*

After the praise of the Lord and mass had been solemnly celebrated,[14] the king went down to the palace and took his place at the marble table, ornate with its royal panoply, where he sat with the bishops and all the people. The dukes served.[15] Duke Gislebert, whose authority encompassed this place,[16] obtained all of the supplies. Eberhard looked after the table.[17] Hermann the Frank served as cup-bearer.[18] Arnulf was responsible for overseeing the horses and choosing the place to make camp.[19] Siegfried, the greatest of

12. The clasps on the cloak were made in the shape of horns that pointed down.

13. Archbishops Hildebert of Mainz and Wigfried of Cologne.

14. This likely means after the singing of the *Laudes,* or praises of the Lord.

15. Widukind is describing each of the four dukes below as undertaking one of the four principal household offices as these had been established under the Carolingians. These offices were seneschal, chamberlain, butler, and constable.

16. Aachen was located in Lotharingia. 17. Duke Eberhard of Franconia.

18. Duke Hermann of Swabia (926–49)

19. Widukind is describing Duke Arnulf of Bavaria as the royal constable without giving him that title.

the Saxons and second only to the king,[20] was brother-in-law of the previous king, and bound to this king by marriage as well.[21] At this time, he oversaw the administration of Saxony so that there would be no attacks by the enemy. He also oversaw the education of the younger Henry, whom he had brought with him.[22] After these festivities, the king honored each of the princes with an appropriate gift according to his royal munificence, and then dismissed the great crowd filled completely with joy.

3. Regarding the war undertaken against Boleslav.

In the meantime, the barbarians were raging to stir up new troubles, and Boleslav[23] killed his brother,[24] a Christian man and, as they say, most devout in the cultivation of God. Boleslav feared having a minor prince nearby[25] who followed the orders of the Saxons, and so waged war against him.[26] So the latter sent a messenger to Saxony to ask for aid. Asik was dispatched to him along with the legion of Merseburgers,[27] and a strong force of men from Hassegau.[28] The Thuringian expeditionary levy also was added to

20. This may have been Count Siegfried of Merseburg, whose brother Gero later would command the entire eastern frontier. Hatheburg, Henry I's first wife, who was the daughter of Count Erwin of Merseburg, was a cousin of Count Siegfried's mother. It is not clear how Siegfried was Henry I's brother-in-law.

21. Suetonius, *Nero,* 35.

22. This is Otto's younger brother Henry.

23. Duke Boleslav of Bohemia (929 or 935 to 972).

24. This is Duke Wenceslaus whose murder is variously identified by scholars in either 929 or 935. We are inclined toward the latter date because of Widukind's decision to discuss Boleslav's murder of Wenceslaus in the context of the Bohemian revolt against Ottonian authority in 936.

25. Widukind does not specify if this *subregulus* was a Bohemian or a minor Slavic prince from another ethnic group.

26. The identity of this *subregulus* has not been established by scholars.

27. The *legio Mesaburiorum,* or Merseburg legion, has attracted considerable scholarly attention as a potentially colorful element in the Ottonian military establishment. See the discussion of the Merseburg legion by K. J. Leyser, "Henry I and the Beginnings of the Saxon Empire," *English Historical Review* 83 (1968): 1–32, reprinted in Leyser, *Medieval Germany and Its Neighbours, 900–1250* (London, 1982), 11–42, here 21–22.

28. Hassegau is a *pagus* or a district in Eastphalia bounded to the east by the Saale river, to the south by the Unstrut, and to the north by the Wipper. The most impor-

Asik's force. The unit from Merseburg was recruited from thieves. King Henry was quite severe with foreigners, but showed mercy to his countrymen in all cases. When he saw that a thief or highwayman was strong and suited to war, Henry spared the man from the punishment that was due, and settled him in a suburb of Merseburg. He gave them fields and arms, and ordered them to spare their countrymen. However, they were to exercise their thievery against the barbarians as much as they dared. When a large number of men of this type had been gathered, Henry created a legion that was fully prepared to go on campaign.

When Boleslav learned of the Saxon army and that the Saxons and Thuringians were marching against him separately, he decided, since he was a very good tactician, to divide his own forces and position them to oppose each of the armies. The Thuringians, when they saw the unexpected approach of the enemy, avoided danger in flight. However, Asik, with his Saxons and other support troops, did not delay at all his attack on the enemy, and killed the greater part of them in battle. He forced the remainder to flee, and returned to his camp as a victor. But Asik was unaware of the army that had pursued the Thuringians, and did not use caution after his victory.

When Boleslav saw that our army was dispersed, with some men taking spoils from the dead, and others resting, and still others busy gathering hay for their horses, he brought together in a single army the forces that had returned and those that had fled.[29] Boleslav then launched a sudden surprise attack against our unprepared men, who were feeling secure because of their recent victory. Boleslav killed the commander[30] and destroyed the entire army. Then, Boleslav marched to the stronghold of the minor prince,

---

tant city in Hassegau was Merseburg. Widukind's use of this regional term to designate this force indicates that the fighting men were drawn from the expeditionary levy rather than consisting primarily of professional fighting men drawn from the military households of local magnates.

29. These are the Bohemian troops who had pursued the Thuringians, and the Bohemians who had been defeated by Count Asik's Saxons.

30. This is Count Asik.

captured it in the first assault, and turned it into a wilderness, which it remains to this day. This war lasted until the fourteenth year of the king's reign.[31] After this point, Boleslav became a faithful and useful dependent of the king.

4. Regarding the king's campaign against the barbarian nations.

The king was little disturbed when he received word from a messenger about what had happened. Rather, fortified by divine strength, he crossed the frontiers of the barbarians to restrain their savagery with his entire army. Otto's father had already waged war against them because they had mistreated the legates sent by his son Thankmar,[32] a matter that we plan to discuss more fully below. The king then decided to establish a new military commander. He chose for this office a noble, diligent, and quite prudent man named Hermann. By bestowing this office, however, Otto aroused the jealousy not only of the other commanders, but also of Hermann's brother Wichmann. It is for this reason that Wichmann pretended some illness and left the army. Wichmann was a powerful and brave man, generous, skilled in war, and possessed of such learning that he was said by his people to have superhuman knowledge.

Herrmann, who was in the front rank of the battle line, found himself in combat against the enemy as he crossed the frontier into their region. He inflicted a grave defeat on them, and, because of this, the jealousy of his enemies burned even hotter. Among them was Ekehard, the son of Liudolf.[33] Ekehard was so enraged by Hermann's success that he swore that he would either do something even greater, or wished to die in the attempt. So Ekehard

31. The fourteenth year of Otto's reign, i.e., 950. Widukind returns to Boleslav in 3.8.

32. Thankmar was Henry I's son from his first marriage to Hatheburg. Thankmar was older than Otto, but was not seen as legitimate because Henry had set aside Hatheburg in 909 in order to marry Mathilda, the mother of Otto. See Thietmar of Mersburg, *Chronicon,* 1.5.

33. It may be that Ekkehard was the son of Liudolf, King Henry I's elder brother, which would make him Otto I's first cousin.

gathered together the ablest men from the entire army and, violating the king's orders, crossed a swamp that was located between the enemy's stronghold and the royal encampment. He immediately attacked but, surrounded by the enemy, he died along with all of his men. Eighteen men chosen from the entire army died there with him. However, the king, after killing many of the enemy, and making the others tributaries, returned to Saxony. This happened on September twenty-fifth.[34]

5. Regarding the Hungarians.

After these events, the Hungarians, the ancient enemy, came to test the mettle of the new king. Having entered through Franconia, they decided, if they could, to invade Saxony from the west. However, when the king received word of this, he did not delay. He went to meet them with a strong army, and caused them to flee, rousting them from his territory.

6. Regarding internal wars.

When these external wars came to an end, civil wars began. For the Saxons, who had been made glorious by the power of their king, refused to obey people of other nations. Moreover, they spurned the idea that they held their offices through the grace of anyone other than the king. For this reason, Eberhard was angered by Bruning.[35] Eberhard mobilized a force and burned down the stronghold of Helmern,[36] killing all of the inhabitants of this fortress. When the king learned about this presumptuous act, he required that Eberhard pay as compensation horses valued at one hundred talents.[37]

34. This campaign took place in 936. See DO I, 2, issued in 936, where the king reports, "We have come in peace to Magdeburg from the province of the Slavs who are called Redarii."

35. Duke Eberhard of Franconia, and a Saxon garrison commander named Bruning.

36. Helmern was located on the eastern slope of the Egge range, which rises in the eastern part of the modern German state of North-Rhine-Westphalia. It stood along the border between Saxon Westphalia and Franconia at the time of this conflict.

37. Widukind uses the Greek term here, which might be construed as a synonym for pound, a unit of account that was current in Widukind's day. This sum amount-

All of the military commanders who had aided Eberhard in this deed were condemned to be shamed by carrying dogs all the way to the royal city that we call Magdeburg.

7. Regarding the relics of the martyr Innocent.

At the same time, the king transferred the relics of the martyr Innocent to this same city.[38] Although he imposed an appropriate punishment on those disturbers of the peace, the king, because he was exceptionally merciful, then immediately received them with compassion. After honoring each of them with a royal gift, the king allowed them to depart in peace. Nevertheless, because their duke had a genial personality, was friendly to his inferiors, and generous in giving gifts, these commanders persisted in carrying out evil deeds on his behalf. Indeed, the duke, using these methods, even won over many Saxons to his side.[39]

8. Regarding Duke Arnulf of the Bavarians.

At this time, Duke Arnulf of the Bavarians died.[40] His sons, in their arrogance, refused the order of the king to attend the royal court.

9. Regarding Siegfried and Thankmar, the son of the king.

At that time Count Siegfried died.[41] Thankmar then sought Siegfried's office for himself, because he was a kinsman. King Henry fathered Thankmar by a woman who was the daughter of Sieg-

ed to two thousand solidi (shillings). To put this figure in perspective, in the late ninth century, a sword in West Francia cost five solidi, so that one hundred pounds amounted to four hundred swords. See Simon Coupland, "Carolingian Arms and Armor in the Ninth Century," *Viator* 21 (1990): 29–50.

38. These relics were a gift from King Rudolf II of Burgundy (912–37) that subsequently were given by Otto I to the monastery of St. Maurice at Magdeburg. Widukind, whose loyalties were to his own house of Corvey, passes over this aspect of the story in silence. For the reference to the grant of the relics to St. Maurice, see DO I, 14 and 15.

39. This is a foreshadowing of Duke Eberhard's successful wooing of Otto I's younger brother Henry.

40. Duke Arnulf died on July 14, 937.

41. Count Siegfried of Merseburg died in December 937.

fried's maternal aunt.[42] When Otto granted this office, by royal gift, to Count Gero, Thankmar was afflicted with a great sadness. However, the king went to Bavaria and, having settled matters there, returned to Saxony.[43]

10. Regarding conflict and the multiplicity of laws.

The dissension between Eberhard and Bruning developed to such an extent that fields were ravaged and burned, and people were killed out in the open. There was also conflict at that time regarding a confusion in the laws. There were some who said that sons of the sons should not be counted among the sons, and that they should not legally receive an inheritance with the sons if, by chance, their fathers died while their grandfathers were still alive.[44] Consequently, the king issued an edict that the entire people[45] should assemble at an estate called Steele.[46] There, it was determined that this matter ought to be investigated and decided by judicial arbitration. However, the king then followed better counsel because did not wish to have noblemen and the elders of the people treated improperly.[47] So, instead, he ordered that this matter be decided by gladiators.[48] In this manner, the side triumphed who wished to include the sons of sons among the sons, and it was confirmed that they would divide

42. King Henry's first wife, Hatheburg, the daughter of Count Erwin of Merseburg, had been married before and then entered a convent when her first husband died.

43. Widukind is telescoping affairs here quite dramatically in order to gloss over Otto I's mishandling of the crisis of 937–38. The king launched an initial campaign into Bavaria in early 938 but failed to impose a settlement. It was only in late 938 that Otto launched a second campaign into Bavaria and drove out Duke Arnulf's sons. See below 2.34; and Adalbert of Magdeburg, *Continuatio, an.* 938.

44. Note that the sons of a man's daughters are not of concern here. The conflict is between nephews and their paternal uncles.

45. Widukind is playing here on Luke 2.1.

46. The assembly at the royal estate of Steele took place on 18 May 938. See DO I, nr. 20.

47. It is not clear how the elders and noblemen would suffer any harm as a result of holding a judicial hearing on this matter.

48. Widukind uses the classical term to denote a public combat between two champions.

the inheritance with their paternal uncles equally under the terms of an eternally valid agreement.

At this assembly, the disturbers of the peace also were made known. They were men who denied that they had done anything against the king's power, but claimed rather that they had avenged an injury in some manner against their fellows.[49] Although the king recognized that they had shown him contempt because they had not deigned to come to this assembly at his order, he nevertheless deferred the use of armed force, and offered them a means of achieving reconciliation. As was his custom, the king was always ready to show mercy. But this delay led many others to do even worse evil. They committed many additional crimes, including treason, murder, perjury, robbery, and arson.[50] At that time, they acted as if there was little difference between good and evil, holiness and wickedness.

11. Regarding Thankmar, Eberhard, Henry, and the civil wars.

Thankmar joined with Eberhard. Then, after he had mobilized a large force, Thankmar besieged a stronghold called Belecke where Henry the Younger was residing.[51] After Thankmar distributed the booty from the fortress to his fellow soldiers,[52] he carried off Henry with him as if he were some kind of vile slave.[53] Gebhard, the son of Udo, Duke Hermann's brother, was killed there. As a consequence of his death, as God orders all matters, the leaders of the Franks were divided among themselves.[54] How-

49. This passage makes clear that the king did not accept the validity of the feud as a legitimate means of solving serious disagreements.

50. Sallust, *Catilinae*, 51.6.

51. Belecke is located on the Möhne river in Westphalia, in the modern German state of North-Rhine Westphalia. Henry was Thankmar's younger half-brother.

52. Widukind uses the term *commilitiones*, which had the connotation in classical sources of a commander who was one of the men, i.e., that he demonstrated concretely his care and concern for the troops under his command.

53. *Hrotsvithae Opera*, ed. Paul von Winterfeld, MGH SRG 34 (Hanover, 1965), here *Gesta Ottonis*, lines 183–84.

54. Udo and Duke Hermann of Swabia were the sons of the Conradine Count Geberhard, and the first cousins of Duke Eberhard of Franconia.

ever, Thankmar's soldiers had been enriched with so many spoils that they were prepared for any task.

After the events at Belecke, Thankmar captured the fortress called Eresburg. He installed a very large garrison there and turned it into a den of thieves. Eberhard kept Henry with him. At this same time, Dedi was killed before the gates of the fortress called Laer, which was held by Eberhard's soldiers.[55] Wichmann, who had at first withdrawn his allegiance from the king, returned to make peace with the king when he learned of this most rebellious deed.[56] And because Wichmann was very intelligent, he remained helpful and loyal to the end of his life.

By contrast, Thankmar, the son of King Henry, who had been born to a noble mother, always was eager for a fight. He had a sharp mind, and was skilled in combat, but did not demonstrate much virtue or honor in war. His mother had extensive possessions. Although Thankmar was enriched with many other properties by his father, he took it very badly when he was deprived of his maternal inheritance. It was for this reason that he took up arms against his lord king to his own ruin and the ruin of his men.

Although he did so unwillingly, the king saw that this matter might lead to an enormous danger, and so marched to Eresburg with his entire military household to vanquish Thankmar's insolence. When the inhabitants of this fortress realized that it was the king who was besieging this city, because he had come with such a powerful force, they opened the gates and allowed his army to enter. Thankmar fled into a church that had been dedicated to St. Peter the Apostle by Pope Leo.[57] The army pursued him to the

55. The location of this fortification is not certain. It has been identified with Laer on the Ruhr near Meschede, Laar near Herford, and Zierenberg northwest of Kassel. Dedi might have been related to the counts of Wettin.

56. This reconciliation is also discussed by Adalbert of Magdeburg, *Continuatio, an.* 939.

57. Pope Leo III came to Paderborn in 799 to beg Charlemagne to restore him to power in Rome. The church at Eresburg was constructed in 785, but there is no other account of it having been dedicated by Pope Leo. For the dedication of the church of St. Peter, see *Annales Laureshamenses, an.* 785, ed. G. H. Pertz, MGH SS 1 (Hanover, 1826).

church, especially Henry's troops, who were angry and wished to avenge the injury done to their lord.[58]

They did not fear to break open the doors with their weapons and to enter armed into this holy building. Thankmar stood next to the altar where he had set down his arms and his golden torque. Then, while he was being driven back on one side by spears, a certain Thiadbold, the illegitimate son of Cobbo, let out a string of curses and struck him a blow. But as soon as the blow fell, Thiadbold was struck in turn by Thankmar, and very soon thereafter Thiadbold died in dreadful pain. But then one of the soldiers named Maincia thrust a lance through a window that was next to the altar, struck Thankmar in the back, and killed him alongside the altar.[59] Later on, this instigator of fraternal discord wretchedly lost his life at the battle of Birten along with the gold that he had wickedly taken from the altar.[60]

When the king, who was absent and ignorant of what had taken place, received word, he disapproved of the rash actions of the soldiers. But as the civil war was now raging, he was not able to punish them. Otto was upset at his brother's fate, and demonstrated his own natural mercy in saying a few words about his brother's honor and energy.[61] Otto then condemned Thiadric and three sons of his father's sister, who had joined Thankmar, and had them hanged according to the law of the Franks.[62] Otto then led his army, which was hungry for battle and enriched by the booty taken at the fortress, to Laer.

58. These were the members of the military household of Henry, Otto I's younger brother.

59. Thankmar was killed on July 28, 938. See *Annales Corbeienses,* MGH SS 3, 4, for the year. For the day of Thankmar's death, see *Die Totenbücher von Merseburg, Magdeburg und Lüneburg,* ed. G. Althoff and J. Wollasch, MGH Libri memoriales et necrologia, n.s. 2 (Hanover, 1983), 29.

60. The battle of Birten took place in the spring of 939. During the battle Henry was wounded while fighting against his brother Otto's soldiers.

61. Vergil, *Aeneid,* 4.337.

62. The specific identity of these men is not known, but it is likely that they were Frankish magnates.

There, the defenders, under the leadership of the fortress commander, bitterly resisted. They did not cease to return stone for stone, and spear for spear. However, worn down by the fighting, they asked for a truce so that they could consult with their duke.[63] After Otto allowed this truce, the duke denied them aid. Therefore, the defenders left the fortress and surrendered themselves into the king's power. During this battle, Tamma the cup-bearer, who was already famous for his many great deeds, earned further renown. When Eberhard received word about the death of Thankmar and the surrender of his soldiers, his spirit was broken. He threw himself at the feet of his captive,[64] and begged for forgiveness so that he might gain reconciliation in this shameful manner.

12. *Regarding Henry, the brother of the king.*

At this time, Henry was still very young and hot-headed.[65] So Eberhard released him, and forged a criminal pact with Henry, who was seduced by his desire to rule. This conspiracy was directed against his lord king and brother so that Henry, if possible, would gain the royal crown for himself.[66] So the pact was made on both sides. Henry freely returned to the king and was received with a purer faith and love than that with which he entered.

13. *Regarding Eberhard and how he obtained mercy.*

At the advice of Frederick,[67] Hildebert's successor as archbishop, an excellent man and highly esteemed for all aspects of his religious life, Eberhard went to the king. Kneeling before him, Eberhard asked for mercy, handing over himself and all of his possessions to the king's judgment. In order that an evil deed of this scale not

63. This is Duke Eberhard of Franconia.

64. Eberhard's captive was Henry, Otto I's younger brother.

65. Henry was born sometime between 919 and 921, which meant that he was seventeen to nineteen years old in 938. He was certainly not very young, particularly in the context of a society in which men of his age and status often already had several years of military experience.

66. See Liudprand of Cremona, *Antapodosis,* 4.21–23.

67. Archbishop Frederick of Mainz (937–54). Hildebert died on May 31, 937.

remain unpunished, Eberhard was sent by the king to the city of Hildesheim as a kind of exile.[68] But shortly thereafter, Eberhard mercifully was received back into the king's grace, and returned to his earlier office.

14. Again regarding the Hungarians, and how they retreated with heavy losses.

Meanwhile, as these events were unfolding, our ancient enemy, the Hungarians, suddenly raided Saxony. Having gathered along the banks of the Bode river,[69] they then spread throughout the region. One of their commanders was dispatched with part of the army at dusk on that day, and marched to the fortress called Steterburg.[70] The defenders saw the enemy was worn down by their journey as well as by the rain, which was a heavy downpour. So they boldly rushed out through the gates. They first let out a terrifying yell, and then charged suddenly into the enemy. Many of the Hungarians were killed, and a huge number of horses and banners were captured. The survivors were forced to flee. But as the defenders of the strongholds along their path realized that the Hungarians were fleeing, they attacked them from all of these places, and killed most of them. When they captured the commander, they buried him in a deep cesspit.

The other part of the army had been led to the north to a place called Drömling through the trickery of a certain Slav.[71] However, discomfited by the difficult terrain, and overwhelmed by armed forces, this army was destroyed. This result frightened the other

68. See Adalbert of Magdeburg, *Continuatio, an.* 938.

69. The Bode, with its sources in the Harz mountains, is a left tributary of the Saale, into which it flows at Nienburg.

70. Steterburg is located about six kilometers northwest of Wolfenbüttel and two kilometers west of the Oker river in the modern German state of Lower Saxony. It is one hundred kilometers as the crow flies from the mouth of the Bode to Steterburg.

71. This is a low-lying area between the Aller and Ohre rivers, north of the modern city of Helmstedt on the border between the modern German states of Lower Saxony and Saxony-Anhalt. *Annales Corbeienses, an.* 938, records that a Hungarian army was destroyed in the *pagus* of Belxa, which reached from Drömling up to the Elbe.

Hungarians.[72] The commander of this army was captured along with a few others. He was led to the king, and then ransomed for a large price. When they learned what had happened, the enemy's entire camp was thrown into confusion, and they sought safety in flight.[73] Nor have they reappeared in Saxony for thirty years.

15. How Henry burned with a desire to rule.

After these events, Henry, who was burning with a desire to rule, organized a festive gathering at a place called Saalfeld.[74] And because he was great and powerful on account of his majesty and royal power,[75] he gave a great many gifts to many men, and, in this manner, gained the support of many for his cause. There were many who believed that it would be better to hide what had occurred so that they would not be judged guilty of stirring up fraternal discord. Nevertheless, they offered counsel to Henry that would bring about war that much more easily. They suggested that he go to the Lotharingians, a people who were unskilled in war, and leave Saxony under the control of his own military forces.[76] And so it happened that King Otto defeated these Lotharingians in a single attack, and wore them down in a single battle.[77]

Following the advice of his fellow soldiers, Henry departed Saxony, leaving garrisons in all of his strongholds in his lands in Saxony and Thuringia, and came to the Lotharingians in person along with his friends. Everyone everywhere was struck with fear

72. The implication is that the loss of this army frightened those Hungarians who had not come on this campaign.

73. It is not clear who remained in the Hungarian camp after the destruction of their two armies in the west and north. It is likely that Widukind is again telescoping events here, so that the camp should be understood as the Hungarian homeland in the Carpathian basin.

74. Saalfeld, in the modern German state of Thuringia, was the site of a royal fortress located along the Saale river.

75. As a member of the royal family and potential heir to Otto I, Henry had significant resources available to him.

76. Suetonius, *Caesar*, 35.

77. Widukind is foreshadowing here the battle of Andernach (939) where Duke Gislebert of Lotharingia and Duke Eberhard of Franconia were killed by forces loyal to Otto I.

when they heard about what Henry had done, because they had no idea at all what caused this sudden abandonment of the king, and the reason for this unexpected war. When the king first heard reports of what was happening, he did not believe them. But when he had confirmed that war was afoot, he led his army without delay in pursuit of his brother. When Otto arrived at the fortress called Dortmund,[78] which was garrisoned by his brother's men, the soldiers there, who were mindful of the fate of Thankmar, did not dare to wait for the king inside the stronghold. They left the fortification and surrendered to the king.

Agina was the man who was supposed to command the fortress on behalf of Henry. The king bound him with a powerful oath that, if possible, Agina was to convince his lord to give up this war and to return to concord and peace, or, at least, come in person to the king. Agina was then dismissed and sent back to his own lord.[79] The army then was led by the king to the banks of the Rhine river.

16. Regarding Duke Gislebert of the Lotharingians.

While Eberhard was fighting his war against the king,[80] Hadald, the king's chamberlain, was sent to Gislebert to discuss concord and peace. But since Gislebert was not yet prepared to side openly with one side or the other, Hadald was received unceremoniously and a response was delayed day after day. Hadald shrewdly recognized the duke's hostility and was no longer willing to accept this behavior. So he said, "I am giving you a royal command in the presence of your people that you present yourself before the king's tribunal on the appointed day, or know for certain that you will be judged an enemy."[81] Gislebert also dishonorably dismissed Bishop Bernhard, whom the king had dispatched to him, without giving

78. Dortmund, located in the modern German state of North-Rhine-Westphalia, was the center of an extensive royal fiscal complex.

79. Agina's lord was Henry, Otto's younger brother.

80. The first phase of this conflict took place in 938.

81. Version C of the *Res gestae* has instead: he said, "I summon you by royal command with the people as my witness."

him a clear answer either.[82] It is also said that Gislebert frequently misused the seals on royal documents.[83] After the legate had spoken, Gislebert began to treat him somewhat better, and had him escorted home in an honorable manner.[84]

17. *Regarding the battle of Birten.*

Preparing their forces for battle, Henry and Gislebert decided to meet the king at the Rhine.[85] Agina, mindful of his oath, preceded the army and, having crossed the Rhine, presented himself to the king. After offering his greetings, he said humbly: "Your brother, my lord, hopes that you are safe and rule over your great and wide realm for a long time. He commends himself to you as one who is hurrying as quickly as possible to join your service."

While the king asked Agina whether Henry was thinking about peace or war, he saw an enormous multitude approaching, with their banners erect, drawing ever closer to the part of his army that already had crossed the Rhine.[86] So Otto turned to Agina and said, "What does this force wish, and who are they?" And Agina answered quietly, "My lord, it is your brother. If he had deigned to follow my advice, he would have come in a different manner. At least I came, as I swore to do."

When the king heard this, he could not hide the pain he felt in his soul. There were no ships there that would allow him to cross the Rhine. This huge river did not offer any means for crossing, nor did the suddenly impending battle offer any time to the men

82. Bishop Bernhard of Halberstadt (924–68). Widukind models his text here on Livy, *Ab urbe condita*, 38.54.9.

83. Widukind is suggesting that Gislebert forged documents and took legitimate royal seals in order to authenticate them. This passage also suggests that far more royal documents were issued to recipients in Lotharingia, including Duke Gislebert, than survive today. The sentence about Bishop Bernhard and the sentence about misusing the royal seals are later interpolations in the text.

84. Suetonius, *Nero*, 34.

85. Birten is located a few kilometers southeast of Xanten in North-Rhine-Westphalia.

86. Otto I's vanguard was dispatched to secure a bridgehead on the other side of the river to protect the main army as it crossed.

on the other side to make any plans other than to die at the hands of the enemy or defend their lives with their arms. So the king, falling to his knees, held up his hands to God and said: "God, creator and ruler of the universe, look upon your people,[87] whom you wished me to rule. Let them be saved from their enemies so that all peoples will know that no mortal can oppose Your decision, You who can do all things, and who live and rule forever."

The king's men on the further bank carried their baggage and other equipment to a place called Xanten. Then they waited, prepared for the enemy.[88] Since there was a fishpond between our men and the enemy, the Saxons divided into two forces. One part attacked the enemy from the front. The other part attacked the enemy from the rear. They crushed the enemy between the two forces so that the few were able to hem in the many. For it is reported that on our side there were not more than one hundred armored men, and the army of the enemy was quite large. But when they were attacked from the front and back at the same time, the enemy did not decide quickly which side ought to be defended with greater strength. In addition, some of our men knew how to speak the Gallic language. They raised up a great shout in Gallic urging their enemies to flee. Since the enemy thought that it was their comrades who had shouted, they fled as they had been called upon to do.

That day, many of our men were wounded and some were even killed. Among them was Ailbert, called the White. He was wounded by Duke Henry's spear and died a few days later.[89] The enemy, however, were either all killed or captured, or certainly driven off. All of the baggage and equipment taken from the enemy was divided up among the victors. It is said that on the Lotharingian side a man named Godfried the Black fought well.[90] But Maincia, whom we mentioned above, fell on that day.[91]

87. Exodus 33.13.

88. Also see Adalbert of Magdeburg, *Continuatio, an.* 939; and Liudprand, *Antapodosis,* 4.24.

89. Widukind is anachronistically identifying Henry as a duke here.

90. This Godofried is not otherwise attested in surviving sources.

91. See 2.11 above.

18. How Dedi cunningly convinced Henry's soldiers to return to the king's side.

Dedi,[92] the Thuringian, sent messages to the garrison commanders in the strongholds located in the eastern parts of Duke Henry's lands, reporting on the victory of the king, and stating that the duke himself had fallen in battle. He did this cunningly so that they would all surrender to the king's authority. Henry, however, did not allow this act to go unavenged.[93] Only two out of all of his fortresses remained under Henry's control, namely Merseburg and Burgscheidungen.[94] Following his victory, the king decided to pursue his brother and brother-in-law.[95]

19. Henry returned to Saxony, but departed again after being defeated by the king.

When Henry, who was shattered by the recent victory of the king, learned about the surrender of his strongholds, he fled with nine armed men. Arriving somewhat later in Saxony, he entered the fortress of Merseburg. When the king learned of this, he also returned to Saxony, and undertook to besiege with his army the fortress where his brother was ensconced. Since he could not resist the stronger and greater power of Otto, Henry surrendered the stronghold after almost two months, and came out to the king. Henry was granted a thirty-day truce in which to gather his soldiers and leave Saxony.[96] If, however, any of these soldiers wished to come to the king, such a man would find mercy. After this, Saxony had a respite from internal wars for a brief while.

92. Dedi, who is also mentioned in 3.16, was a count in Hassegau in the region around Merseburg. See DO I, nr. 114.

93. Dedi was stripped of his offices and banned by King Otto in 953 at the urging of Henry.

94. These two fortresses are located about thirty kilometers apart, as the crow flies. Burgscheidungen was situated along the Unstrut river, and Merseburg was constructed on the Saale.

95. Henry and Duke Gislebert.

96. This siege took place during April and May of 939.

20. How the barbarians sought to kill Gero, and dragged out the war for a long time.

The barbarians were delighted by our misfortunes, and did not cease their arson, murder, and devastation. They also considered cunning ways to kill Gero, whom the king had assigned to govern them. But Gero, anticipating their trickery with his own, killed almost thirty leading men of the barbarians in one night after they were drunk from wine and buried in sleep following an excellent feast.[97] But Gero did not have sufficient forces to fight against all of the barbarian peoples. Indeed, at this time, the Obodrites were rebelling, after having annihilated our army, and killed its commander named Haika. So the king often led the army in person, striking against them, inflicting substantial losses on them, and finally driving them almost to the point of complete defeat.[98] Nevertheless, they chose war instead of peace, putting aside all thoughts of misery in the pursuit of costly freedom.

They were a tough people, and able to endure hardship. Accustomed to a poor way of life, the Slavs desire those things that seem heavy burdens to us. There was truly a long struggle between the two sides, with one fighting for glory and a great and broad empire,[99] and the other fighting for liberty or against the worst kind of slavery. In those days, the Saxons were afflicted by many enemies, the Slavs from the east, the Franks from the south, the Lotharingians from the west, and the Danes and Slavs from the north. It is for this reason that the barbarians carried on the war for so long.[100]

21. Regarding the Slav, who was released by King Henry.

There was a certain Slav, released by King Henry, who by paternal right of succession was to be the lord of those people who are

97. Widukind does not identify these leaders more precisely, but it seems likely that they were Hevelli. The passage is reworked from Vergil, *Aeneid*, 11.265.

98. This is a polite way of saying that King Otto was not able to defeat the Obodrites at this time in 939.

99. Sallust, *Jugurtha*, 94.

100. The implication here is that the Saxons could have overcome one enemy quickly, but that with enemies on all sides, the wars necessarily lasted longer.

called the Hevelli. His name was Tugumir. Having been convinced by a great deal of money, and persuaded by the promise of even more, Tugumir agreed to betray his own land. And so acting as if he had escaped in secret, he came to the fortress of Brandenburg. He was acknowledged by the people, and received as their lord. A short time later, he fulfilled his promise. For he invited his nephew, who had gained a dominant position among all of the leaders of his people, to visit him. After Tugumir captured his nephew through trickery, he killed him and delivered his fortress along with the entire region to the king.[101] After this was done, all of the barbarian nations up to the Oder river subjugated themselves to royal tribute in a similar manner.[102]

22. *How the king's army was led against Henry.*

When Henry departed Saxony, he went again to the Lotharingians. Henry, along with his soldiers, remained with his brother-in-law, namely Duke Gislebert, for some time. Then, the king again led his army against Gislebert. After ravaging the lands of the Lotharingians with fire, the king again brought them under his authority. Gislebert, who was being besieged in the fortress of Chièvrement, slipped out and made his escape.[103] However, since the king could not bring the siege to a successful conclusion because of the difficulties in attacking the place,[104] he devastated the surrounding region, and returned to Saxony.[105]

101. Tugumir surrendered Brandenburg to King Otto I.

102. Widukind is condensing at least a decade of struggle against the Slavs into this one incident. Tugumir's ascension at Brandenburg may be dated to 939, if Widukind's discussion of this incident in the context of the civil war between Otto I and Henry is intended to place it in its proper chronological context. However, it is clear that Otto I was still campaigning against a number of Slavic peoples west of the Oder, including the Redarii and the Ukrani, well into the 950s.

103. This fortress at Vaux-sous-Chèvrement is located southeast of Liège in modern Belgium. Also see Liudprand, *Antapodosis,* 4.34; and Flodoard, *Annales, an.* 939, who emphasizes Louis IV's role in this conflict, and particularly the support that he offered to the Lotharingian magnates who were rebelling against Otto I.

104. Sallust, *Jugurtha,* 46.

105. Otto issued a charter on September 11, 939, at Werla. See DO I, nr. 22. It is

23. Regarding Immo and Gislebert.

Knowing that Gislebert had a close adviser named Immo who was astute and exceptionally sly, Otto decided that it was better to use this man's cunning rather than to fight with arms.[106] Immo, as he was quite shrewd, gave in to one who was superior and more powerful, and took up arms against the duke.[107] The duke took this particularly badly because Immo had always supported him, and because Gislebert had trusted his counsel and loyalty. The duke's indignation grew even worse as a herd of his pigs was captured cunningly by Immo. For when the duke's swineherds passed in front of the gates of Immo's stronghold, the latter had a piglet chased in front of his gate, and then captured the entire herd of pigs as they came into his fortress through the open gates.

The duke, who did not wish to accept this loss, mobilized an army and besieged Immo. But the latter is said to have had many beehives. Breaking them apart, Immo had them thrown at the mounted men. The bees struck the horses with their stingers and drove them insane, so that the riders were in danger. When Immo, standing on the wall, saw the results, he threatened an attack alongside his men. The duke, after being tricked many times by Immo's stratagems, broke off the siege. As he was departing, the duke was reported to have said: "When Immo was with me, I was able to maintain the loyalty of all of the Lotharingians easily. Now, even with all of the Lotharingians, I am not able to capture him, while he stands alone."

24. Regarding Eberhard and Gislebert.

When Eberhard saw that the war had gone on for a long time, he no longer remained neutral. Having scorned the king,

---

approximately five hundred kilometers, or about a three-week journey, from Liège to Werla, which means that Otto must have abandoned his siege of Chièvrement no later than the third week of August 939.

106. Widukind does not use Otto I's name or title in this chapter, although it is clear that the king is the one who has decided to gain the support of the unsavory Immo against Gislebert.

107. The reference here is to Duke Gislebert, Immo's own lord.

and spurned the bonds of his oath, Eberhard joined forces with Gislebert, as in the beginning, and they plotted together to start a war. Nor were they content with the western kingdom alone. They plunged into the lands east of the Rhine with their army to devastate the fields there. When word of this reached the king's camp, for at this time he was besieging Breisach and other fortresses that were loyal to Eberhard,[108] many of the king's supporters abandoned him because they no longer had hope that the Saxons would continue to rule.[109] The king, however, practiced such constancy and command during this time of trouble, despite having a small army with him, that it seemed he faced no difficulties at all. This was so even though the high priest abandoned him, leaving behind this tents and all manner of supplies.[110]

25. Regarding Bishops Frederick and Rothard.

It is not for me to discuss the reason for their desertion, or to reveal royal secrets.[111] We have decided that history must suffice.[112] Whatever sins we have committed in this section, may they be forgivable. The high priest was sent to Eberhard to discuss terms for making peace and achieving concord, since he was most desirous of these things.[113] The former gave his oath to uphold the agree-

108. Breisach is located along the Rhine, halfway between Freiburg and Colmar, in the modern German state of Baden-Württemberg. At the time of this siege, Breisach was located on an island in the Rhine. See A. von Hofmann, *Das deutsche Land und die deutsche Geschichte* (Stuttgart, 1930), 3.26–27.

109. See Adalbert of Magdeburg, *Continuatio, an.* 939; and Liudprand, *Antapodosis,* 4.24.

110. The deserters were Archbishop Frederick of Mainz and Bishop Rothard of Straßburg (933–50).

111. It would appear that Widukind is playing on the word *misteria* here, which can have the meaning of secret, as we have translated the text, but also of archives, which would permit the perceptive reader to understand Widukind's ability to gain detailed information about the activities of the royal court.

112. By "history" Widukind means here a description of what took place, rather than an analysis of the motives of the main actors.

113. The high priest is Archbishop Frederick of Mainz, who was dispatched by Otto I to negotiate with Eberhard. Frederick was the brother of Duke Gislebert, and so may have been seen as a useful intermediary with strong connections to both sides

ment that had been made, and, it is reported, he said that he could not withdraw from it. But the king responded in a manner appropriate to his office that he would not be bound by what the bishop had done without the king's authority. But because he did not wish to be subject to the king as the preeminent power, against the authority of God,[114] the high priest left the king's presence and went to the city of Hamburg as if in exile.[115] The king sent Bishop Rothard to New Corbie.[116]

26. Regarding the deaths of Dukes Eberhard and Gislebert.

Duke Hermann[117] was dispatched with an army to crush the arrogant dukes. He found them along the banks of the Rhine with the greater part of their army absent, having already crossed the river with their booty.[118] Duke Eberhard himself was surrounded by soldiers and received many wounds, manfully returning them as well. He finally fell after being struck by a spear. Gislebert, who fled, climbed into a boat with many other men. But it then sank, succumbing to the enormous weight. The duke drowned with many others and was never found.[119]

When the king received word of the victory won by his soldiers and the death of the dukes, he gave thanks to omnipotent God whose timely aid he often had received. He placed Otto, the son of Richwin, in charge of the Lotharingians with the task of guiding the king's nephew, the son of Gislebert, a small boy with

---

in this conflict. Adalbert of Magdeburg, *Continuatio, an.* 939, presents the archbishop and bishop as preparing to join Eberhard and Gislebert in order to betray the king.

114. Widukind is playing here on 1 Peter 2.13, "submit for the Lord's sake to every human authority, whether a king as a preeminent power...." The implication is that Archbishop Frederick was in the wrong because he did not follow the biblical dictate.

115. According to Adalbert of Magdeburg, *Continuatio, an.* 939; and Liudprand, *Antapodosis,* 4.33, Archbishop Frederick of Mainz was sent into captivity at Fulda.

116. This is Widukind's monastery of Corvey.

117. Duke Hermann I of Swabia (926–49).

118. Adalbert of Magdeburg, *Continuatio, an.* 939, records that it was troops under the command of Hermann's brothers Udo and Conrad who defeated Dukes Gislebert and Eberhard at Andernach.

119. Also see *Annales Corbeienses, an.* 939.

a hopeful future named Henry.[120] The king then returned to Saxony. The boy's mother married King Louis.[121] The king's brother Henry departed from the Lotharingians and went to the kingdom of Charles.[122] The death of the dukes was followed by a bitter winter, and the winter was followed by a very hard famine.[123]

27. Again regarding Immo.

After these events, Immo took up arms against the king, although I do not know whether this was real or illusory. So, in the middle of the winter, he was surrounded by an army and surrendered himself as well as his stronghold. From that point on he remained faithful and useful.[124]

28. Regarding Gislebert's nephews, Ansfrid and Arnold.

Gislebert's nephews subjected themselves to the king's service, and so retained the strongholds that they had held.[125] Chièvrement was possessed up to this time by Ansfrid and Arnold.[126] Immo

120. Count Otto of Verdun (923–43) was the most important political figure in Upper Lotharingia. He served as duke of Lotharingia from 939 to 942. Gislebert's son Henry was the nephew of Otto I, born to his sister Gerberga. Gislebert's decision to name his son Henry likely resulted from his marriage to the daughter of King Henry I.

121. Gerberga, the wife of Gislebert and sister of Otto I, married King Louis IV of West Francia (936–54) and bore him eight children, including Lothar IV of West Francia (941–86) and Charles, duke of Lower Lotharingia (953–93).

122. This is the kingdom of Charles the Bald, i.e., West Francia.

123. The severity of the winter and the concomitant famine also are discussed by *Annales Sangallenses maiores, an.* 940, ed. G. H. Pertz, MGH SS 1 (Hanover, 1826); and *Annales Colonienses, an.* 939, ed. G. H. Pertz, MGH SS 1 (Hanover, 1826).

124. Widukind uses the phrase *fidelis et utilis* regularly to denote the behavior of those whom Otto I defeated and then forgave.

125. Ansfrid and Arnold were the sons of Gislebert's sister, who had married Nivelong, the son of Count Ricfrid of Betuwe. Regarding the family relationship between the counts of Betuwe and the Gislebert's family, see Hein H. Jongbloed, "Immed 'von Kleve' (um 950). Das erste klevische Grafenhaus (c. 885–c. 1015) als Vorstufe des geldrischen Fürstentums," *Annalen des historischen Vereins für den Niederrhein* 209 (2006): 13–44.

126. This Ansfrid is likely Count Ansfrid, who was identified by Thietmar of

sent a message to them saying: "I have no views of myself other than the views that you hold. However, it is well known that you are leaders of this people. There is no doubt that a man with two hands can do more than a man with one. It is even more certain that three surpass one in strength. What necessity compels us to serve the Saxons other than our own conflicts? When they overcame you by force of arms, surely they did not enjoy the victory? It is shameful to serve the victors. I deserted the best of all men,[127] who raised me as a boy and always kept me among his friends, and who was illustrious because of his great power. I took up with the Saxons at great danger to myself. As you know, instead of the honor that I deserved from this act, I have been afflicted with insults. I am surrounded by armed men, and have been transformed from a free man almost into a slave.[128] Therefore, you ought to know that I wish to offer counsel for the common good. Ansfrid, I will marry my one daughter to you so that you will not regard me as having a single ounce of treachery. Set a place for us to meet together so that you can test my loyalty in person, which you have not yet been able to test through my messenger."

Although they had hearts of iron, and long had mistrusted Immo, they gave in to his great cunning, and were softened by his persuasive words.[129] And so they set a place to meet in person. But Immo, who had hidden armed men in suitable places, captured both of them by trickery, and sent them under guard to the king. He also sent a message as follows: "The taller one,"[130] he said, "is softer and does not require either chains or beatings. He will reveal everything that he knows if threatened. Ansfrid, however, is harder

Merseburg, *Chronicon*, 4.31, as the son of Queen Mathilda's brother, and hence Otto I's first cousin. For a useful survey of the sources relating to Count Ansfrid and his nephew, Bishop Ansfrid of Utrecht (995–1010), see Jean Baerten, "Les Ansfrid au Xe Siècle," *Revue belge de philology et d'histoire* 39, no. 4 (1961): 1144–58.

127. This is Duke Gislebert.

128. This passage may indicate that Otto I stationed his own troops as a garrison in Immo's stronghold.

129. Sallust, *Jugurtha*, 71.

130. The taller brother was Arnold.

than iron. If the harshest torments are used to question him, that would be best."

The king received them, and punished them for some time by keeping them in captivity. However, after he had gained their loyalty through the leniency of his grace, the king released them in peace.[131] Since the causes and events are so jumbled together that it is not possible to disentangle the order in which they happened, let no one accuse me of changing around the times for having placed the later events before the earlier ones.[132]

29. *How Henry received mercy.*

Therefore the king, who was always prone to clemency, felt compassion for the great suffering of his brother.[133] The king granted him some fortresses for his own use, and permitted him to live in the land of the Lotharingians.[134]

30. *Regarding Gero, the frontier commander.*

At this time, the war against the barbarians was raging. When the soldiers, who had enlisted in Gero's forces,[135] were worn down by the frequent campaigns, and were receiving less in the way of pay and booty, because the tribute was not being paid,[136] they de-

131. Ansfrid eventually became a prominent count under Otto I. He is mentioned by name in DO I, 370. Thietmar of Merseburg, *Chronicon,* 4.31, observed that Ansfrid held fifteen counties.

132. Widukind's comment on his own text provides a useful insight into his conception of what a historical work entails. Clearly, Widukind believes that events should be presented in the order in which they occurred. However, affairs in Lotharingia, at least, were so complex that Widukind could not establish a clear pattern from the information that he was able to obtain.

133. Vergil, *Aeneid,* 1.597.

134. Fortresses in the Ottonian period were the centers of extensive fiscal districts. So by granting a number of fortresses to his brother Henry, the king was, in effect, giving him the revenues that were associated with these strongholds. Flodoard, *Annales, an.* 940, records that Otto I made his brother Henry duke of Lotharingia at this time.

135. Widukind frequently uses the term *praeses* to indicate the office of frontier commander (German *Markgraf*).

136. This is the tribute that Henry I and Otto I had imposed on the Slavic peoples living east of the Elbe river.

veloped a seditious hatred of Gero. But the king always stood by Gero for the common good of the state.[137] So it happened that the soldiers were so riled up that they turned their hatred of Gero against the king as well.

31. Again regarding Henry, and how many people plotted with him against the king.

These circumstances were well known to Henry. And, as is often the case when something sweet is offered to embittered souls, he easily persuaded men of this type to join with him. He again hoped that he would rule, knowing that the army was upset with the king. So, after dispatching numerous emissaries and exchanging gifts, Henry gathered to his side almost all of the soldiers in the eastern lands.[138] Matters grew to such evil proportions that they made a plan to kill the king during Easter, which was fast approaching, while Henry himself was at the palace,[139] and then to place the royal crown on Henry's head.

Although no one publicly betrayed these plans, shortly before Easter the plot was revealed to the king,[140] who was always protected by God. So the king had himself surrounded day and night with a protective guard of loyal soldiers, and did not diminish in any way his royal dignity or majesty before the people during this holy day. But he did terrify his enemies.

After this holy day, the king took counsel, mostly with the Franks who were there with him at that time, namely Hermann, Udo, and Conrad, called the Red, and secretly ordered them to capture or kill the plotters.[141] The first of these plotters was Erich. Aside from this one evil act, he had demonstrated his great bravery and become illustrious through his many other virtuous

137. Widukind uses the term *res publica* in the Roman sense of the institution of the state.

138. It is likely that Widukind is referring here to the Eastphalian region of Saxony.

139. This is the royal palace of Quedlinburg.

140. Acts 9.24.

141. These were Duke Hermann I of Swabia, his brother Udo, and Conrad the Red, future son-in-law of King Otto I and future duke of Lotharingia.

achievements.[142] When he realized that armed men were coming toward him, and knowing why, he mounted his horse, and took up his arms. Surrounded by a crowd of enemies, and mindful of his earlier virtue and nobility,[143] he chose to die rather than to submit to the domination of his enemies. He fell, struck by a lance. This man was beloved and honored by his fellow citizens for his every virtue and his sense of purpose. The other participants in the conspiracy were held for another week. Then, according to the law, they paid the penalty due for their evil deeds and were beheaded. However Henry fled, departing from the kingdom.

32. *Regarding the portents.*

That same year some portents appeared, namely comets.[144] They were seen from the eighteenth of October up to the first of November. Many people were terrified at the sight of the comets, fearing that there would be a great pestilence or at least a change in ruler since great prodigies were seen before the death of King Henry. For example, the light of the sun could hardly be seen outdoors because of the dark sky, but inside sunlight poured red as blood in through the windows of houses. Moreover, it is said that the mountain where the lord of the world is buried[145] emitted flames in many different places. The left hand of a certain man, which had been cut off with a sword, was restored almost completely a year later while he was sleeping.[146] As a sign of this miracle, a blood-colored line was observed at the point where the flesh

142. Erich was the father of Bishop Hildiward of Halberstadt (968–98). See Thietmar of Merseburg, *Chronicon,* 2.21, who lists Erich along with a number of other Saxon magnates, who were executed by King Otto at this time. Thietmar's own grandfather Liuthar was spared execution, but suffered the loss of extensive properties and was sent into captivity in Bavaria.

143. Sallust, *Catilinae,* 58 and 60.

144. Portents also were mentioned in the *Annales Corbeienses, an.* 941; and *Annales Sangallienses maiores, an.* 941.

145. This is the burial site of King Henry I on a steep hill at Quedlinburg abbey. See 1.41.

146. See Flodoard, *Annales, an.* 944, who places this event some years after Widukind.

was joined. But the comets were followed by a great flood, and the flood was followed by a pestilence among the cattle.[147]

33. Regarding Otto, the guardian of the Lotharingians.

When Otto, the guardian of the Lotharingians,[148] had died along with Henry,[149] the king's nephew, the ducal office in this region was granted to Conrad.[150] The king married his only daughter to him.[151] Conrad was an intelligent man and brave. Excellent both in the management of civil affairs and war, Conrad showed great kindness to his fellow soldiers.[152]

34. Regarding Berthold, the brother of Arnulf.

In those days, Berthold, the brother of Arnulf,[153] administered Bavaria.[154] He fought against the Hungarians and emerged victorious, becoming renowned for this celebrated triumph.[155]

147. Flodoard, *Annales, an.* 942, also describes a cattle pestilence, but three years after the battle of Andernach.

148. In this case, Widukind uses the term *praeses* to indicate that Count Otto of Verdun held the preeminent office in Lotharingia. However, the author assiduously avoids denoting this office as the *ducatus* or Otto as *dux,* the title that he accorded to both Gislebert and Conrad the Red, Otto's predecessor and successor, respectively. It may be that Otto of Verdun's role as the guardian of Gislebert's son Henry made it untenable for the king to grant him the title of duke.

149. Flodoard, *Annales, an.* 944; and Adalbert of Magdeburg, *Continuatio, an.* 944, both place the death of Otto of Verdun in 944.

150. This was Conrad the Red.

151. Otto I's daughter Liutgard (died 954) who married Conrad in 947.

152. Widukind's use of the term *commilitones* indicates that Conrad the Red was seen by his men as an ideal soldier as well as commander.

153. Following the revolt by Duke Arnulf of Bavaria's sons in 938, Otto I appointed Arnulf's younger brother Berthold to serve as duke in Bavaria (938–47).

154. Widukind uses the term *procurabat,* i.e., administering as a *procurator,* which has the implication that Berthold was not in fact duke of Bavaria but rather was merely Otto's agent in the duchy.

155. The reference here is to Berthold's victory over the Hungarians at the battle of Wels on August 12, 943. See *Herimanni Augiensis Chronicon a. 1–1054,* ed. Georg Pertz, MGH SS 5 (Hanover, 1844), 113; *Annales Magdeburgenses,* ed. Georg Pertz, MGH SS 16 (Hanover, 1859), 144; and Adalbert of Magdeburg, *Continuatio, an.* 944, who attributes the victory to the Carantanians rather than to the Bavarians; and below 2.36.

35. How the king defeated another Hugh by force of arms.

As the king grew stronger from day to day, he was no longer content with his father's kingdom. So he marched to Burgundy and brought under his authority its king along with the kingdom.[156] The king overcame the other Hugh by force of arms, and made him his subject.[157] Hugh made a gift to the king of his golden brooch, marvelously sparkling with a variety of gems, which we saw on the altar of the protomartyr Stephen.[158]

36. Regarding the harmony between the brothers, their manner of life, and their characters.

Once all of the kingdoms had been pacified under Otto, and all of his enemies had submitted to his power, he was reminded through the urging and intercession of his holy mother about his brother, now worn down by his many misfortunes.[159] So, now that Berthold had died, Otto established Henry in the kingdom of the Bavarians.[160] Otto made peace and established harmony with Henry, which the latter maintained up through the end of his life. For Lord Henry was married to the daughter of Duke Arnulf, a women distinguished by her beauty, and exceptional for her intelligence.[161] This concord and peace between the brothers was pleasing to God and beloved by man, and soon became celebrated throughout the world, as the two men together enriched the state, defeated their enemies, and exercised paternal power over their people. Having accepted the ducal office in Bavaria, Henry dem-

156. King Conrad I of Burgundy (937–93). Otto I's campaign into Burgundy took place in 940. See Flodoard, *Annales, an.* 940.

157. This is Hugh the Black, duke of Burgundy (923–52), the younger brother of King Raoul of West Francia (923–36).

158. St. Stephen was venerated at Widukind's monastery of Corvei, where our author likely saw this jewel-encrusted golden brooch.

159. King Otto I was urged by his mother, Mathilda, to forgive and rehabilitate his brother Henry, who had been deprived of any major role in the Ottonian government since the conspiracy discussed in 2.31.

160. Berthold died in November 947.

161. This was Judith (died c. 985).

onstrated consistent energy. He went on campaign and captured Aquileia,[162] defeated the Hungarians in two battles,[163] crossed the Ticino river and captured a huge quantity of booty in the lands of the enemy, and brought his army back safely.[164]

We do not have the ability to set out fully the way of life of such distinguished and great men, their characters, and their appearance; men whom the highest mercy[165] provided for the delight and glory of the earth. But we certainly cannot hide completely the true devotion that we feel toward them. Otto, the lord of the world, the greatest and best of the brothers by birth, is distinguished first by his piety. He is the most steadfast of men in his labors, and, aside from the terror of royal punishment, he is always friendly. He is generous in giving gifts, limited in his sleep,[166] and always talking even while asleep so that it appears he is still awake.[167] He denies nothing to his friends, and shows them superhuman loyalty. For we have heard that some men, although charged and appearing guilty, had Otto as their advocate and intercessor since he did not believe they had committed the crime. Moreover, afterward, he treated them as if they had not sinned against him in any way.

His intelligence is exceptional. For after the death of Queen Edith,[168] he learned his letters, which he had not done previously, and did so well that he can now easily read and understand books.[169] Furthermore, he knows how to speak the Romance and

162. The capture of Aquileia is not attested in any other surviving source.

163. *Annales Hildesheimenses, an.* 950, MGH SS 3, 58, records a major battle between the Bavarians and the Hungarians.

164. In 948 Henry defeated the Hungarians near Floß on the Entenbühl mountain, located in the Oberpfälzer Wald, along Bavaria's eastern frontier with Bohemia. Two years later, in 950, Henry won another victory over the Hungarians at Ticino in modern Switzerland.

165. The highest mercy is God.

166. Lucan, *Pharsalia,* 9.590.

167. Widukind appears to have modeled this portrait of Otto I on Einhard's depiction of Charlemagne, which is itself, modeled on Suetonius's depiction of Augustus.

168. Queen Edith died in January 946.

169. Einhard, *Vita Karoli Magni,* ch. 25, commented on Charlemagne's failed effort

Slavic languages.[170] But it is rarely the case that he finds it useful to do so. He frequently goes hunting, and loves table games.[171] He also gracefully practices his horsemanship in a weighty royal manner. He has grown into a large body that shows his full royal dignity. His head is covered with white hair.[172] His glittering eyes emit a certain splendor that has the effect of a rapid lighting strike. He has a red face and a bushy beard, which goes against the old custom. His chest is covered with hair like the mane of a lion.[173] He has a moderate-sized belly, and a quick gait, which has slowed down somewhat. He dresses in the clothing of his homeland, and never puts on foreign garb.[174] Whenever he has to wear his crown, it is reported accurately that he always fasts beforehand.

Henry had a more dour character. For this reason, people who did not know him thought that he was less merciful and friendly. However, he had a constancy of spirit, and was loyal to his friends. Indeed, Henry honored a soldier of limited means by marrying him to the sister of his wife, making him both his comrade and his friend.[175] He was very tall, and from his youth gained popularity with everyone because of his good looks.

The youngest of the brothers was Lord Brun, who had a great intellect and was exceptional for his learning, energy, and every virtue. The king placed him over that indomitable people, the Lo-

---

to learn how to compose letters with a pen. It should be noted that Widukind does not enter into the question of Otto I's ability to write, which was a task usually undertaken by an amanuensis, but rather focuses on the ruler's ability to read texts, presumably in Latin.

170. It is not clear here whether Widukind is referring to Old French or Latin. Flodoard, *Annales, an.* 948, records that at the synod at Ingelheim, a letter issued by Pope Agepitus II was read out loud before the assembled bishops as well as Otto I and Louis IV, and many of their secular magnates. Flodoard records that the letter was then translated into *Teudisca lingua,* but does not specifically say that this was done for Otto rather than for other native German speakers in attendance.

171. Widukind does not specify which games, but they may have included chess.

172. Ovid, *Metamorphoses,* 8.568.

173. Pliny, *Naturalis historia,* 38.10, 54.

174. Einhard, *Vita Karoli Magni,* 23.

175. This was Count Burhard, the father of Bishop Henry of Augsburg (973–82), who married Judith's sister, whose name does not appear in surviving sources.

tharingians. Brun then cleansed the land of highwaymen, and imposed such discipline on the Lotharingians, following the law, that exceptional order and peace took hold in that region.

37. Regarding the persecution of monks.

When the civil and external wars came to an end, both divine and human laws now prevailed with the force intended by their authors. In those days, the monks began to suffer severe persecution because some bishops claimed that they thought it better for a few men to live distinguished lives rather than for many half-hearted men to dwell in the monasteries. They forgot, unless I am mistaken, the views of the head of the household who prohibited the servants from gathering the weeds, noting that it was necessary to allow both weeds and wheat to grow until the harvest.[176] So it happened that many, who were aware of their own weakness, set aside their habits and departed the monasteries in order to avoid the even heavier burden of priesthood.[177] There were some who judged that the highest priest Frederick[178] had not acted out of pure motives, but rather for some contrived purpose so that he could harm in some way that venerable man who was always loyal to the king, Abbot Hadamar.[179]

38. Regarding Abbot Hadamar.

He was a man remarkable for his knowledge and industry. In his day, the famous church at Fulda was destroyed by fire.[180] He restored it, and made it much more magnificent.[181] Hadamar held a bish-

176. Matthew 13.27–30.

177. Widukind is commenting here on the growing practice of having monks ordained as priests.

178. Archbishop Frederick of Mainz.

179. Abbot Hadamar of Fulda (927–56) had extensive conflicts with Archbishop Frederick of Mainz over jurisdictional and financial matters. Widukind's mention of Hadamar's loyalty to the king is intended as a contrast with Frederick's abandonment of the king at the siege of Breisach, and his later dalliance with the rebels in 953.

180. *Annales Corbeienses, an.* 937.

181. The church at Fulda was consecrated in 948. See Flodoard, *Annales, an.* 948.

op in custody, who was guilty of conspiracy for a second time.[182] At first, the bishop was held honorably. But when Hadamar seized some letters written by the bishop, the captivity became somewhat more harsh. When the bishop sought revenge after being released, the law could not prevail against such a man. He used his power against the most humble of monasteries in the same way as he acted against the most exalted. But his many plots were in vain. For the abbot retained the grace and friendship of the king. So, as events intervened, the bishop was not able to implement his plans.

39. Regarding King Louis and his sons.

The sister of the king bore three sons to King Louis,[183] namely Charles, Lothar, and Karlmann.[184] However, King Louis himself was betrayed by his military commanders and captured by the Northmen. At the suggestion of Hugh, Louis was brought to Laon and placed in public custody.[185] The Northmen took Louis's elder son Charles with them to Rouen, where he died.[186] When the king learned about the misfortune of his friend,[187] he became quite upset and ordered an expedition to Gaul against Hugh to take place the next year.

40. Regarding the hostages from Boleslav.

At that time, while the king spent some time in forested regions hunting, we saw the hostages sent by Boleslav,[188] whom the king

182. This is Archbishop Frederick of Mainz.

183. King Louis IV of West Francia.

184. Otto I's sister Gerberga, who previously had been married to Duke Gislebert of Lotharingia. Charles died in 945. Lothar IV ruled as king of West Francia (954–86). Karlmann is not identified in other contemporary sources.

185. This is Hugh the Great, Otto I's other west Frankish brother-in-law. These events took place in 945. See Flodoard, *Annales, an.* 945.

186. Charles was not the elder son, but rather the second-born son. In addition, he did not die at that time. Version C of the *Res gestae* corrects this passage, replacing Charles with Karlmann, i.e., *Carlomannum* in place of *Carolum,* since Charles (died 991) was still living at that time, and had been duke of lower Lotharingia since 977.

187. The reference here is to Otto I learning about Louis IV's captivity.

188. Duke Boleslav I of Bohemia.

ordered to be presented to the people.[189] The king was very happy about them.

41. Regarding the death of Queen Edith.

This year was noteworthy because of a terrible calamity for the whole people, namely the death of Queen Edith of blessed memory, whose last day was celebrated on the twenty-sixth of January with moans and tears of all Saxons. She was an Angle by birth and was distinguished no less by her piety than by her royal descent from such a powerful family. She shared in the rule of the kingdom for ten years and died in the eleventh. She lived in Saxony for nineteen years.[190] She left behind a son named Liudolf whose strength of spirit and body was second to no one in that age. She also left behind a daughter named Liutgard who married Duke Conrad. Edith was buried facing east in the new basilica in the city of Magdeburg.

Here ends book two.

189. This is one of the few instances in which Widukind interjects his own eyewitness testimony into the text. Otto I issued a charter in December 945 at Königsdahlum some fifty-five kilometers east of Corvey, and issued a charter on behalf of Corvey at Frose, near Magdeburg, in May 946. Widukind may well have been in attendance at the royal court on one or both of these occasions. Whether Duke Boleslav I sent hostages at such an early date is not clear. Otto undertook a major expedition against Bohemia in 950. See 3.8. Consequently, if Boleslav did send hostages in either 945 or 946, relations between the two rulers deteriorated significantly after this date.

190. Widukind is off by a year here. Edith actually died in the tenth year of her marriage to Otto and in the eighteenth year of her residence in Saxony.

BOOK THREE

Preface Book Three

To Lady Mathilda, daughter of the emperor, here begins the preface to book three.

Just as the appearance of heaven and earth, and the voices, faces, and traditions of men, although they might vary in a thousand ways in harmonious disagreement, nevertheless are compelled by the wisdom of the all-ruling God toward the guidance and understanding of a single light, so too does the imperial honor, which has poured out in you as the most serene excellence and the most brilliant gem in the world, require a single arbiter of justice and one standard of rectitude in both public and private affairs.[1] Therefore, I humbly ask that the product of our labor, although it might be understood to have a range of meanings by men of diverse character because it lacks the clarity of brilliant discourse, nevertheless be taken into the bosom of your glorious mercy, and that greater weight be given to our devotion than to our foolishness.

End preface

Book three begins

1. How the king selected his son Liudolf to succeed him as king.

After the death of Queen Edith, the king transferred all of his love from the mother to his only son, Liudolf. After making a testa-

1. The phrase *mille modis concordi discordia* is taken from St. Augustine's letter to Maximus of Madauros. See Paolo Mastandrea, *Massimo de Madauros: Agostino, Epistulae 16 e 17* (Padua, 1985), 30–31.

ment, he chose his son to rule as king after him. The youth, at this time, was still untried, not yet having reached the age of sixteen.[2]

2. Regarding the campaign in Gaul, and the struggle of the king with Duke Hugh, and also concerning King Louis.

The king set out on a campaign in Gaul.[3] After mobilizing his army at Cambrai, the king hurried to enter the kingdom of Charles[4] to avenge the injury done to his brother-in-law Louis.[5] When Hugh[6] received word of these events he sent an emissary through whom he swore on the soul of his now long-dead father, who had rebelled against God and his own king, that he would mobilize a larger force of troops than Otto had ever seen.[7] Hugh went on, in his swollen vanity, to say about the Saxons that they were useless in war, and that he could easily swallow seven Saxon spears in a single gulp. To this claim, the king famously responded:

VERSION B

It will be necessary to show him a greater multitude of straw hats than either he or his father has ever seen. And this is what

2. The naming of Liudolf as heir took place in 946.

3. Otto was in Magdeburg on July 29. See DO I, nr. 79. As the crow flies, Magdeburg is 625 kilometers from Cambrai, which would require three weeks for a fast-moving mounted column to cover. The earliest, therefore, that Otto could have begun his campaign was mid-August. This campaign also is recorded by Flodoard, *Annales*, *an.* 946.

4. The kingdom of Charles likely refers here to the lands once ruled by Charles the Bald, who received the western kingdom following the Treaty of Verdun in 843. Widukind's observation that Otto's army departed from Cambrai, located in Lotharingia, to enter the kingdom of Charles conforms with his general view that Henry I, Otto I's father, had successfully and permanently incorporated Lotharingia into the eastern kingdom.

5. Louis IV (920–54) was the Carolingian ruler of West Francia. He was the son of Charles III (879–929) and Eadgifu, the daughter of Edward the Elder of Wessex (900–924). Thus he was the nephew, by marriage, of Otto I, whose wife, Edith, was a daughter of Edward the Elder. Louis IV married Otto I's sister Gerberga in 939.

6. Hugh the Great was the brother-in-law of Otto I, having married his sister Hadwig.

7. Hugh's father was King Robert I, who died in the battle of Soissons fighting against Charles III, the father of Louis IV.

happened. Although the army was immense,[8] numbering thirty-two legions, not a single man was found without a straw hat except for the abbot of Corvey, named Bovo, along with his three companions.[9] He was a wise and illustrious man, whom God only gave to us on loan, rather than for a long time.[10] The grandfather of his father, named Bovo, became famous for reading Greek in the presence of King Conrad.[11] Bovo also had a grandfather of the same name, who surpassed him not only in age, but also in virtue and wisdom. The first Bovo was the nephew of Warin, who became a monk after a career as a soldier.[12] He was the first of all of those at New Corbei to be elected as abbot in a manner consistent with the rule.[13] He was admirable for his sanctity. Redounding to his own virtue and blessed memory, he brought a sacred treasure to Saxony, namely the relics of the worthy martyr Vitus.[14] Louis, after he was freed, hurried to the king, and joined his forces to Otto's army.

VERSION C

It will be necessary to show him a greater multitude of straw hats than either he or his father has ever seen. And so it happened. Although the army was enormous, comprising thirty-two legions, almost no one could be found who did not have a hat of this type. When it became clear that the king was coming, Hugh, driven by fear, freed Louis.

8. Widukind draws here on 1 Maccabees 6.41 to provide a sense of the enormous size of the army mobilized by Otto I.

9. Widukind tends to use the term *legio,* which we have translated as legion, to indicate a unit of fighting men who served under a single commander.

10. This is in reference to the short reign of Abbot Bovo III of Corvey (942–948).

11. Abbot Bovo I of Corvey (879–90). Widukind is confusing this abbot with Bovo II of Corvey (900–916). King Conrad I visited Corvey on February 3, 913. See *Die Urkunden Konrad I., Heinrich I. und Otto I.,* ed. Theodor Sickel (Hanover, 1879–84), DK I, nr. 14.

12. This is Bovo I, who was the nephew of Abbot Warin of Corvey (826–56). Again, it appears that Widukind is confusing Bovo II with Bovo I.

13. This is the Rule of St. Benedict.

14. See *Historia translationis S. Viti,* MGH SS 2 (Hanover, 1829), 576–85.

3. How the king came to the cities of Laon, Paris, and Rheims.

The king arrived at Laon with his army, and undertook to capture it by storm. From here, he marched to Paris and besieged Hugh. He also venerated the memory of St. Denis in every possible manner. The army was then led to the city of Rheims where Hugh's nephew had been installed as bishop against all practice and divine law, although the legitimate prelate was still alive.[15] Otto captured the city by storm, and expelled the unjustly elevated priest, restoring the legitimate bishop to his church and see.[16]

4. How the king came to Rouen and then returned to Saxony.

The king then chose a picked force of soldiers from the entire army and marched to Rouen, the city of the Danes.[17] However, the difficulty of the region, and the onslaught of harsh winter weather battered them. So, after three months, the still strong and healthy army returned to Saxony with their work incomplete.[18] The cities of Rheims and Laon, as well as the others that were captured by their arms, were handed over to King Louis.[19]

5. How Hugh came to the king beyond the Chiers river.

Hugh, after he had experienced the power of the king and the strength of the Saxons, did not wait for them to invade his lands again. Instead, he hurried to Otto as the latter was setting out the following year to resume his campaign, and met the king on the

15. Bishop Artold (931–61) was driven out by Hugh of Vermandois (920 to after 961) in 941. See Flodoard, *Annales, an.* 941.

16. Otto I issued a charter from Rheims on September 19, 946. See DO I, nr. 81.

17. Charles III made an agreement in 911 with the Viking leader Rollo, granting the latter control of the region around the mouth of the Seine, including Rouen, in return for guarding the river against other Viking raiders. This siege is discussed by Dudo of St. Quentin from an early eleventh-century Norman perspective in his *De moribus et actis primorum Normanniae ducum*, ed. Jules Lair (Caen, 1865), bk 4, chs. 96–99. Also see *Dudo of St. Quentin, History of the Normans*, trans. Eric Christiansen (Woodbridge, 1998), 128–36.

18. Otto was at Frankfurt on November 28, 946. It required a minimum of eighteen days to cover the 530 kilometer distance from Rouen to Frankfurt, meaning that Otto ended his campaign no later than November 10, 946.

19. Adalbert of Magdeburg, *Continuatio, an.* 946.

far side of the Chiers river.[20] Here, he gave his hand to Otto, and entered into a pact in a manner dictated by the king. He remained helpful to the king from this point forward.

6. *Regarding Liudolf, the son of the king, and how he marched to Italy.*

The king, seeing that his son Liudolf had become a man,[21] gave him an exceptionally noble and wealthy wife. This was Ida, the daughter of Duke Hermann.[22] A short time after they were married, Liudolf's father-in-law died. The duchy and all of Hermann's possessions then came to Liudolf. After he had gained this power, however, Liudolf discarded the peaceful spirit that he had borne in his youth. He led a military force into Italy where he captured and garrisoned some cities before returning to Franconia.[23]

7. *Regarding Berengar, king of the Lombards.*

At this time a fierce and greedy man named Berengar ruled in Lombardy.[24] Having usurped the royal power, he put all justice up for sale for money.[25] He feared the strength of the singularly prudent queen whom King Louis had left a widow.[26] He harried her in multifarious ways so that by these means he could extinguish her blazing glory, or, at least, obscure it.

8. *How the king led an army against Boleslav.*

At that time, the king campaigned against Boleslav, the king of the Bohemians.[27] After he had captured the fortress called "New,"

20. The Chiers (German Korn) is a right tributary of the Meuse. Flodoard, *Annales, an.* 947, dates this meeting to August.

21. Liudolf (930–57) married Ida some time before the death of Duke Hermann of Swabia in 949. The year of Liudolf's marriage is not known.

22. Duke Hermann I of Swabia.

23. This campaign took place in the summer of 951, before Otto I's own larger expedition in September of that year.

24. Berengar II of Italy (950–63).

25. Berengar drove out Hugh of Arles, who was king of Lombardy (924–48).

26. Widukind misidentifies the king as Louis rather than Lothar. The queen is Adelheid (931–99), the daughter of King Rudolf II of Burgundy (912–37) and the widow of King Lothar of Italy (born 926, king 931–50).

27. Duke Boleslav I of Bohemia.

in which Boleslav's son had been one of those who was besieged, the king, following prudent advice, ended the fighting.[28] He did so to avoid having any of his soldiers fall prey to danger while seizing spoils from the enemy. After he had taken stock of the great strength of the king, and the enormous size of his army, Boleslav departed from his city, preferring to subject himself to such great majesty rather than suffer ultimate ruin.[29] So, standing under the banners, listening to the king, and giving answers, he earned mercy. After he had achieved glory through this complete victory, the king returned to Saxony.

9. How the king married the queen, and how Liduolf then departed in tears.

Since the virtues of the aforementioned queen[30] were not hidden from Otto, he decided to set out under the pretext of a journey to Rome.[31] When the king arrived in Lombardy, he tried to strengthen the queen's love for him with gifts of gold. After the king determined that she was loyal, he married her, and captured the city of Pavia, which was the royal seat. When his son, Liudolf, saw what had occurred, he departed in sadness from the king, and set out for Saxony. He stayed for some time at Saalfeld, a place that was disgraced by conspiracies.[32]

10. After celebrating his marriage, the king returned to Saxony. Berengar followed him in order to make peace.

After he had celebrated his marriage in Italy in magnificent royal style, Otto set out for Saxony to hold Easter with all of the

28. This is the fortress of Nimburg (Czech Nymburk) on the Elbe, approximately forty kilometers west of Prague. Otto issued a charter here on July 16, 950. See DO I, nr. 126. Duke Boleslav I's son was Boleslav II (972–99).

29. The city is Prague.

30. This is Adelheid, the widow of King Lothar of Italy.

31. The implication here is that Otto set out to obtain Queen Adelheid under the pretext of visiting Rome. See Flodoard, *Annales, an.* 952.

32. See book 2.15 for the conspiracy against Otto I by his brother Henry (919–55), which was organized at Saalfeld.

splendor of a new marriage, bringing joy and great cheer to his fatherland. Moreover, Duke Conrad, who had been left in command of the garrison to guard Pavia, persuaded King Berengar to follow the king to Germany, to make peace with him, and to follow all of the commands that the king gave him.[33] As Berengar approached the royal city, he was met a mile from the city by the dukes, magistrates, and important members of the court, received in a manner befitting a king, led to the city, and ordered to remain in quarters that had been prepared for him.[34] He was not permitted to enter the presence of the king for three days.[35] Conrad, who had brought Berengar here, took this ill. Liudolf, the son of the king, felt the same way. The two of them believed that Henry, the brother of the king, had a hand in this turn of events. They avoided his company, treating him as if he had been motivated by some long-standing jealousy. Henry, knowing that Liudolf now lacked the support of his mother, began to show contempt for him.[36] Henry even went so far as to insult him. In the meantime, the king spoke with the king.[37] Berengar received the grace of the king and the queen. He promised to accept their authority. He also set a day for entering freely into a pact with them at the city of Augsburg.[38]

11. Concerning the public assembly at Augsburg and the miracle that occurred there.

When the assembly had commenced, Berengar placed the hands of his son Adalbert within his own hands and, although he had already once subjected himself to the king when he was fleeing Hugh, nevertheless renewed his oath of loyalty before the entire army.[39] He bound himself as well as his son to the service of the

33. Duke Conrad the Red of Lotharingia (945–53).

34. The royal city is Magdeburg on the Elbe. Widukind is recording an *adventus* ceremony here.

35. The king here is Otto I.

36. Suetonius, *Augustus*, 93.

37. Otto I and Berengar II.

38. Augsburg was the traditional starting point for German kings heading over the Brenner Pass into northern Italy.

39. This is Hugh of Arles, the king of Lombardy. When Berengar fled Lombar-

king. After this act, he was dismissed and returned to Italy with grace and peace. There was then an enormous thunderstorm that produced such an enormous hailstone that it seemed to be a miraculous event to the numerous onlookers.

12. Regarding the sons of the king.

Of the sons born to the king by the most serene queen, the firstborn was Henry, the second was Brun, and the third was designated by the majesty of his father's name.[40] Now, the whole world hopes for him to be lord and emperor after his father. A daughter also was born and given the name of Otto's saintly mother.[41] We do not presume to say anything further about her because her brilliance exceeds anything that we might be able to say or write.

13. Regarding the ambushes that they prepared for the king.

When the king was traveling around the regions and cities of the Franks,[42] he heard that ambushes were being prepared for him by his son and son-in-law.[43] Whereupon the archbishop was summoned from the rather more austere style of life that he was accustomed to practice among the hermits and solitaries in the period before Easter. He received the king at Mainz, and provided

---

dy in 945, he was received at Otto I's court and given protection. Berengar's son was Adalbert (932–75).

40. The third son was Otto II (955–83). Henry apparently was born in 953. See Flodoard, *Annales, an.* 953. According to the *necrologia* of Merseburg, this young Henry died on April 7, perhaps as early as 954. See *Die Totenbücher von Merseburg, Magdeburg und Lüneburg*, 29. Brun died on September 8, 957. See *Annales necrologici Fuldensis*, ed. Georg Waitz, MGH SS 13 (Hanover, 1881), 198.

41. Otto I's mother, Mathilda (895–968), was alive while Widukind was composing the first version of the *Res gestae.* Widukind dedicated the present work to Otto's daughter Mathilda, who was named after her grandmother. The younger Mathilda's birth is noted by the *Annales Quedlinburgenses, an.* 955.

42. King Otto was traveling in the duchy of Franconia. Adalbert of Magdeburg, *Continuatio, an.* 951, records that Otto intended to celebrate Easter at the royal palace at Ingelheim, which was located a few kilometers from Frankfurt.

43. These are Otto I's son and son-in-law, respectively Liudolf and Conrad the Red.

for his needs there for some time.[44] When the son and son-in-law realized that their evil plans had been discovered, they followed the advice of the bishop and sought and received an opportunity to purge themselves of their crime.[45] Then, although they clearly were guilty of crimes, the king accepted each of their arguments because of the difficult place and circumstances in which he found himself.[46]

14. Regarding the preparations for Easter.

When the time came to organize the celebration of Easter at Aachen, the king learned that nothing fitting had been prepared for him.[47] So, he was then properly cared for with maternal joy and kindness, and magnificently took up in his fatherland the royal majesty that he almost had lost in Franconia.[48]

15. Regarding the son and son-in-law of the king, as well as Bishop Frederick.

Comforted by the presence of his friends and his own people, Otto declared void the agreement, which he claimed was forced upon him. His son and son-in-law were ordered to hand over for punishment the perpetrators of this crime. Otherwise the king would know that his son and son-in-law were public enemies. The

44. Archbishop Frederick of Mainz (937–54).

45. This is Archbishop Frederick. Liudolf and Conrad came to Mainz and confronted Otto I there. Widukind's use of the phrase *petunt et inpetrant* here recalls Jerome's letter, written in 412, to Principia regarding Marcella and the sack of Rome. See *Select Letters of St. Jerome,* ed. Frederick Adam Wright (London, 1933), letter 127, ch. 10.

46. Widukind is emphasizing here that Conrad and Liudolf held Otto in their power.

47. Adalbert of Magdeburg, *Continuatio, an.* 953, records that Otto originally planned to celebrate Easter at Ingelheim. However, after meeting with Liudolf and Conrad at Mainz, Otto traveled first to Cologne and then to Dortmund where he celebrated Easter.

48. Widukind is referring here to the settlement imposed on Otto by Conrad the Red and Liudolf at Mainz, and Otto's subsequent celebration at Dortmund. See Adalbert of Magdeburg, *Continuatio, an.* 953.

bishop spoke on behalf of the earlier agreement as if he were offering advice about concord and peace.[49] For this reason, the king came to suspect him because Frederick was scorning all of Otto's friends and advisers. We do not believe that it is proper for us to render a rash judgment concerning the bishop. We also do not believe that it is appropriate to remain silent about those matters we know for certain about him. The bishop spent a great part of every day and night in prayer, was generous in giving alms, and highly skilled in preaching. With regard to accusations against him, it is the Lord who will judge.[50]

16. Regarding the public assembly at Fritzlar, and Counts Dado and William.

Since these matters were not brought to an end there,[51] a public assembly was ordered to be held at the estate called Fritzlar to discuss the aforementioned charges.[52] When Henry, the brother of the king, arrived, he raised many grave charges against the bishop. From this point on, the bishop incurred the enmity of the king and almost the entire army. On the basis of what Henry had said, they believed that the bishop was completely guilty.[53] Furthermore, the king, who was very angry because of the indignity that he had just suffered, sentenced some very eminent men to go into exile under his brother's control. This group included some men who had been quite dear to him, and who had served him loyally in the battle of Birten.[54] They had tried to justify themselves after they were accused, but were not able to demonstrate their in-

49. The use of the genitive object with *consulare* is a classical usage, rather than the more common accusative found in postclassical texts.

50. Adalbert of Magdeburg, *Continuatio, an.* 953, presents Archbishop Frederick as acting in concert with Liudolf and Conrad the Red.

51. This refers to the place where Otto celebrated Easter, i.e., Dortmund.

52. It is approximately 130 kilometers from Dortmund to Fritzlar as the crow flies.

53. After this point, Archbishop Frederick no longer appears as arch-chancellor in royal charters.

54. These were men who had remained loyal to Otto while Henry had joined with the rebel dukes Gislebert of Lotharingia and Eberhard of Franconia in 939.

nocence. Among them were Thuringian counts named Dedi and William.[55] After this was done, many others, who had knowledge of the plot, were terrified.[56] When the assembly was dissolved, and the mass of people was dismissed, the king headed east.

17. Regarding the battle of the Lotharingians against Duke Conrad.

When the Lotharingians learned that Conrad had offended the king, they rose up in arms against him.[57] They had long been hostile to him because Conrad exercised his ducal authority over them against their will. But Conrad was undeterred, having the spirit of a lion. He turned his banners against theirs, and shed the blood of an incredible multitude of them with his own hand.[58] Conrad's savage fury was whetted even further by the blood of his friend Conrad, the son of Eberhard, whom he had lost in the battle.[59] Conrad was supported strongly by his troop of brave soldiers. At the same time, the enemy army was constantly gaining strength. The battle dragged on from midday to dusk. The fighting was brought to a close by night, and no one enjoyed a victory.

18. Regarding the siege of Mainz and the conflict between Henry and Liudolf.

Around the first of July, the king mobilized his army and marched out to find his son and son-in-law. The king either captured or accepted the surrender of the fortresses of his opponents

55. Count Dedi of Hassegau and Count William of South Thüringgau. See above 2.18 for Dedi's role in the civil war of 939 on Otto's side. Widukind consistently uses the term *praefectus* as a synonym for *comes,* i.e., count.

56. This is the plot of Liudolf and Conrad the Red against Otto I.

57. The leader of the revolt against Conrad the Red was Count Ranier III of Hainault. *Annales Lobienses,* ed. Georg Waitz, MGH 13 (Hanover, 1881), 224, identifies the fighting as taking place along the Maas; and Flodoard, *Annales, an.* 953, notes that Ranier attacked Conrad in order to force the rebel duke to break off his siege of one of the count's fortifications.

58. Widukind draws here on Lucan, *Pharsalia,* 1.6.

59. It is not clear who this Conrad is. However, on the basis of his name, he may have been a member of the powerful Conradine family, and one of Conrad the Red's cousins.

until he reached Mainz, which his son had entered with his own army. Awful to say, he waited in armed expectation for his father. From this point the war began, worse than a civil war, or any other calamity.[60] Numerous engines were brought up to the walls, but they were destroyed or burned by the defenders of the city. There was considerable fighting before the gates, but only rarely were the guard stations atop the walls overwhelmed by the attackers from the outside. Everyone remained frozen by hesitation as they feared the lord of the kingdom outside, and his successor who was within the walls.[61]

When the siege had gone on for almost sixty days,[62] peace discussions began. Eckbert, a cousin of the king, was sent into the city as a hostage.[63] It seemed that a clear path had opened in camp to anyone who wished to purge his guilt, and discuss making peace, and reestablishing concord. The son and son-in-law entered the camp and prostrated themselves before the king's feet. They were prepared to accept every punishment for their crime if their friends and supporters were received in good faith and did not suffer any punishment. However, the king, who did not see how he could impose the appropriate punishment on his son, demanded the accomplices in the plot. The son and son-in-law, who were constrained by mutual oaths, and also were bound, in some way, by the wiles of the ancient enemy, refused utterly to do this.[64] In the meantime, a huge wave of joy rose up in the camp. The rumor spread all around the camp that the son and son-in-law never would have left the city unless they were prepared to obey all of the commands of the king. This hope was born in vain. For when the son and son-in-law would not obey the king's commands, Henry grew enraged at the youth saying: "You claim that you have done nothing against my

60. Lucan, *Pharsalia,* 1.1.

61. These are Otto I and his son Liudolf, respectively.

62. Flodoard, *Annales, an.* 953, notes that the siege occupied all of July and August.

63. Eckbert and his brother Wichmann were the sons of Friderun, the sister of Queen Mathilda, Henry I's wife. They were also the nephews of Hermann Billung, who had received the military command of eastern Saxony in place of their father Wichmann the Elder in 936.

64. The ancient enemy is Satan.

lord king, but behold the entire army knows that you are a usurper and invader of the kingdom.[65] If I have been accused of some crime, if I am guilty, why do you not lead your legions against me? Lead your banners against me!" Then picking up a stick from the ground, he added, "You cannot take from me and from my power anything worth even this much. What led you to believe that you should disturb your father with matters of this kind? You are acting against the highest divine power when you fight against your father. If you know something, or wish something, then vomit out your anger against me, for I do not fear your anger." The youth did not respond to this at all. Instead, after he heard what the king had to say, he returned with his men into the city.

19. Regarding Eckbert, the cousin of the king.

Eckbert, the cousin of the king who was sent into the city as a hostage, was corrupted by persuasive words, and turned against the king. Earlier, Eckbert had been angry with the king because he blamed Otto for entering unprepared into a battle in which Eckbert had lost an eye.[66]

20. Regarding the Bavarians and how they joined Liudolf.

The next night, while all of this was going on, the Bavarians, who had accompanied the king's brother, left Henry and joined with Liudolf. The latter escaped with them, and then captured the royal city, which is called Regensburg, along with other very strong fortifications in the region. Liudolf divided all of the duke's money among his own soldiers. He then forced the wife, children, and friends of his uncle to leave the city, and, indeed, the region, entirely.[67] We believe that God allowed all of this to happen so that one who wished to rule as a most illustrious king over many people and nations would learn that he could achieve very little on his own, but could achieve everything through God.[68]

65. This is Duke Henry of Bavaria, Otto I's brother.

66. It is not clear which battle Widukind is referring to here.

67. Duke Henry's wife was Judith, the daughter of Duke Arnulf of Bavaria.

68. Widukind is implying here that God was testing Otto and showing the king

21. Regarding Arnulf and his brothers, and that the army sought and received permission to depart.

However, it was the younger Arnulf, along with his brothers,[69] who had devised this plan against Henry, because Arnulf had been replaced in his father's kingdom,[70] and had been deprived of his father's office. Furthermore, the army also was exhausted by its lengthy labor, so that it sought and received permission to depart. Then the king, along with a small force, pursued his son to Bavaria to the extent that he could.

22. Regarding the king, and that many abandoned him.

The king, himself, was inured to this effort to a greater extent than one might believe of a man who had such a pampered upbringing.[71] After so many men had abandoned their loyalty, there were few left, indeed, who remained on the king's side. Among these was Adalbert, and a small number of others who were with him.[72]

23. Regarding the army from Saxony that was marching to Mainz.

While the king was campaigning against Mainz, Hermann governed Saxony as duke. When it came time to dispatch a new army

---

that it was only divine rather than human strength that determines human fate. This is a subtle criticism of Otto, and a suggestion that the king had acted in an arrogant manner up to this point.

69. These were the sons of Duke Arnulf of Bavaria. Otto I selected their uncle Berthold to rule in Bavaria following the elder Arnulf's death, and subsequently chose his own brother Henry to serve as duke following the death of Berthold.

70. Widukind is using the standard Carolingian political and administrative designation of Bavaria as a kingdom (*regnum*), i.e., as a subordinate kingdom within the broader Carolingian Empire.

71. This observation could be understood as a subtle criticism of Henry I, who did not provide the kind of rough-and-ready upbringing for Otto that was the norm for the Saxons in the so-called heroic age described by Widukind in the first book of the *Res gestae*. This passage is modeled on Sallust, *Catilinae*, 5.

72. Adalbert may have been the Swabian count who aided Bishop Ulrich of Augsburg during the Swabian phase of the 953–955 civil war. See *Herimmani Augiensis chronicon*, 114; and Gerhard of Augsburg, *Vita Sancti Uodalrici*, ed. Walter Berschin and Angelika Häse (Heidelberg, 1993), 1.10.

from Saxony to reinforce the earlier army, the command was given to Thiadric[73] and the younger Wichmann.[74] When the army reached the border of Franconia, it suddenly was surrounded by Liudolf and Duke Conrad, and the Saxons were forced to enter a certain deserted fortification.[75] But when the former pressed their attack, a wheel that had been launched took off the flag-bearer's arm right in front of the gates.[76] After this occurred, the battle ended, and a three-day truce was agreed so that the relief army could return to Saxony.

24. Regarding Thiadric and Wichmann.

Thiadric was tempted by Liudolf's extravagant promises, but Wichmann was fully seduced. The latter began to denounce his paternal uncle,[77] to say that he had stolen his paternal inheritance, and to call him the thief of his inheritance.[78] Hermann was fully aware of this intrigue. It is difficult to describe completely the great wisdom and prudence that he employed in guarding against his kinsmen, who also were his open enemies.

73. This may be the Count Thiadric who became margrave of the Nordmark following the death of Margrave Gero in 965.

74. This Wichmann was the nephew of Duke Hermann. Widukind likely is presenting events out of order here. The relief army probably was dispatched while the siege of Mainz was still ongoing, i.e., before the escape of Liudolf to Bavaria and Otto I's subsequent decision to pursue him.

75. It is probably the case that the army was attacked by forces loyal to Conrad and Liudolf rather than by the two leaders in person.

76. The gates were the weakest part of any fortification, and it is here that attackers generally concentrated their assaults, particularly when they lacked siege equipment. Apparently, in this case, one of the heavy objects that was cast at the attackers was a wagon wheel.

77. This is Hermann Billung, who served as the commander of the northeastern Saxon frontier against the Slavs, and as Otto I's regent in Saxony.

78. Wichmann's father, Wichmann the Elder, had been passed over by Otto I in 936 in favor of Hermann when the frontier command structure in Saxony was reorganized. Both father and son Wichmann believed that they had been deprived of offices that should have been theirs.

25. Regarding Eckbert, Wichmann, and Duke Hermann.

Eckbert joined with Wichmann, and they rose up with the same intentions against the duke, giving him no peace.[79] Hermann, however, broke the furor of these youths through his noble patience. He took care that there was no increase in violence while the king was absent in those parts.[80]

26. Regarding the king's arrival in Bavaria.

Faced with the king's sudden arrival,[81] the Bavarians neither turned to peace, nor did they dare to face him in open battle. Instead, enclosed behind their walls, they readied a great labor for the army, but destitution for their region.[82] Since it was making no progress, the army acted without compassion and devastated everything without restraint.

27. Regarding Bishop Frederick and other bishops.

In the meantime, the highest priest,[83] as he himself said, set aside his episcopal office because of his fear of the king, and began to lead the life of a hermit among the solitaries. Also, there was considerable dithering among the other bishops in Bavaria in making a choice between the opposing sides, now aiding the king, and now offering support to his enemies. They could not abandon

79. Eckbert was Wichmann the Younger's brother, and so also a paternal nephew of Hermann, whom Widukind is calling a *dux* in the sense of a military commander rather than as duke of Saxony.

80. The reference here is to Otto's absence on campaign, first in Franconia and then in Bavaria.

81. The term *adventus* has an important ideological component, since it is used to describe the triumphal entry of a ruler into a city. Widukind's readers likely understood his point here that although this campaign was not a complete success, Otto's status as the true and ultimately triumphant king was not in doubt.

82. Otto I's army would have to undertake grueling siege operations to capture Bavarian fortress cities and other strongholds, but could, nevertheless, ravage the countryside with relative ease. Adalbert of Magdeburg, *Continuatio, an.* 953, records that Otto I's army undertook a siege of Regensburg.

83. Archbishop Frederick of Mainz.

the king without danger, nor could they remain loyal to him without loss.

28. How the king returned to Saxony with his task uncompleted.

The king operated for three full months in these regions after departing from Mainz. Around the beginning of January, he returned to Saxony with this affair still unresolved.[84] He had lost two of his most important and distinguished men, Immed and Mainwerk.[85] Both of them were killed by arrows, the former at Mainz, and the latter during the march to Bavaria.

29. Regarding the conflict between Hermann and his nephews.

When Hermann and his nephews had discussed their conflict in the presence of the king, all those who held to justice praised the judgment of the duke, and judged that the youths ought to be punished. However, the king, out of love, spared them, and had Wichmann handed over to a military guard within the palace.[86]

30. The Avars joined with the Bavarians. The king hurried to confront them with a powerful force.

In the meantime, the king received word that the Avars had entered Bavaria,[87] joined his adversaries, and had deployed in such a manner as to encourage him to meet them in a battle in the field.[88]

84. Adalbert of Magdeburg, *Continuatio, an.* 953, records that the royal army maintained its siege of Regensburg almost up to Christmas. If this is correct, then Otto's forces likely were on their way back to Saxony by early January.

85. It is not clear who Meinwerk was. Immed is mentioned by Adam of Bremen, *Gesta Hammaburgensis ecclesiae pontificum*, 3rd ed., ed. B. Schmeidler, MGH SRG 2 (Hanover, 1917), 2.45. See in English translation, *History of the Archbishops of Hamburg-Bremen*, trans. F. J. Tschan (New York, 2002).

86. Wichmann and his brother Eckbert were the nephews of Otto, through his wife Mathilda, so the expression of love here should be understood in the context of family obligations.

87. Widukind is using Avars here as a synonym for Hungarians.

88. The entrance of the Hungarians into the civil war is also discussed by Adalbert of Magdeburg, *Continuatio, an.* 954; and Flodoard, *Annales, an.* 954, who provide a

But the king was not at all disturbed by this difficulty, nor did he forget that he was lord and king by the grace of God. Instead, he mobilized a powerful force, and marched against the bitter enemy. But they avoided him. After obtaining guides from Liudolf, they spread throughout all of Franconia and inflicted enormous losses, particularly among their own friends. Unbelievable as it may sound, among all the other captives, they also took as prisoners more than a thousand dependents belonging to a man named Ernst, who belonged to the party opposing the king.[89] The Hungarians were received publicly at Worms on the Sunday before Easter, and given abundant gifts of gold and silver.[90] The Hungarians then departed for Gaul, and returned to their fatherland along a different route.[91]

31. The Bavarians, who were worn down by war, discussed terms for peace.

The Bavarians were worn down by both internal and external armies—for once the Hungarians departed, they were pressed by the royal army—and were forced to discuss terms for peace. So it happened that they were granted peace up to the sixteenth of June.[92] Langenzenn was chosen as the place where they would give their explanations, and where a response would be given to them.[93]

---

broader perspective, and Heriger, *Translatio S. Landoaldi sociorumque*, ed. O. Holder-Egger, MGH SS 15.2 (Hanover, 1888), ch. 9; John of St. Arnulf, *Vita Iohannis Abbatis Gorziensis*, ed. Georg Pertz, MGH SS 4 (Hanover, 1841), ch. 136; Sigibert of Gembloux, *Vita Wicberti*, ed. Georg Pertz, MGH SS 8 (Hanover, 1858), 14; Folcuin, *Gesta abbatum Lobiensium*, ed. Georg Pertz, MGH SS 4 (Hanover, 1841), 25; and *Gesta episcoporum Cameracensium Liber I. II. III. Usque ad a. 1051*, ed. L. C. Bethmann, MGH SS 7 (Hanover, 1846), bk 1, ch. 75, who are focused more on the Hungarian attacks in the lower Rhineland and Lotharingia.

89. This may be Count Ernst of Sualafeld.

90. Easter in 954 fell on March 26, so the public meeting between Conrad the Red and the Hungarians took place on March 17, 954.

91. It was during this return home that the Hungarians launched a number of unsuccessful attacks against fortified monasteries and episcopal cities along their line of march. See Adalbert of Magdeburg, *Continuatio*, *an.* 954; and Flodoard, *Annales*, *an.* 954, who both comment on the route taken by the Hungarians.

92. Although Widukind uses the term *pax* here, the context suggests that this was a truce rather than a peace agreement.

93. Langenzenn is located approximately twenty kilometers west of Nuremberg in Bavaria.

32. Regarding the royal assembly at Langenzenn.

When the entire people had gathered at the place that had been arranged, the king gave the following address: "I would have endured it," he said "if the provocation of my son and the other participants in this plot had tormented me, alone, and had not troubled the entire Christian people. It would have been bad enough if they only had invaded my fortresses and stripped lands from my power like thieves, and not also sated themselves on the blood of my kinsmen and my dearest companions. Behold, I sit here bereft of sons while I suffer to have my son as my greatest enemy.[94] Behold that one, whom I loved above all, and whom I raised up from his mediocre status to the highest level and greatest honor.[95] He has turned my one son against me. Even this I could have borne if they had not introduced the enemies of God and man into this business.[96] They have left my kingdom desolate, captured or killed my people, destroyed my fortresses, burned down my churches, and murdered my priests. The roads are now flooded with blood. The enemy of Christ now returns home, loaded down with my gold and silver with which I enriched my son and son-in-law. I cannot imagine what kind of evil, what kind of perfidy is still to come."

After he said this, the king was silent. Henry, who praised the king's views, added that the enemy,[97] who had been defeated twice in open battle, subsequently, in a most foul and evil way, had been provided another opportunity to inflict damage. He added that he would have preferred to suffer any calamity or adversity rather than that they had ever joined with the common enemy.[98] Af-

94. Otto I's son Brun did not die until 957, so this is technically not accurate in 954.

95. Here, the king is discussing Conrad the Red, whom he raised up to be duke of Lotharingia. From the royal perspective, even a count such as Conrad could be considered a *mediocris.* Widukind would appear to have developed this passage from Suetonius, *Caesar,* 72.

96. The implication is that Otto could have borne all of these evils if Liudolf and Conrad had not allied themselves with the Hungarians.

97. The reference here is to the Hungarians.

98. Here again, Liudolf and Conrad are being condemned for having made common cause with the Hungarians.

ter this was said, Liudolf came forward and spoke: "I admit that I gathered money for those who were led against me so that they would not harm me or my dependents.[99] If I am declared guilty in this matter, let the whole people know that I did not do this freely, but rather was forced by extreme necessity."

Finally, the high priest entered to explain himself.[100] He promised that he would demonstrate by whatever form of judgment the king commanded that he had never been opposed to the king, and that he had never wished to do or actually done anything against the king. Overcome by fear, he had left the king because he realized that the king was angry with him. But he was innocent although overwhelmed by such grave charges. Moreover, he would preserve his loyalty through every possible kind of oath. The king responded to these claims: "I do not demand an oath from you except that you will aid my efforts for concord and peace to the extent that you are able." When this oath was given, the king dismissed him in good faith and peace.

33. Regarding Bishop Frederick and Duke Conrad.

Because the bishop, along with Duke Conrad, were not able to convince the youth[101] to submit himself to his father, and, having accepted his judgment, to support his father, they abandoned him and joined God and the king.

34. Regarding Liudolf, who angrily departed from his father, and the king who pursued him.

The next night, Liudolf and his supporters departed from the king, and entered the city of Regensburg with his army. The king, however, who was following his son, came upon a fortress called Roßtal, and besieged it.[102]

99. See Ruotger, *Vita Brunonis,* ch. 25, who blames Liudolf and Conrad for bringing in the Hungarians.

100. Archbishop Frederick of Mainz.

101. This is Liudolf.

102. Roßtal, located twenty kilometers south of Nuremberg, was held by Li-

35. The battle at Roßtal.

There was a battle, and no mortal had ever seen harder fighting around the walls. Many were killed on both sides, and even more were wounded. The darkness of night brought the fighting to an end. The army, which was weakened during the indecisive battle, withdrew the next morning. With weightier matters at hand, it did not seem advisable to delay there any longer.

36. Siege of the city called Regensburg.

It was a three-day march to Regensburg. They occupied the places for their camps, and surrounded them with fortifications. Then the siege of the city began in earnest. But because the great multitude of defenders made it impossible to bring engines up to the walls, there was intense fighting between the two sides outside the walls.[103] The long-drawn-out siege forced the besieged to undertake some military action. For they decided that it would be worse to be tortured by hunger, if it came to this, than to die bravely in battle.

udolf's ally, the count of Hammerstein. See the discussion of the powerful defenses at Roßtal by Peter Ettel, "Der Befestigungsbau im 10. Jahrhundert in Süddeutschaldn und die Rolle Ottos des Großen am Beispiel der Burg von Roßtal," *Europa im 10. Jahrhundert: Archäologie einer Aufbruchszeit,* ed. Joachim Henning (Mainz, 2002), 365–79. This fortification also is noted by the anonymous author of the *Annales Hildesheimenses, an.* 953.

103. Regensburg was constructed on the south side of the Danube as a Roman legionary camp, and the imperial walls of the city, rebuilt in the fourth century, were still in use in 954. They comprised a rectangle measuring two thousand meters in length, enclosing an area of 24.5 hectares. Between 920 and 936 the walls of Regensburg were massively expanded to the west by Duke Arnulf to enclose both the merchant district and the monastery of St. Emmeram. The fortified addition measured approximately three thousand meters and enclosed an additional forty hectares. The new walls also were protected by a substantial ditch. It is not known, however, whether this was filled with water diverted from the Danube. See Carlrichard Brühl, *Palatium und Civitas: Studien zur Profantopographie spätantiker Civitates vom 3. bis 13. Jahrhundert,* vol. 2 (Cologne, 1990), 219–55. Widukind's comments here about the number of defenders prohibiting the deployment of engines suggests that in the face of concentrated missile fire from the walls, it was not possible to fill in the defensive ditch and so provide an avenue to bring forward rams, towers, and other siege equipment.

So it was ordered that mounted troops would burst out of the west gate as if making an attack on the camp.[104] Others were to board ships and launch an attack on the deserted camp by using the river that flowed alongside the city,[105] while the battle among the mounted troops was going on. The marshaled defenders set forth when the agreed-upon signal from a bell had been given. But the use of this signal was not unknown in the camp. As a result, they were not caught unprepared. While the mounted force encountered a delay in making its attack, the fleet slipped ever further from the city. As they disembarked from the ships and rushed into the camp, they encountered armed men.

Fearful, they considered fleeing, but were surrounded and cut down on all sides. Some rushed back to the ships, but driven by fear, they lost their way and were swallowed by the river. Others, in greater numbers, boarded the ships, but swamped them. As a consequence, hardly anyone from this large force survived. The mounted troops were worn down and defeated by the king's mounted forces. Many were wounded, and forced back into the city. The royal troops returned victorious to the camp.[106] They brought back with them just one man who was struck a mortal wound before the gates.[107] The entire herd of cattle from the city had been set out to pasture in a grassy area, which was located between the Regen and Danube rivers.[108] This herd was captured by Henry, the brother of the king, and divided among his companions. The defenders, who were worn down by numerous battles, now also began to suffer from hunger as well.

104. This is the royal camp positioned outside the west gate of the city. See Sallust, *Jugurtha,* 99 for a similar description of an attack through a gate that may have influenced Widukind's text here.

105. This river is the Danube.

106. Widukind's use of the term *regius miles* here to denote the king's troops, who emerged victorious in the battle among the mounted forces, suggests that he was calling specific attention to Otto I's military household of professional fighting men.

107. Vergil, *Aeneid,* 9.580.

108. The Regen is a left tributary of the Danube that joins the main stream at Regensburg. Consequently, the grassy area described here likely was near the eastern gate of the city.

37. Liudolf sues for peace, but does not receive it. Also regarding the death of Arnulf.

Consequently, Liudolf departed the city in the company of his leading men, and asked for peace. But he did not receive it because he refused to obey his father. So he returned to the city, and then launched an assault against Gero, a man distinguished by his victories that equaled in number his battles, who was besieging the east gate. The battle raged fiercely from nine in the morning until noon. A horse fell before the gates as did its rider Arnulf.[109] Stripped of his arms, he was struck through by spears, and died.[110] His death was made known two days later by a woman who fled the city because of hunger. The matter had been uncertain up to this point.[111] The defenders were distressed at his death, and now were ready to make a peace agreement.

38. Liudolf was granted peace, and the king returned to Saxony.

With the leading men acting as intermediaries,[112] Liudolf again exited the city with his companions. The siege had lasted an entire month and a half. He received peace until an appointed day when his case would be judged. The place selected for this assembly was Fritzlar. The king then returned to his fatherland.[113]

39. Henry came to the new city.

Henry gained the new city.[114] The following night, Regensburg burned down almost completely.

109. This is the count palatine, who was the son of Duke Arnulf of Bavaria. He was killed on July 22, 954. For the date, see *Necrologia Germaniae: Dioceses Brixinensis Frisingensis Ratisbonensis*, ed. F. L. Baumann (Berlin, 1905), 80.

110. Vergil, *Aeneid*, 11.395.

111. It is likely that Arnulf's weapons had been recognized by one of Gero's officers after the battle, but no one had examined the corpses on the field to see whether Arnulf had been killed.

112. Widukind appears to be referring here to Bavarian magnates who had been loyal to Arnulf, rather than to Liudolf's Swabian or Saxon supporters.

113. Otto I's homeland was Saxony.

114. The new city at Regensburg consisted of the portions enclosed within walls by Duke Arnulf during the 920s and 930s.

40. How the king received his son with mercy.

While the king was hunting for the sake of exercise in a place called Saufeld,[115] the son cast himself with bare feet before his father.[116] Overcome by a profound sense of penance, he first brought forth tears from his father with his own tearful speech, and then wrenched tears from all the others who were present. So it happened that he again received the grace of his father's love, and promised that he would always obey and agree to his father's will in all matters.

41. Regarding the death of Bishop Frederick.

In the meantime, it was announced that the bishop had grown ill and given up hope. Therefore, the royal assembly was delayed for a short time. Those who were present said that the high priest's end was praiseworthy.[117] After the bishop died, an assembly of the entire people was held.[118] Mainz, along with all of Franconia, surrendered to the king after a year and a half. The son and son-in-law, having received his grace, served him loyally until their deaths.[119]

42. How the Ukrani were defeated by Gero.

In that year, the Slavs, who are called Ukrani,[120] were defeated by Gero with great glory because Duke Conrad was dispatched to

115. This lodge was located in modern Thangelstedt on the Ilm in the district of Weimar in Thuringia. Gerhard, *Vita Uodalrici*, 1.12, suggests that Bishop Ulrich was the principal figure in negotiating the settlement between Liudolf and Otto, and that the final meeting between the two took place in Swabia rather than in Thuringia.

116. Liudolf humbled himself before Otto by laying face-down on the ground in front of his father.

117. Archbishop Frederick of Mainz died on October 25, 954. His death also is mentioned by the author of the *Annales Corbeienses, an.* 954.

118. This assembly took place on December 17, 954 at Arnstadt, which is located south of Erfurt. See Ruotger, *Vita Brunonis*, ch. 35.

119. Both Liudolf and Conrad the Red remained loyal to Otto, and died in royal service.

120. The Ukrani were members of the Weleti confederation who lived in the

provide aid to him. They captured an enormous quantity of booty, and great happiness reigned in Saxony.

43. How Regensburg surrendered and the king restored the region to his brother.

The king celebrated the next Easter with his brother, and then led an army against Regensburg. He again subjected the city to his arms and engines. Since they now lacked the aid of the Saxons, and were suffering from hunger, the defenders came out of the gates of the city, and surrendered themselves to the king. He condemned their leaders to exile, but spared the remaining multitude. Having gained glory from this victory, he returned to his fatherland, having restored the entire region of Bavaria to his brother.

44. Regarding the famous triumph that the king achieved over the Hungarians.

When the king entered Saxony around the beginning of July,[121] he met legates from the Hungarians, who presented themselves as if they had come to see him because of their established good faith and friendship.[122] In truth, however, as it seemed to some people, they had come to learn about the outcome of the civil war. The king kept them with him for a few days and then sent them back in peace, bearing some minor gifts. But he then learned from messengers sent by his brother, that is the duke of the Bavarians, that: "Behold numerous Hungarians have invaded your lands and stand pre-

region comprising the Uckermark district of the German state of Brandenburg and the Uecker-Randow district of Mecklenburg-Vorpommern. The main seat of the Ukrani was at Drense. See Volker Schmidt, *Drense: Eine Hauptburg der Ukrane* (Berlin, 1989).

121. The triumph described in this chapter is the battle of the Lechfeld fought on August 10, 955. The basic account of this battle and its context is now Charles R. Bowlus, *Battle of Lechfeld and Its Aftermath, August 955: The End of the Age of Migrations in the West* (Aldershot, 2006).

122. In light of the participation of the Hungarians in the civil war the previous year, it seems likely that the Hungarian leadership was ostensibly disavowing the men who had participated in the raids in Franconia and Lotharingia.

pared for battle with you." As soon as he heard this, the king, acting as if he had not endured any labor in the war just ended, began to march against the enemy. He took a small force with him, and particularly few from among the Saxons, because they were now threatened by a war with the Slavs.

He established his camp near the city of Augsburg,[123] and was joined by an army of Franks and Bavarians. Duke Conrad entered the camp with a powerful mounted force.[124] The soldiers were cheered by his arrival and now did not wish to put off the battle. For Conrad was by nature bold. But, what is even more rare among bold men, he also gave good counsel. Whether he went mounted into battle or on foot, he was an unstoppable warrior. He was solicitous of his companions in both peacetime and in war.

So it happened that the soldiers in both armies could see each other not far in the distance. A camp-wide fast was called for, and everyone was ordered to prepare for battle on the next day. Rising at dawn the next day, they gave and received peace.[125] Then, the men promised under oath first to their commanders, and then to each other, that they would do their duty. Then, with their banners raised, they left the camp organized as if there were eight legions.[126] The army was led through uneven and difficult ground. Since our extensive formations were protected by tree cover, the enemy would not be given an opportunity to disrupt them with their arrows, which they used with deadly results. The first, second, and third legions were comprised of Bavarians, who were led

123. Augsburg was located on the border between Swabia and Bavaria in the valley of the Lech river.

124. Widukind is naming Conrad a duke here out of courtesy since the latter had been stripped of his office in 953. The forces led by Conrad were raised, most likely, from his private lands, which were quite extensive.

125. This means that whatever ongoing hostility there might be among the men in Otto's army, they would put this aside for the duration of the battle, and focus all of their attention on the enemy.

126. Widukind is not commenting here on the numerical strength of the army, but rather indicating that the total force was organized into eight distinct units, the composition of which differed considerably. The royal *legio*, as will be seen below, was the largest, while the eighth *legio*, of Bohemians, is specifically identified by Widukind as having one thousand men.

by Duke Henry's officers. Henry himself was not at the battle because he was suffering from a bodily ailment from which he subsequently died.[127] The fourth legion was comprised of Franconians whose leader and commander was Duke Conrad. The prince himself[128] was surrounded by the fifth legion, which was the largest and called the royal legion. It was comprised of a picked force chosen out from among all the thousands of soldiers, and the eager youth.[129] The victory-bringing angel, surrounded by a dense formation, marched in front of the legion.[130] The sixth and seventh legions were composed of Swabians, who were commanded by Burchard, who was married to the daughter of the brother of the king.[131] In the eighth legion were the Bohemians, one thousand select soldiers, better equipped with arms than with good fortune.[132] All of the baggage and equipment also was with this legion, because the rearmost position was supposed to be the safest place. But matters turned out differently than they thought.

For the Hungarians did not delay in crossing the Lech river. Coming behind our army, they began to assault the last legion with their arrows. They then attacked with a great shout. After killing some and capturing others, they seized the entire baggage train. They forced the remaining armed men of the legion to flee. They attacked the seventh and sixth legions in a similar manner. They killed many of the men and forced them to turn in flight. However, when the king realized that the battle was going against him, and that battle line right behind him was being threatened, he dispatched the duke with the fourth legion, who recovered the captives, regained the booty, and overwhelmed the thieving forc-

127. Duke Henry of Bavaria, Otto I's younger brother, died on November 1, 955.

128. That is King Otto.

129. Here, Widukind appears to be distinguishing between grizzled veterans and relatively inexperienced young men. He returns to this distinction below.

130. This is likely a reference to a battle flag, probably bearing the image of the archangel Michael.

131. Duke Burchard II of Swabia (954–73) married Hadwig, the daughter of Duke Henry of Bavaria, and consequently the niece of Otto I.

132. Flodoard, *Annales, an.* 955, records that Duke Boleslav I of Bohemia was present at the battle.

es of the enemy. Duke Conrad then returned to the king under his conquering banners. And it was an amazing thing to the veteran soldiers, accustomed to the glory of victory, that Conrad had achieved this triumph with new troops, who had so little experience of war.[133]

45. Regarding Thiadric's battle against the Slavs.

While these events were going on in Bavaria, Thiadric[134] fought with mixed luck against the barbarians.[135] While attempting to capture one of their strongholds, Thiadric pursued the enemy up to the entrance of the gate, forcing them inside the wall. He captured the fort and burned it. All of those who were outside the walls were either captured or killed. He returned when the fire died out. Half of his soldiers crossed through a swamp that was adjacent to the fort. When the Slavs realized that our men were in a tight spot because of the difficulty of the terrain, and that they did not have enough men to fight, and did not have anywhere to flee, they attacked our men from the rear with a great shout. They killed about fifty of our men, and the remainder of our force shamefully fled.

46. Regarding the portents that occurred in the meantime.

Meanwhile, a great fear invaded all of Saxony because of this reverse, and there was also concern about the king and his army. Additional unusual portents also terrified our people. Churches in many places were struck by powerful storms that terrified those who saw or heard them. Religious of both sexes were killed by lightning strikes.[136] Many other things happened at that time, about which it is horrible to speak, so we will pass over them.

133. After Conrad the Red was stripped of his ducal office, it is likely that he also lost most of the professional soldiers who had served in his military household. These new men, whom he led in battle, probably were those who had chosen to serve under the former duke since he reconciled with the king in the summer of 953.

134. This is Count Thiadric of the *pagus* of North Thuringia.

135. This may be the same Count Thiadric who led a relief army from Saxony to Mainz in 953, mentioned at 3.23.

136. Widukind uses the unusual phrase *utriusque sexus sacerdotes,* literally, "priests of

The king, realizing that the entire weight of the battle had turned against him, addressed his companions in the following manner in order to encourage them:[137] "You can see for yourselves, my soldiers, that it is our task to be of good spirit in this time of difficulty. You face an enemy that is not far off, but rather positioned directly before us. Up to now, I have always employed your energetic hands and ever-victorious arms beyond my lands and empire, and everywhere I have conquered. Should I now flee in my own land and my own kingdom? I know that we are overmatched in numbers, but not in strength and not in our arms. We know that most of them are completely lacking in armor. What is of even greater consolation to us, they lack the aid of God. Audacity is their only protection.[138] For us, it is the hope of divine shelter. It would be shameful for us, who are now the lords of almost all of Europe, to surrender to the enemy. It is better to die gloriously in battle, my soldiers, if this should be our end, than to live as slaves subject or our enemies, or rather that we suffer torture like evil beasts. I would say more, my soldiers, if I believed that I could increase the strength and boldness of your spirits with words. But let us begin this conversation with swords rather than with words."[139]

After he had spoken, the king raised up his shield and the holy lance.[140] He was the first to turn his horse toward the enemy, fulfilling his duty as the bravest of soldiers and the best of emperors.[141] The bravest of the enemy at first resisted. But when they saw that their companions had fled, they stood stunned, and then

both sexes." He certainly does not mean that there were female priests, but rather is calling attention to the deaths of nuns, priests, and perhaps monks as well.

137. The following speech draws on images found in Sallust, *Catilinae,* ch. 58.

138. Sallust, *Catilinae,* 58.

139. The battle and particularly its aftermath also are described by Gerhard, *Vita Sancti Uodalrici,* 1.12. For the idea that saying more would be of little use and the time for action had come, see Sallust, *Jugurtha,* 85, and *Catilinae,* 58.

140. This is a reference to the lance used by the Roman soldier Longinus to pierce Jesus's side during the crucifixion. A piece of this lance served as one of the central elements of regalia of the Ottonian kings.

141. Sallust, *Catilinae,* 60.

were killed as our men mixed among them.[142] Some of the others, as their horses grew tired, entered nearby settlements. They were surrounded by armed men, and were burned along with the buildings. Others swam across the nearby river. But the higher bank on the opposite side did not permit them to climb up, so they were enveloped by the river and died. That same day[143] their camp was captured and all of the captives were recovered. On the second and third day, the remaining multitude was utterly destroyed by the nearby strongholds.[144] None or only a very few of them escaped. But the victory over this savage people was not without some cost in blood.

47. Regarding the death of Duke Conrad.

Duke Conrad, who certainly fought bravely, became overheated by the passion of his spirit and the heat of the sun, which was quite excessive that day. So when he loosened the clasps of his helmet[145] and sucked in air, he was struck by arrows, and died from a wound in his neck. At the king's order, his body was gathered up honorably, and carried to Worms. Here, this man, who was great and renowned for every virtue of his spirit and body, was buried to the mourning and weeping of all of the Franks.[146]

48. Regarding the three leaders of the Avars.

Three leaders of the Hungarian[147] people were captured and led before Duke Henry. They were sentenced to a bad death, which they deserved. For their necks snapped from being hanged.[148]

142. Livy, *Ab urbe condita,* 10.20.8.

143. August 10, 955.

144. Widukind is making clear here that the Hungarians were killed by forces who were stationed in fortifications along their lines of retreat.

145. Widukind says only that Conrad loosened the clasps (*vinclisque solutis*). But given the site of the wound, it is likely that Conrad removed his helmet.

146. Worms was a main seat of the Conrad the Red's branch of the Conradine family. His death also is recorded in the *Annales Corbeienses, an.* 955.

147. Widukind is again using "Avars" as a synonym for Hungarians.

148. Widukind uses the term *crepere* here to denote the fate of the Hungarians.

49. Regarding the triumph of the king.

The king, made glorious by this celebrated triumph, was named father of the fatherland and emperor by his army. Then he decreed that worthy honor and praise be given to God in every church. He had word of his triumph sent by messenger to his sainted mother, and then, with great happiness and joy, he returned to Saxony as a victor, and was received most warmly by his people. No king in the two hundred years before him had celebrated a victory of this size.[149] The Saxons had not been present at the battle with the Hungarians, having been held in reserve for the battle against the Slavs.[150]

50. Regarding the king and Wichmann's cunning.

As we recorded above, Wichmann was confined inside the palace when he was unable to justify his actions against his paternal uncle.[151] When the king planned to go to Bavaria, Wichmann refused to undertake the journey, excusing himself with a feigned illness. Whereupon he was reminded by the emperor that when Wichmann lost his mother and father,[152] the emperor had given him a place alongside his own sons, had given him a liberal education, and had elevated him to his father's office. The emperor now asked that Wichmann not harm him when he already was burdened by so many other difficulties. When he did not receive

---

This word is not usually associated with death, but rather with loud noises, including passing gas and cracking. Consequently, it seems likely that Widukind is drawing the attention of his readers to the sounds made when a man's neck is broken by hanging. These events are also discussed in *Chronicon Eberspergense*, ed. Wilhelm Arndt, MGH SS 20 (Hanover, 1878), 12.

149. Widukind may perhaps be thinking here of Charles Martel's triumph over the Muslims at the battle of Poitiers in 732 as a victory that was an equal of Otto I's achievement.

150. This last sentence was removed from the C version of the text.

151. Wichmann's paternal uncle was Hermann, Otto I's frontier commander in the northeast and his viceroy in Saxony. It is not clear in which palace Wichmann was confined.

152. Wichmann the Elder died in 944.

a worthy response to his comments, the emperor departed, and placed Wichmann under the supervision of Count Ibo.[153]

After Wichmann had spent several days in Ibo's company, he asked that he be permitted to go into the forest to go hunting. He gathered some of his companions, who had hidden there, and returned to his fatherland. After occupying some fortifications, he was joined by his brother Eckbert, and raised up arms against the emperor. However, Duke Hermann's efforts easily suppressed them, and forced them across the Elbe. When they realized that they could not oppose the duke, they joined forces with two minor barbarian kings, who had been troubling the Saxons for a long time, namely Nacco and his brother.[154]

51. Regarding the army that almost captured Wichmann in the stronghold of Suitleiscranne.

An army commanded by the duke found them in a stronghold that was called Suithleiscranne.[155] They were almost captured along with the fort. But they were warned by the shouting and hastened to arm themselves. Forty armed men were killed before the gates of the fort, and Duke Hermann departed loaded down with spoils taken from the dead men. Henry, the frontier commander,[156] and his brother Siegfried,[157] aided him. Both of them were prominent and powerful men, excelling equally in both war and in peace. This action took place at the beginning of the forty-day period of fasting.[158]

153. This count is not otherwise identified in the surviving sources.

154. Nacco and his brother Stoinef were leaders among the Obodrites in the region of the modern German state of Mecklenburg-Vorpommern.

155. This fortification has not been identified by scholars.

156. Widukind describes Henry as a *praeses*, a term that he generally uses to denote one of Otto's frontier commanders (German *Markgraf*). DO I, nr. 205, issued in 959, describes the areas under the authority of the frontier commander Henry as including the districts (German *Gaue*) of Helinge and Moside, which correspond to region along the left (west) bank of the Elbe, with important centers at Buxtehude and Stade, and the region west of the Luhe (a tributary of the Elbe) and south of the Elbe.

157. This is likely Count Siegfried of Stade.

158. This is the beginning of Lent in 954.

52. *How the fortress of the Cocarescemi was captured.*

Just after Easter that year,[159] the barbarians raided the region.[160] They were guided by Wichmann in this action, although he was not their commander. Hermann did not delay. He brought up military forces to resist them. However, when Hermann saw that the enemy army was large, and that his own forces were small as a result of the demands of the ongoing civil war, he decided that it would be better to put off battle under these adverse conditions. He also ordered the great multitude of people, who had fled into one fortress, because they did not trust the others, to ask for peace under whatever terms they could obtain. Hermann's soldiers were opposed to this plan, especially Siegfried, who was an exceptionally powerful warrior. But the people of the Cocarescemi did as the duke had ordered and made peace under the following conditions:[161] the free men along with their wives and children should climb up onto the wall, unarmed. They were to leave behind all of their slaves and other goods in the middle of the fort for the enemy. However, when the barbarians rushed into the stronghold, one of them recognized the wife of a certain free man as his slave. When the barbarian tried to seize her from the hands of the man, the barbarian was struck and then shouted that the agreement had been broken by the Saxons. So it happened that all of the enemy turned to killing, and they left no one behind. They killed all of the adults, and took the mothers and children away as captives.

53. *How the king avenged this raid.*

The emperor, who was eager to avenge this evil deed now that he had achieved victory over the Hungarians, invaded the lands of the barbarians. He took counsel regarding the Saxons who had

159. The disturbances described in this section took place in 954–55.

160. Easter fell on April 15 in 955.

161. It should be noted that the Cocarescemi were Slavs who lived under Ottonian rule. These were not Saxon settlers in erstwhile Slavic lands. Although the Cocarescemi have not been identified by scholars, it is almost certainly the case that these events took place east of the Elbe river.

conspired with the Slavs, and judged it fitting that Wichmann and Eckbert be declared public enemies. However, he would spare the others insofar as they were willing to return to their own people. A legation from the barbarians was present announcing that they wished to pay their tribute in the customary manner, but that they wished to have the dominant position among the other peoples of their region. Under these conditions, they wished peace. Otherwise, they would fight for their liberty. The emperor responded to them in this manner: he had no desire to deny them peace. But under no circumstances could he give them peace unless they purged themselves in an honorable manner for the injury they had caused, and provided compensation.

The emperor then led an army throughout their lands,[162] burning and devastating everything,[163] until finally establishing his camp along the Recknitz river, which was very difficult to cross because of the swamps.[164] Here the army was surrounded by enemies. From the rear the path was blocked by powerful trees that were defended by a force of armed men.[165] Directly in front of them, the river, the swamp adjacent to the river, and a huge army of Slav warriors blocked the work as well as the path of the army. The army was bothered by other difficulties as well, namely sickness and hunger in equal measure. After operating under these conditions for several days, Count Gero was dispatched to the leader of the barbarians, who was called Stoinef, to give him a chance to surrender to the emperor. The emperor thus offered to receive him as a friend, and not to test him as an enemy.

162. These are the lands of the Obodrites in the regions north and east of the Havel river in modern Mecklenburg-Vorpommern.

163. The devastation wrought by Otto I's army during this invasion has been confirmed by excavations. See, e.g., Jens Ulrich, "Der Burgwall von Klempenow, Lkr. Demmin," *Archäologische Berichte aus Mecklenburg-Vorpommern* 11 (2004): 28–38, here 33.

164. The likely location of this camp was nearby the modern town of Ribnitz-Damgarten in Mecklenburg-Vorpommern, some 240 kilometers north-northeast of Magdeburg.

165. The Obodrites felled trees along the route traveled by the advancing Ottonian army in order to cut off their line of communication back to imperial territory.

54. Regarding the frontier commander Gero.

Gero excelled in many areas. He was skilled in war, and offered good counsel in peacetime matters. He was quite eloquent, and very learned.[166] He preferred to demonstrate his prudence through deeds rather than through words. He showed great energy in gaining wealth, and generosity in giving it away. But best of all, he showed zeal for the worship of God. Therefore, the frontier commander greeted the barbarians over the swamp and the river, which was adjacent to the swamp. A Slav responded to him similarly. The frontier commander then addressed him in the following manner: "It would be enough if you waged war against one of the servants of my lord, and not against my lord king himself. What kind of army do you have, what kinds of arms that you would presume to do such a thing? If you have any strength, if you have the skill, if you have sufficient bravery, give us room to cross over to you. Or do you wish to cross over to us so that the strength of the fighters might be seen on even ground?"

But the Slav raged at him in the barbarian way and, vomiting out curses, mocked Gero, the emperor, and the whole army, knowing that they were burdened by many problems. Gero, who grew angered by this because he had such an ardent spirit, said: "Tomorrow the day will make clear whether you and your people are strong or not. Let there be no doubt that tomorrow you will see us attacking you." Gero, who for a long time had achieved renown for his many great deeds, was especially celebrated at this point because he had defeated the Slavs, called the Ukrani, with such great glory.[167]

Gero returned to camp and reported what he had heard. The emperor, who rose while it was still night, ordered that bows and other machines be deployed for battle as if he wished to cross the river and swamp in force. Following the warning of the previous

166. In drawing up this list of attributes, Widukind may have taken inspiration from Sallust, *Jugurtha,* 28.

167. Regarding Gero's defeat of the Ukrani, see 3.42.

day, the Slavs did not think that this preparation boded anything else. So they prepared for battle, defending the path with all of their forces.[168] But Gero, along with his allies the Ranen,[169] traveled almost a mile downstream from the camp, without the enemy realizing it, and quickly constructed three bridges. Gero then sent a messenger to the emperor summoning the entire army. When the barbarians realized what had happened, they hurried to meet the legions. But the foot soldiers of the barbarians had to run a longer route before entering the battle. Thus, overcome by fatigue, they quickly gave way before the soldiers. They were immediately cut down as they sought the safety of flight.[170]

55. Regarding Stoinef, the king of the barbarians, and the soldier who killed him.

Stoinef waited on events with some mounted troops atop a high hill. Recognizing that his companions were fleeing, he also took flight. But he was discovered in a certain wood, along with two of his bodyguards, by a soldier whose name was Hosed. After being overcome in combat, Stoinef was stripped of his arms, and beheaded. One of his bodyguards was captured alive. The soldier presented him along with Stoinef's head and the spoils taken from that minor king[171] to the emperor. Through this act, Hosed became renowned and distinguished. The reward for this famous deed was an imperial grant with an income equivalent to twenty farms.[172]

168. They deployed all of their men in defensive positions to deny Otto I's army the ability to cross the river, likely over a ford.

169. The Ranen (German Rugier) likely lived in the region around the island of Rügen along the coast of the Baltic Sea in modern Mecklenburg-Vorpommern.

170. The author of the *Annales Sangallienses maiores, an.* 955, places the date of the battle on October 16, i.e., the feast of St. Gall.

171. Widukind's use of the term *regulus* here should be understood as a mark of his contempt for Stoinef rather than a comment on the power that he wielded while still alive. Indeed, Widukind's characterization of Stoinef's army as huge permits the inference that this Obodrite ruler was quite powerful indeed.

172. Widukind uses the term *hoba,* which is the German equivalent of a *mansus.* The size of a *hoba* or *mansus* is a matter of some scholarly debate, but, in general, is

That same day, the enemy camp was attacked, and many men were killed or captured. The killing went on far into the night. The next morning, the head of this minor king was placed in a field. Around it, seven hundred prisoners were beheaded. The eyes of his adviser were torn out, as was his tongue. He was then left helpless in the midst of the corpses. Wichmann and Eckbert, conscious of their evil deeds, left for Gaul and escaped to Duke Hugh.[173]

56. Regarding the king who was made glorious through many victories.

The emperor, who had attained fame and glory through his many victories, awakened both fear and support among many kings and peoples. As a consequence, he received many emissaries from the Romans, Greeks, and Saracens.[174] Through them came a wide range of gifts: golden and silver vessels, bronze works that were distinguished by an amazing variety of types, glass vessels, and even ivory vessels, all manner of rugs, balsam, every kind of dye, and animals never before seen by the Saxons. These included lions, camels, apes, and ostriches. The hope of all Christians everywhere rested in him.

57. Regarding Liudolf, and that he departed his fatherland for the sake of his friends.

However, when Liudolf, the son of the emperor, wished to preserve his loyalty to his friends, he departed his fatherland and went with them to Italy.[175] After operating there for almost an entire year, he died.[176] His death inflicted a heavy loss on the entire empire of the Franks. His funeral was arranged with all due honor by

---

agreed to represent a quantity of land that is able to produce enough income to support a family, including dependents, for a year.

173. This is Hugh the Great, brother-in-law of Otto I.

174. These emissaries came from the pope, from the Byzantines, and likely Caliph Al-Hakam II (961–76), the Muslim ruler of Cordoba.

175. Liudolf departed for Italy sometime in 956.

176. Liudolf died on September 6, 957 as he was returning from his Italian campaign. His death is also recorded by the *Annales Corbeienses, an.* 957.

his soldiers. His body was carried from Italy to Mainz, and buried in the basilica of Alban the martyr,[177] to the great mourning and weeping of many people. He left behind a son marked with his father's name.[178]

58. Regarding the letter that reported his death.

A letter bringing news of his death was carried to the emperor while he was on campaign, fighting against the Redarii.[179] He poured out many tears on account of his son's death. As for the rest, he remained faithfully committed to God, the guide of all things,[180] who had ordained his empire up to now.

59. Regarding Wichmann who secretly entered Saxony.

At that time Wichmann, who knew that Saxony was empty of fighting men, secretly entered Saxony from Gaul, and returned to his home and wife. He then again joined the foreigners. Eckbert, however, was again received in the king's grace through the intervention of the great bishop Brun.[181]

60. How Wichmann gained Gero's trust.

When an army was led against Wichman for the third time,[182] he succeeded, after great difficulty, in gaining the trust of Gero and his son[183] so that they would gain the consent of the emperor

177. St. Alban was a missionary with a base at Mainz who is thought to have been martyred by the Vandals in 406. The monastery of St. Alban was located on a hill south of Mainz, outside the city walls.

178. This is Liudolf's son Otto, born in 954. See Adalbert of Magdeburg, *Continuatio, an.* 954. This Otto subsequently obtained his father's former office as duke of Swabia (973–82).

179. Adalbert of Magdeburg, *Continuatio, an.* 957, records Otto I's campaign against the Slavs.

180. Esther 15.5.

181. Eckbert, Wichmann's brother, and Brun, archbishop of Cologne and duke of Lotharingia.

182. See 3.51 and 3.53.

183. Count Gero's son Siegfried died in 959. Gero subsequently established the convent of Gernrode in memory of his son and established the latter's widow Hathui

for him to enjoy his fatherland, and his wife's patrimony, with the emperor's grace. He freely gave a fearsome oath that he would never do anything evil, by word or by deed, against the emperor or the emperor's rule. After Wichmann gave this oath, he was dismissed in peace, and was raised up by the emperor with promises of good things to come.[184]

61. *Regarding the prodigies that appeared on clothing.*

That same year,[185] after the slaughter of the barbarians had come to a close, prodigies appeared, most notably crosses in the clothing of many people.[186] After these prodigies were seen, many people were struck by a healthy fear and worried about what would happen to them, and so atoned for their way of life. There were some who interpreted this as leprosy in the clothing, meaning that leprosy would follow and taint many people. However, wise people said that the sign of the cross prefigured safety and victory, and we offer our faithful agreement to these conclusions.

62. *Regarding the emperor's illness.*

At that time, the emperor grew ill. However, through the merits of the saints, to whom he continually demonstrated his faithful obedience, and most of all to the illustrious patron, the martyr Vitus to whom he prayed, the emperor recovered. And so the world was granted all the same grace and delight as when the clearest sun arises after the night.

63. *Regarding the king's second expedition into Italy.*

When affairs had been put in proper order in Franconia, Saxony, and among the neighboring peoples, and those living all around,

---

as its first abbess. See Thietmar of Merseburg, *Chronicon,* 2.19; and the royal charter confirming the establishment of this house, DO I, nr. 229.

184. The implication here is that Wichmann was promised that if he behaved, he would be rewarded in the future.

185. This event took place, according to Widukind, in 955.

186. A similar observation is made by the author of the *Annales Corbeienses, an.* 959.

the king issued orders to set out for Rome, and to arrive in Lombardy. As I said at the beginning of this history, it is beyond our meager ability to describe how he besieged Berengar, the king of the Lombards, for two years,[187] and sent him as a captive with his wife and sons into exile, defeated the Romans in two battles,[188] and stormed Rome, defeated the dukes of Benevento, overcame the Greeks in Calabria and Apulia,[189] opened up silver mines in Saxon lands,[190] and, along with his son, grandly expanded his empire.[191] It should be enough that I have set forth this much with faithful devotion.

As for the rest, may this humble work glorify on behalf of your splendor and serenity the exalted status of your father and brother, which has provided every honor to the fatherland and solace to us. But let the end of the civil war be the end of this little book.[192]

64. *Regarding Wichmann and how he rebelled again.*

Wichmann, who had been allowed to return to his fatherland, kept the peace as long as he had an expectation that the emperor would return. But when the king delayed his return, Wichmann traveled north in order to stir up a war along with Harald, the king

187. The actual siege of the fortress of St. Leo, near St. Marino, lasted for only half a year, from May through December 963. See Adalbert of Magdeburg, *Continuatio, an.* 963.

188. These two battles took place on January 3 and June 23, 964. See Liudprand, *Historia Ottonis,* ch. 16; and Adalbert of Magdeburg, *Continuatio, an.* 963.

189. These campaigns also are noted by *Annales Corbeienses, an.* 963.

190. These include the well-known Rammelsberg mine near Goslar in Saxony.

191. These events, which took place between 961 and 964, are described in considerable detail in other contemporary chronicles. See *Annales Sancti Nazarii,* ed. C. L. Bethmann, MGH SS 17 (Hanover, 1861), *an.* 962; Adalbert of Magdeburg, *Continuatio, an.* 961–65; *Vita Brunonis,* ch. 41; *Benedicti Sancti Andrea Chronicon,* ed. G. Zucchetti (Rome, 1920), in *Fonti per la Storia d'Italia* 55, ch. 56–57; Liudprand, *Historia Ottonis;* and *Annales Magdaburgensis, an.* 963.

192. Chapter 63 of Book Three, which takes the account up to 968, was intended intended to be a final addition to the work, which was completed sometime after Otto I's second campaign in Calabria and Apulia in 968. The final paragraph of chapter 63 is characterized by the same kind of elevated style that Widukind used in the introduction to each of the three books.

of the Danes.[193] Harald made clear to Wichmann that if he killed the duke,[194] or some other leader, he would know that Wichmann wished to join him without any trickery. Otherwise, Harald would be certain that Wichmann had acted deceitfully.[195] In the meantime, Wichmann's banditry was discovered by a traveling merchant. Some of Wichmann's companions were captured and lost their lives, having been condemned by the duke to be hanged for their actions against the state.[196] Wichmann and his brother barely escaped.[197]

65. Regarding the Danes, and how they became Christians.

In times past, the Danes were Christians, but nevertheless continued to worship idols in their traditional manner. But then there was a dispute in the presence of the king during a feast regarding the worshipping of their gods. The Danes affirmed that Christ was a god. But they claimed that there were other, greater gods, who manifested themselves to people through even more powerful signs and prodigies. Against this, a certain cleric named Poppo,[198] who is now a bishop and leads a religious life, proclaimed that there is one true God, the father, along with his only begotten son, Jesus Christ, and the Holy Spirit. The images, he proclaimed, were of demons and not gods. King Harald, who it is said was quick to listen but slow to speak,[199] asked if Poppo wished to demonstrate this faith

193. King Harald Bluetooth (958–85).

194. This is Duke Hermann, Wichmann's uncle.

195. Widukind would have his audience believe that Harald feared Wichmann was put up to this act, perhaps by Otto I, to justify an attack on Denmark.

196. Widukind employs the term *res publica* here in the traditional Roman manner. The duke in this case is undoubtedly Wichmann's uncle, Hermann.

197. Presumably, this was Wichmann's brother Eckbert.

198. The identity of Poppo is not certain. In the twelfth century, he was identified as the bishop of Aarhus by Saxo Grammaticus, *Gesta Danorum,* ed. Karsten Friis-Jensen (Copenhagen, 2005), ch. 15; in English translation, *Saxo Grammaticus: The History of the Danes, Books I–IX: 1. English Text; II. Commentary (Bks. 1–9),* ed. and trans. Hilda Ellis Davidson and Peter Fisher (Rochester, N.Y., 1998). Writing in the later eleventh century, Adam of Bremen, *Gesta Hammaburgensis,* 2.35, identified Poppo as bishop in the Schleswig region.

199. James 1.19.

through his own person. Poppo responded without hesitation that he wished to do so. The king then ordered that the priest be placed under guard until the next day. When morning came, the king ordered that a very heavy piece of iron be heated in the fire. He then ordered the cleric to carry this glowing iron for his Catholic faith. The confessor of Christ seized the iron without any fear at all, and carried it far as the king had ordered. The priest then showed everyone his unharmed hand, and gave proof to everyone there of his Catholic faith. As a result, the king became a Christian and decreed that God alone was to be worshipped. He ordered all of his subjects to reject idols, and gave all due honor to the priests and servants of God.[200] But these events also are to be ascribed to the virtues and merit of your father by whose efforts the churches and orders of priests shined forth in these regions.[201]

66. *Gero, because of his oath, released Wichmann.*

Not unmindful of his oath, when Count Gero saw that Wichmann had been accused, and recognized that he was guilty, he released him back to the barbarians from whom he had acquired him. They happily received Wichmann, who then wore down the barbarians, who lived even further away, with numerous battles. Wichmann defeated King Miesco,[202] who ruled over the Slavs called the Licicaviki, in two battles, and killed his brother. He then extorted a great quantity of booty from them.

200. See Ruotger, *Vita Brunonis,* ch. 40, who also claims that King Harald rejected idols.

201. As early as 948, Otto I had made claims at the synod of Ingelheim to supervise the development of a diocesan organization in Denmark under the jurisdiction of the archbishops of Hamburg-Bremen. These claims subsequently were authorized by the papacy. See, e.g., the discussion by Helmut Beumann, "Magdeburg und die Ostpolitik der Ottonen," *Die historische Wirkung der östlichen Regionen des Reiches: Vorträge einer Tagung zum vierzigjährigen Bestehen der Bundesrepublik Deutschland* (Cologen, 1989), 9–29.

202. Miesco I (964–92) of Poland, the first ruler whose name has survived in the written record of the people that came to be known as the Poles.

67. *How Gero conquered the Lutizi.*

During this time, the frontier commander Gero badly defeated the Slavs who are called the Lutizi,[203] and compelled them to accept the heaviest burdens of servitude.[204] This victory, however, was not accomplished without Gero having suffered a serious wound, and the death of his nephew, who was among the best of men, and the deaths of many other outstanding men.

68. *Regarding two minor kings and Wichmann.*

There were two minor kings under the jurisdiction of Duke Hermann who had inherited enmity toward each from their fathers. One was named Selibur and the other Mistav. Selibur ruled the Wagrians.[205] Mistav ruled the Obodrites.[206] They frequently brought accusations against each other. Finally, however, Selibur was convicted after an investigation by the duke, and condemned to pay fifteen talents of silver.[207] Taking this fine very badly, Selibur decided to raise arms against the duke. But since he did not

203. The Lutizi were the inhabitants of the northern parts of Lusatia (German Lausitz). This is the district between the Bobr and Kwisa rivers and the Elbe in the modern German states of Saxony and Brandenburg and in southwestern Poland (Lower Silesian Voivodeship) and the northern Czech Republic. The upper and lower regions of Lusatia were separated by the Grenzwall, a belt of dense forests that dominated the region throughout the Middle Ages. The population of Upper Lusatia during the Ottonian period consisted of the Milceni.

204. Adalbert of Magdeburg, *Continuatio, an.* 963, dates the conquest of the Lutizi to this year. These heavy burdens likely refer to extensive tribute payments, and also the requirement to build and to support the numerous fortifications that were established by the Ottonians in this region.

205. The Wagrians were members of the Obodrite confederation who lived in the region of eastern Holstein in modern Germany.

206. This is unlikely to be correct. The Obodrites were a broad confederation of Slavic peoples living to the east of the Elbe and north of the Havel. It is more likely that Mistav, like Selibur, was the ruler of one of the constituent peoples, which comprised the Obodrite confederation, but that Widukind did not know the name of his people.

207. Widukind uses the classicizing term *talentis.* He might be indicating the sum of fifteen pounds of silver, as the pound was the largest unit of account in use under the Ottonians.

have sufficient forces to fight against him, Selibur sent a messenger to ask Wichmann for aid against the duke. Wichmann, who thought that there was nothing more pleasant than to have some means of troubling his paternal uncle, immediately set out with his companions to join with the Slav. However, as soon as Wichmann gained entry into the stronghold, it was immediately laid under siege by the enemy, who surrounded it with a wall.[208] An army commanded by the duke also besieged the fort. In the meantime, whether by chance or by prudent counsel, Wichmann left the stronghold along with a few others, pretending as if they were going to seek aid from the Danes.

Within a few days, the food for the fighting men and the fodder for the baggage animals began to give out. There were those who said that the Slav had only undertaken a sham rather than a true war. It seemed incredible that a man, who had been accustomed to war from his youth,[209] could have made such bad preparations. They argued that this was, instead, a plan conceived by the duke so that he might be able to overcome his nephew by whatever possible means, so that he could recover him safely in his fatherland rather than allowing him to perish utterly among the pagans. So the garrison, burdened by hunger and by the stink of their cattle, was forced to exit the stronghold.

The duke spoke bitterly to the Slav about his treachery, denounced him as wretched because of his actions. The duke then received this response from the Slav: "Why do you accuse me of treachery?" he said. "Behold, here are the men whom neither you nor your lord emperor were able to overcome. They stand here unarmed because of my treachery." The duke was silent after receiving this answer. He deprived the Slav of the lands that he held un-

208. The enemy, in this case, would appear to be Mistav. Widukind uses the term *vallatur* to describe the siege. Generally, this implies that the besieging army built a wall around the stronghold to ensure that no one could get in or out. It is not entirely clear in this case, however, whether the besieging army actually undertook this engineering operation. The fortress in question may be Stargard (German Oldenburg), which was made into an episcopal seat no later than 968.

209. Vergil, *Aeneid,* 9.201.

der the duke's authority. The duke then handed this territory with full authority to the son of the Slav, whom the duke earlier had received as a hostage. The duke imposed a range of punishments on Wichmann's soldiers, and gave the booty from the stronghold as a gift to his own soldiers. On his victorious return to the fatherland, the duke brought forth an idol of Saturn made of bronze, which he had found among the other spoils in the fort, as a great spectacle for his people.[210]

69. *Regarding the death of Wichmann.*

When Wichmann learned that the fort had been captured and that his companions had been punished, he went east and again joined with the pagans. He took up with the Slavs called the Wuloini,[211] who wished to wage war against Miesco, the friend of the emperor,[212] something that was not hidden at all from Miesco. Consequently, Miesco sent a request to King Boleslav of the Bohemians, who was his father-in-law,[213] and received two units of mounted troops from him. When Wichmann led his army against Miesco, the latter first dispatched his foot soldiers against him.[214] However, at the duke's order, they gradually withdrew before Wichmann so that he was pulled ever further from his fortified encampment. Then, when Miesco had sent his mounted troops to attack from the rear, he used a signal to order the foot soldiers, who had been withdrawing, to advance against the enemy.

When he was being pressed from the front and from the rear, Wichmann attempted to flee. But he was accused of betrayal by

210. Widukind would seem to be playing here on the idea of a triumph, in which the spoils of war were exhibited to the cheering populace.

211. Their place of settlement included the island of Wollin, which is located off the coast of modern Poland in the lagoon area at the mouth of the Oder river.

212. Widukind uses the term *amicus* here in the traditional Roman manner, meaning subordinate political ally.

213. Miesco had married Boleslav's daughter Dobrawa. See Thietmar of Merseburg, *Chronicon,* 4.55.

214. This battle took place on September 21, 967, and Wichmann was killed on the following day. For the date of his death, see *Die Totenbücher von Merseburg, Magdeburg und Lüneburg,* 33.

his companions. Although he had convinced them to go into battle, when it became dangerous, he did not hesitate to try to flee on his horse. After being forced to dismount, Wichmann joined with his companions on foot, and entered the battle. He fought very bravely that day, defended by his armor. The next morning, worn down by hunger and the long road that he had traveled, fully armed, through the entire night, he and a few others entered a building belonging to some man.

When some leading men among the enemy found him, they recognized from his arms that he was an important man. When they asked who he was, he responded that he was Wichmann. They demanded that he lay down his arms. They swore that they would present him safe to their lord, and that he would see to it that Wichmann was returned unharmed to the emperor. Wichmann, who now found himself in dire straights, was not unmindful of his earlier nobility and strength, and disdained surrendering to such men. So he asked that they bring word to Miesco that he would lay down his arms and surrender to him. While they set off to find Miesco, an enormous crowd surrounded Wichmann, bitterly attacking him. Although he was exhausted, Wichmann struck down many of them. At last, he raised up his sword,[215] and said the following to one of the more capable of his enemies: "Take this sword, and carry it to your lord. Let him have this as a symbol of his victory, and send it to his friend the emperor so that he might know that he can laugh at the death of an enemy, but should weep at the death of a kinsman." After he said this, Wichmann turned to the east and prayed in his mother tongue, as best he could, to the Lord, and poured out his soul, filled with many misfortunes and troubles, to the mercy of the Creator of all things.[216] This was the end of Wichmann, and such also was the

215. Widukind uses the term *gladius* here, which is technically a short thrusting sword, rather than one that would be used in a slashing motion described in this passage.

216. The implication here is that Wichmann confessed his sins before God, and did so in Saxon.

end for almost all of those who raised arms against your father. Here ends book three.[217]

70. After he had received Wichmann's arms, the emperor, who was now certain [of his death], wrote a letter to be dispatched throughout Saxony.

After the emperor[218] received Wichmann's arms, and was certain of his death, he wrote a letter[219] to the military commanders and counts of Saxony in the following manner:[220]

"Otto, august emperor by divine grace, to Hermann, Thiadric,[221] and the other counts of our state,[222] every friendly greeting. By the will of God, I am well, and all of my affairs are advancing without pause. Furthermore, messengers have come to us from the king of Constantinople,[223] very distinguished men, who, as I understand, are very interested in seeking peace. However this matter turns out, they certainly will not dare, God willing, to test us with war.[224] Unless we can come to an agreement, I will gain from them

217. This is the text of version A. The final two chapters dealing with Wichmann form a kind of epilogue for the entire book. In versions B and C, the reference to "your father" and the mention of this as the end of Book Three both are dropped.

218. Otto was crowned emperor on February 2, 962.

219. This letter is published separately as DO I, nr. 355.

220. Widukind uses the terms *duces* and *praefecti* here to denote the officials in Saxony, who were the recipients of Otto I's letter. In general, Widukind has used the term *dux* to describe either the leader of a people, i.e., Miesco, or to denote the office held by high officials such as Hermann Billung. It is clear that from an administrative perspective, there was only one "duke" in Saxony, or at least only one man serving in this capacity in the absence of Otto I, and this was Hermann. Consequently, the use of the plural *duces* should be understood in the traditional sense as high-ranking military commanders. As is his practice, Widukind uses the term *praefectus* as a synonym for *comes*, i.e., count.

221. Thiadric was one of five military commanders who were given command over the regions previously held by Gero. Thiadric's main area of responsibility was the Saxon north march (965–83), which would eventually be known as the Altmark.

222. Widukind is again using the term *res publica* in the traditional Roman manner.

223. Widukind uses the royal title for the Byzantine ruler, in contrast to Otto I's imperial title.

224. Otto I fought two important campaigns against the Byzantines and their allies in southern Italy in 968 and 969, with mixed results. See *Chronicon Salernitanum*, ed U. Westerbergh (Stockholm, 1956), cc. 172–73.

the provinces of Apulia and Calabria, which they have held until now. However, if they accept our will, we will send our wife and our like-named son this summer to Francia,[225] and we promise you that, with God's aid, we shall go on campaign to Frainet, to destroy the Saracens.[226] Furthermore, we wish, if the Redarii have indeed suffered very heavy losses, as we have heard—you know how often they have broken their oaths and what injuries they have inflicted—that they shall have no peace from you. Discuss these matters with Duke Hermann, and attack with all of your forces, so that you can bring about their final destruction. If it is necessary, we shall march against them, ourselves. On the nativity of the Lord, our son received the crown, as a sign of the imperial office, from the blessed apostle.[227] Written on 18 January at Capua in Campania."

When this letter was read aloud to the assembled leaders and a great crowd of common people, who had gathered at the assembly, which was being held at a place called Werla, it seemed appropriate to keep the peace that had been made with the Redarii, since there was a threat of war against the Danes at that time,[228] and because they did not have sufficient forces to wage two wars at the same time.

71. *Regarding the legates from the Greeks and their deceit.*

The emperor, having sufficient faith in the Greeks,[229] dispatched part of his army along with many leading men to the afore-men-

225. The reference here is to Otto II (973–83).

226. This was the site of a Muslim-held fortress in what is now La Garde-Freinet, near Saint Tropez. Regarding the deployment of troops against the Muslims at Frainet, see Liudprand, *Antapodosis*, 2.49; and Ekkehard IV, *Casus Sancti Galli*, ed. Hans F. Haefele (Darmstadt, 1980), 244.

227. Otto II was crowned emperor on December 24, 967 at the age of 12 by Pope John XIII (965–72).

228. The threat from the Danes is remarked upon by the author of *Annales Althahenses maiores*, MGH SRG 4 (Hanover, 1890), 12, which he dates to 973.

229. The chronology in this chapter is incorrect. The Byzantine offensive in Apulia that Widukind describes took place in 968 and early 969. The Ottonian counteroffensive culminated in a crushing defeat of the Byzantines in late 969. See *Chronicon Salernitanum*, c. 172–73. It was only in 972, following the death of Emperor Nikephoros

tioned place,[230] and consistent with the promises of the legates, the girl was handed over, and escorted honorably by his son.[231] However, the Greeks then turned back to their traditional methods. From the beginning, they were lords of almost all of the peoples of the world. Those whom they could not defeat by strength, they overcame by guile. Without warning, they attacked those who were unprepared, and did not even suspect that anything would happen. They destroyed forts, killed many people, and captured many others whom they presented to their emperor at Constantinople. When they were able to flee, they returned to the emperor and reported what had been done.[232]

72. Regarding Gunther and Siegfried.

The emperor was greatly disturbed by these events. In order to avenge this act of aggression, he dispatched Gunther and Siegfried, prominent men who had often gained renown in both domestic and foreign affairs, along with a large force into Calabria.[233] The Greeks, who were elated by their previous victories and acted without caution, fell into their hands. A great multitude of them were killed. Gunther and Siegfried captured those who survived, and permitted them to return to New Rome only after cutting off their noses.[234]

in December 968 and extensive negotiations with his successor John Tzimiskes, that a marriage was arranged. See Thietmar of Merseburg, *Chronicon,* 2.15.

230. This is a reference to the previous chapter.

231. The girl was Theophanu, who arrived in Rome from Constantinople in 972, around Easter, and subsequently married Otto II. The negotiations for a marriage between the Ottonian and Byzantine imperial families is discussed by Adalbert of Magdeburg, *Continuatio, an.* 967; and Liudprand of Cremona, *Legatio,* 7.

232. These are the supporters of Otto I who made their reports to him.

233. The commanders of this force were Count Gunther of Merseburg (965–76, 979–82) and Siegfried, who may have been the count of Hassegau (961–80). They commanded an army of Saxon and Swabian troops, who were joined by forces from the duchy of Spoleto. See *Chronicon Salernitanum,* c. 173, which identifies a Swabian count named Cono (Conrad) as commander of this army.

234. *Chronicon Salernitanum,* c. 173, records that 1,500 Byzantine soldiers under the command of the *patricius* Abdila were killed in battle outside the fortified town of Ascoli-Satriano on the frontier between Campania and Apulia. New Rome is Constantinople.

They then extorted tribute in Calabria and Apulia, and returned to the emperor having been made illustrious[235] through their victory, and rich through the spoils taken from the enemy.

73. Regarding the people of Constantinople and their emperors.

When the people of Constantinople heard that their men had fought poorly, they rose up against their emperor, and through the scheming of his own wife, and the plotting of a certain soldier, they killed him.[236] They then designated this soldier as the emperor in place of their lord. After being made king, he immediately released the captives, and sent the girl, along with a large army and splendid gifts to the emperor.[237] The emperor immediately handed her over to his son. After celebrating the marriage in magnificent style, he traveled all the way through Italy to Germany in great joy at what had occurred. During this time, while these events were taking place in Italy, the high priest William, a wise and prudent man, pious and friendly to all, ruled the Frankish empire, which was committed to him by his father.[238]

74. Regarding Mathilda, the mother of the emperor, and the deaths of Bishops Bernhard and William.

His mother, although a foreigner, nevertheless came from a noble line.[239] He heard that the mother of the emperor, a woman of remarkable sanctity named Mathilda, had become ill. While await-

235. Widukind is playing on the term *vir inluster,* a title widely used in the later Roman Empire, and later used in the entitulature of the Merovingian kings.

236. Widukind is referring here to Emperor Nikephoros Phokas (963–69), who was murdered and replaced by his nephew, the general John Tzimiskes (969–76).

237. Widukind returns here to the proper chronology, describing the dispatch by John Tzimiskes of Theophanu along with appropriate gifts to Otto I.

238. Archbishop William of Mainz (954–68) was the illegitimate son of Otto I and a Slav princess. He died long before Theophanu came to Rome in 972, and even before the victorious campaign by Gunther and Siegfried mentioned in 3.72.

239. Widukind is discussing here the mother of Archbishop William of Mainz, Otto I's illegitimate son. See the discussion of her origins by Thietmar of Merseburg, *Chronicon,* 2.35. According to Adalbert of Magdeburg, *Continuatio, an.* 928, William was born in this year.

ing her death, he met his own death before she had died.[240] If we wished to say something in praise of her[241] we would fail because the virtue of such a great woman overcomes every effort of our meager intellect. Who could describe in a worthy manner her commitment to the service of God. Every night she filled her little chamber with the melodies of divine music of every kind and type.[242] She had a little cell near the church, where she briefly rested. She left it every night and entered the church, while male and female singers were organized in three groups in order to praise and bless God's mercy, inside her little chamber, before the doors, and along the road. She remained in the church, keeping vigil and praying, while she awaited the celebration of mass. Whenever she heard that there were sick people nearby, she visited them, and offered what they needed. She extended her hand to the poor. She generously received the ever-present visitors. She never sent anyone away without a kind greeting, and almost no one departed without some small gift, or some help that he needed. She often sent necessities to travelers, whom she saw in the distance from her little cell.

Although she was very humbly engaged in works of this type day and night, she did nothing that would diminish the honor of the king. As it is written, although she sat as a queen with the people standing all around, she was always and everywhere a consoler of those in mourning.[243] She instructed the household servants, both the men and the women, in a variety of skills, and also taught them their letters.[244] She herself knew her letters, which she had

240. The archbishop died on February 2, 968. See Thietmar of Merseburg, *Chronicon,* 2.18.

241. That is, in praise of Otto I's mother, Mathilda.

242. Mathilda's religiosity and manner of life are also described in some detail in *Vita Mathildis reginae,* ch. 10, in MGH SS 4 (Hanover, 1841), 290. This text is available in English translation as *Queenship and Sanctity: The Lives of Mathilda and the Epitaph of Adelheid,* ed. and trans. Sean Gilsdorf (Washington, D.C., 2004).

243. Widukind is playing here on Job 29.25.

244. This could mean several things, including to read Latin, to write in Latin, or merely to understand Latin when it was read outloud.

learned very well after the death of the king.[245] If I wished to list all of her virtues, I would run out of time. Even if I had the eloquence of Homer or Maro,[246] this would still not be enough. She returned her soul to Christ on the fourteenth of March,[247] full of years, replete with every honor, and filled with good works and charity after distributing all of her royal wealth among the servants and maidens and paupers of God.

During this period, Bernhard, who was praised by all the people as the most worthy priest of his age, also had his last day.[248] Let no one condemn us for having revealed their pious reputation since we have not succumbed to the danger of veering from the truth. For we have heard from a certain hermit that he saw, whether in spirit or in clear sight we do not know, the soul of the queen and of the bishop being carried up to heaven with unspeakable glory in the company of an infinite multitude of angels.

75. Regarding the return of the emperor from Italy, and his death.

When the emperor heard about the death of his mother and his son, and of the other important men, for Gero, that great and powerful man had already died,[249] he decided to break off his campaign against Frainet. Then, after putting affairs in Italy in order, he returned to his fatherland. He was agitated by a report that many of the Saxons wished to rebel. But since it would not serve any purpose, we do not believe it is worthwhile to discuss this further. So he departed from Italy with great glory, having captured the king of the Lombards, overcome the Greeks, and defeated the Saracens. He entered Gaul with his victorious forces, and then crossed into Germany where he would celebrate the coming Easter in that famous place, Quedlinburg. A great multitude of diverse peoples gathered there, and celebrated with great joy the return of

245. That is after the death of Henry I in 936.

246. This is Publius Vergilius Maro, i.e., Vergil.

247. 968.

248. Bishop Bernhard of Halberstadt (924–68) died on February 3, about six weeks before Mathilda. See Thietmar of Merseburg, *Chronicon*, 2.18.

249. Gero, who had served as one of Otto I's most important military commanders since 936, died on May 20, 965.

the father along with his son. Remaining there for not longer than seventeen days,[250] he then departed to celebrate the Ascension of the Lord at Merseburg.[251] However, his journey through this region was a sad one because of the death of that great man Duke Hermann,[252] who left to his fellow men an eternal memory of his prudence, justice, and remarkable vigilance in internal and external affairs. Thereafter, the king received legates from Africa, who were waiting for him with gifts worthy of his royal status, and had them stay with him. On the Tuesday before Pentecost,[253] he came to a place called Memleben.[254]

The following night, as was his custom, he rose from bed at the break of dawn, and participated in the night and morning prayers.[255] After this, he rested for a short time. Then, following the celebration of mass, he made some offerings, as was his custom, to the poor. He then ate a little bit, and again rested in his bed. When it was time, he got up, happy and cheerful, and took his place at the table. He was present through the completion of the office of vespers.[256] But while the canticle of the evangelist[257] was being sung, he began to grow feverish and tired. When the leading men, who were standing near, understood what was happening, they lay him down on a bench. His head was drooping as if he were already dead, but they revived him. After he sought and received the sacrament of the divine body and blood, he gave over his final breath to the mercy of the creator of all things, without a groan and at peace, to the sounds of the divine office.[258]

250. Otto was present at Quedlinburg from March 19 to April 4, 973.

251. Ascension is celebrated forty days after Easter Sunday. In 973, Ascension fell on May 1.

252. Duke Hermann died on March 27, 973.

253. Otto arrived at Memleben on May 6.

254. Memleben was the site of an important royal palace and monastery, where Henry I had died.

255. This is matins, the prayer service said in the early hours of the day, before morning.

256. This is the evening prayer service.

257. This is the Magnificat, also known as the Canticle of Mary, which is taken from Luke 1:46–55.

258. Otto I died on May 7, 973.

He was carried into his bed chamber. Although it was now late, his death was announced to the people. The people said a great deal in praise of him and remembered that he had governed his subjects with paternal mercy, and had freed them from their enemies. He had conquered with arms his arrogant enemies, namely the Avars, Saracens, and Danes. He had subjugated Italy. He had destroyed the shrines to the gods among the neighboring peoples. He established churches and orders of priests. They recalled many other good things, as they participated in the royal funeral.

76. *How the people chose the son as their ruler in place of his father.*

When morning came, although he had already been anointed as king, and designated as emperor by the pope, they eagerly gave their hands to the son of the emperor, the unique hope of the entire church, as they had done before, promised their loyalty and support against all of his adversaries, and confirmed this with military oaths.[259] Thus, he was elected anew by the entire people as their ruler. He transferred his father's body to the city, which the father, himself, had built, called Magdeburg. So died the emperor of the Romans, the king of peoples, on the seventh of May, the Wednesday before Pentecost. He left behind for posterity a great many glorious monuments in both religious and secular affairs.

Here ends book three.

259. Widukind's use of the phrase *sacramenta militaria* should not be confused with some kind of "feudal" oath. Rather, Widukind is explicitly drawing on the Carolingian, and indeed Roman, tradition that all soldiers (*milites*) had to take a specific oath of loyalty to the ruler in addition to whatever oaths they had already taken to their individual commanders.

Bibliography

MGH = Monumenta Germaniae Historiae; SRG = Scriptores rerum germanicarum in usum Scholarum; SS = Scriptores.

EDITIONS

Annales Witichindi Monachi Corbeiensis familiae Benedictinae. Frankfurt, 1577.

Die Sachsengeschichte des Widukind von Korvei. Edited by Albert Bauer and Reinhold Rau. In *Quellen zur Geschichte der sächsischen Kaiserzeit,* vol. 8. Darmstadt, 1971.

Widukindi, Res gestae Saxonicae. Edited by Georg Waitz. MGH SRG. Hanover, 1839; 2nd ed, 1866; 3rd ed. 1882.

Widukindi monachi Corbeiensis rerum gestarum Saxonicarum. Edited by Andrew Kehr. MGH SRG. Hanover, 1904.

Widukind von Corvei: Die Sachsengeschichte. Edited by H.-E. Lohman and Paul Hirsch. Hanover, 1935.

Widukind von Corvey: Res gestae Sasonicae, Die Sachsengeschichte. Edited by Ekkhart Rotter and Bernd Schneidmüller. Leipzig, 1986.

Witichindi monachi Corbeiensis, familiae Benedictinae Annalium libri tres. In vol. 1 of *Rerum Germanicarum Tomi Tres, Dissertationes historicas varii argumenti et chronica monasteriorum Saxoniae nonnulla continens,* edited by Heinrich Meibom. 3 vols. Helmstadt, 1688.

Witichindi Saxonis rerum ab Henrico et Ottone I imp. Gestarum libri iii. Basel, 1532.

TRANSLATIONS

Cousin, Louis. *Histoire de l'Empire d'Occident.* 2 vols. Paris, 1689.

Giraud, Cédric, and Benoît-Michel Tock. *Rois, reines et éveques: L'Allemagne aux Xe et XIe siècles: Recueil de textes traduits.* Turnhout, 2009.

Hirsch, Paul. *Widukind von Korvei: Sächsische Geschichten auf Grund des Textes der Scriptores rerum Germanicarum und nach der Übersetzung von Rheinhold Schottin in der Ausgabe von W. Wattenbach.* Leipzig, 1931.

Pollmächer, Christian Salomon. *Geschichte König Heinrich des Ersten und Kaiser Otto des Grossen, nach den Annalen Wittekinds von Korvei mit historisch-geographischen Anmerkungen.* Dresden, 1790.

Schottin, Rheinhold. *Widukinds Sächsische Geschichten, nach der Ausgabe der Monumenta Germaniae.* Leipzig, 1852; reprinted 1882.

Wood, Raymund F. "The Three Books of the Deeds of the Saxons, by Widukind of Corvey, Translated with Introduction, Notes and Bibliography." Unpublished Ph.D. dissertation, University of California at Los Angeles, 1949.

OTHER PRIMARY SOURCES

Adalbert of Magdeburg. *Reginonis abbatis Prumiensis Chronicon cum continuatione Treverensi.* Edited by F. Kurze. MGH SRG 50. Hanover, 1890.

Adam of Bremen. *Gesta Hammaburgensis ecclesiae pontificum.* 3rd ed. Edited by B.Schmeidler. MGH SRG 2. Hanover, 1917.

Annales Alamannici. Edited by G. H. Pertz. MGH SS 1. Hanover, 1826.

Annales Althahenses maiores. MGH SRG 4. Hanover, 1890.

Annales Colonienses, an. 939. Edited by G. H. Pertz. MGH SS 1. Hanover, 1826.

Annales Corbeienses. Edited by G. H. Pertz. MGH SS 3. Hanover, 1849.

Les Annales de Flodoard. Edited by Ph. Lauer. Paris, 1905.

Annales Hildesheimensis. Edited by G. H. Pertz. MGH SS 3. Hanover, 1849.

Annales Iuvavenses maximi. Edited by Harry Bresslau. MGH SS 30.2. Leipzig, 1934.

Annales Laureshamenses, an. 785. Edited by G. H. Pertz. MGH SS 1. Hanover, 1826.

Annales Lobienses. Edited by Georg Waitz. MGH 13. Hanover, 1881.

Annales Magdeburgenses. Edited by Georg Pertz. MGH SS 16. Hanover, 1859.

Annales necrologici Fuldensis. Edited by Georg Waitz. MGH SS 13. Hanover, 1881.

Annales Pragenses. Edited by G. H. Pertz. MGH SS 3. Hanover, 1849.

Die Annales Quedlinburgenses. Edited by Martina Giese. Hanover, 2004.

Annales Sancti Nazarii. Edited by C. L. Bethmann. MGH SS 17. Hanover, 1861.

Annales Sangallenses maiores, an. 940. Edited by G. H. Pertz. MGH SS 1. Hanover, 1826.

The Annals of Flodoard of Rheims 916–919. Translated and edited by Steven Fanning and Bernard S. Bachrach. Peterborough, 2004.

Aurelius Victor. *Livre de Cesars (Liber de Caesaribus).* Edited by Pierre Dufraigne. Paris, 1975.

Bede. *Bede's Ecclesiastical History of the English People.* Edited by Bertram Colgrave and R. A. B. Mynors. Oxford, 1969.

Benedicti Sancti Andrea Chronicon. Edited by G. Zucchetti. Rome, 1920.

Catalogus abbatum et nomina fratrum Corbeiensium. Edited by O. Holder-Egger. MGH SS 13. Hanover, 1881.

Chronicon Eberspergense. Edited by Wilhelm Arndt. MGH SS 20. Hanover, 1878.

Chronicon Salernitanum. Edited by U. Westerbergh. Stockholm, 1956.

Commentary on the Dream of Scipio by Macrobius. Translated by William Harris Stahl. New York, 1952.

The Complete Works of Liudprand of Cremona. Edited and translated by Paolo Squatriti. Washington, D. C., 2007.

De moribus et actis primorum Normanniae ducum. Edited by Jules Lair. Caen, 1865.

Dudo of St. Quentin, History of the Normans. Translated by Eric Christiansen. Woodbridge, 1998.

Einhard. *Vita Karoli Magni.* Edited by Georg Waitz. MGH SRG. Hanover, 1905.

Ekkehard IV. *Casus Sancti Galli.* Edited by Hans F. Haefele. Darmstadt, 1980.

Ermoldus Nigellus. *In honorem Hludovici imperatoris.* Edited by E. Dümmler. Poetae Latini aevi Carolini 2. Berlin, 1884.

Eutropius. *Brevarium ab urbe condite.* Edited by H. Droysen. MGH Auctores antiquissimi 2. Berlin, 1879.

Folcuin. *Gesta abbatum Lobiensium.* Edited by Georg Pertz. MGH SS 4. Hanover, 1841.

Frutolf. *Chronicon Universale.* Edited by G. H. Pertz. MGH SS 6. Hanover, 1844.

Gerhard of Augsburg. *Vita Sancti Uodalrici.* Edited by Walter Berschin and Angelika Häse. Heidelberg, 1993.

Gesta episcoporum Cameracensium Liber I. II. III. Usque ad a. 1051. Edited by L. C. Bethmann. MGH SS 7. Hanover, 1846.

Gildas. *De excidio Britanniae.* Edited by Theodor Mommsen. In MGH Auctores antiquissimi 13: *Chronica minora saec. IV. V. VI. VII.* Berlin, 1898.

Gregory of Tours. *Libri Historiarum X, editionem alteram.* Edited by Bruno Krusch and Wilhelm Levison. MGH Scriptores rerum Merovingicarum 1. Berlin, 1951.

Gumpold. *Vita Vencezlavi Ducis,* ch. 19. Edited by Georg Watiz. Hanover, 1841.

Hegesippus. *De Excidio Urbis Hierosolymitanae.* PL 15.

Heriger. *Translatio S. Landoaldi sociorumque.* Edited by O. Holder-Egger. MGH SS 15.2. Hanover, 1888.

Herimanni Augiensis Chronicon a. 1–1054. Edited by Georg Pertz. MGH SS 5. Hanover, 1844.

Hincmar of Rheims. *Ad Carolum Calvum regem pro Ecclesiae libertatum defensione.* PL 125.

Historia translationis S. Viti. Edited by G. H. Pertz. MGH SS 2. Hanover, 1829.

History and Politics in Late Carolingian and Ottonian Europe: The Chronicle of Regino of Prüm and Adalbert of Magdeburg. Edited and translated by Simon MacLean. Manchester, 2009.

History of the Archbishops of Hamburg-Bremen. Translated by F. J. Tschan. New York, 2002.

Hrotsvithae Opera. Edited by Paul von Winterfeld. MGH SRG 34. Hanover, 1965.

Isidore of Seville. *Etymologiarum sive originum libri xx.* Edited by W. M. Lindsay. Oxford, 1911, reprint 1957.

John of St. Arnulf. *Vita Iohannis Abbatis Gorziensis.* Edited by Georg Pertz. MGH SS 4. Hanover, 1841.

John the Lydian. *De Magistratibus. On the Magistracies of the Roman Constitutions.* Translated by Thomas Francis Carney. Lawrence, 1971.

Jordanes. *De origine actibusque Getarum.* Edited by Theodor Mommsen. MGH Auctores antiquissimi 5. Berlin, 1882.

Leges Saxonum und Lex Thuringorum. Edited by Claudius Freiherr von Schwerin. In *Fontes Iuris Germanci Antiqui in usum Scholarum separatism editi.* Hanover, 1918.

The Life of Saint Martin of Tours. Translated by F. R. Hoare. In *Soldiers of Christ: Saints and Saints' Lives from Late Antiquity and the Early Middle Ages,* edited by Thomas F. X. Noble and Thomas Head, 31–74. London, 1995.

Liutprand of Cremona. *Liudprandi Cremonensis Opera Omnia: Antapodosis, Homelia Paschalis, Historia Ottonis, Relatio de Legatione Constantinopolitana.* Edited by P. Chiesa. Turnholt, 1998.

Lucius Ampelius. *Liber Memorialis.* Edited by Eduard von Woelfflin. Leipzig, 1873.

Macrobius. *Comentarii in Somnium Scipionis.* Edited by J. Willis. 2nd ed. Leipzig, 1970.

Necrologia Germaniae: Dioceses Brixinensis Frisingensis Ratisbonensis. Edited by F. L. Baumann. Berlin, 1905.

Nennius. *Historia Brittonum.* Edited by Theodor Mommsen MGH Auctores antiquissimi 13. Berlin, 1888.

Orosius. *Histoires contre le païens.* 3 vols. Edited and translated by Maire-Pierre Arnaud-Lindet. Paris, 1990–91.

Ottonian Germany: The Chronicon of Thietmar of Merseburg. Edited and translated by David A. Warner. Manchester, 2001.

Passio Sancti Viti. Acta Sanctorum 20, no. 2 (June 15 [no year]): 1021–23.

Paul the Deacon. *Historia Langobardum.* Edited by Ludwig Bethmann and Georg Waitz. MGH Scriptores rerum Langobardicarum et Italicarum. Hanover, 1878.

———. *Historia Romana.* Edited by H. Droysen. MGH Auctores antiquissimi 2. Berlin, 1879.

Queenship and Sanctity: The Lives of Mathilda and the Epitaph of Adelheid. Edited and translated by Sean Gilsdorf. Washington, D.C., 2004.

Rabanus Maurus. *De invention linguarum.* Patralogia Latina 112.

Rudolf of Fulda. *Translatio s. Alexandri.* Edited by G. H. Pertz. MGH SS 2. Hanover, 1829.

Ruotger. *Vita Brunonis.* Edited by Walter Berschin and Angelika Häse. Heidelberg, 1993.

Saxo Grammaticus. *Gesta Danorum.* Edited by Karsten Friis-Jensen. Copenhagen, 2005.

Saxo Grammaticus: The History of the Danes, Books I–IX: 1. English Text; II. Commentary (Bks. 1–9). Edited and translated by Hilda Ellis Davidson and Peter Fisher. Rochester, 1998.

Sigibert of Gembloux. *Vita Wicberti.* Edited by Georg Pertz. MGH SS 8. Hanover, 1858.

Thietmar of Merseburg. *Chronik.* Edited and translated by Werner Trillmich. 8th ed. Darmstadt, 2002.

Die Totenbücher von Merseburg, Magdeburg und Lüneburg. Edited by G. Althoff and J.Wollasch. MGH Libri Memoriales et Necrologia, n.s. 2. Hanover, 1983.

Translatio Sancti Alexandri. Edited by Bruno Krusch. In "Die Übertragung des Heiligen Alexander von Rom nach Wildeshausen durch den Enkel Widukinds 851: Die älteste niedersächsische Geschichtsdenkmal." *Nachrichten von der Gesellschaft der Wissenschaften zu Göttingen, philosophische-historische Klasse* 2 13 (1933): 405–36.

Die Urkunden Arnolfs. Edited by Paul Kehr. MGH Diplomata regum Germaniae ex stirpe Karolinorum 3. Berlin, 1940.

Die Urkunden Konrad I., Heinrich I. und Otto I. Edited by Theodor Sickel. Hanover, 1879–84.

Vita Mathildis reginae, ch. 10. In MGH SS 4. Hanover, 1841.

SECONDARY SOURCES

Althoff, Gerd. *Amicitia und pacta: Bündnis, Einung, Politik und Gebetsgedenken im beginnenden 10. Jahrhundert.* Hanover, 1992.

———. "Widukind von Corvey: Kronzeuge und Herausforderung." *Frühmittelalterliche Studien* 27 (1993): 253–72.

———. "Der frieden-bündnis—und gemeinschaftstiftende Charakter des Mahles im früheren Mittelalter." In *Essen und Trinken in Mittelalter und Neuzeit,* edited by Irmgard Bitsch, Trude Ehlert, and Xenja von Ertzdorff, 13–25. Sigmaringen, 1997.

Bachrach, Bernard S. "Early Medieval Military Demography: Some Observations on the Methods of Hans Delbrück." In *The Circle of War,* edited by Donald Kagay and L. J. Andrew Villalon, 3–20. Woodbridge, 1999.

———. *Early Carolingian Warfare: Prelude to Empire.* Philadelphia, 2001.

———. "Gregory of Tours as a Military Historian." In *The World of Gregory of Tours,* edited by Kathleen Mitchell and Ian Wood, 351–63. Leiden, 2002.

Bachrach, B. S., and David S. Bachrach. "Saxon Military Revolution, 912–973? Myth and Reality." *Early Medieval Europe* 15 (2007): 186–222.

Bachrach, David S. *Religion and the Conduct of War c. 300–c. 1215.* Woodbridge, 2003.

———. "The Military Organization of Ottonian Germany, c. 900–1018: The Views of Bishop Thietmar of Merseburg." *Journal of Military History* 72 (2008): 1061–88.

———. "Exercise of Royal Power in Early Medieval Europe: The Case of Otto the Great, 936–973." *Early Medieval Europe* 17 (2009): 389–419.

Baerten, Jean. "Les Ansfrid au Xe Siècle." *Revue belge de philology et d'histoire* 39, no. 4 (1961): 1144–58.

Bairoch, Paul, Jean Batou, and Pierre Chèvre. *La Population des ville européennes: Banque de données et analyse sommaire des résultats, 800–1850.* Geneva, 1988.

Beumann, Helmut. *Widukind von Korvey: Untersuchungen zur Geschichtsschreibung und Ideengeschichte des 10. Jahrhunderts.* Weimar, 1950.

———. "Die Historiographie des Mittelalters als Quelle für die Ideengeschichte des Königtums." *Historische Zeitschrift* 180 (1955): 449–88.

———. "Historiographische Konzeption und politische Ziele Widukinds von Corvey." *La storiografia altomedievale: Settimane di studio del centro italiano di studi sull'alto medioevo* 17 (1970): 857–94.

———. "Imperator Romanorum, rex gentium. Zu Widukind III 76." In *Tradition als historische Kraft: Interdisziplinäre Forschungen zur Geschichte des früheren Mittelalter,* edited by Norbert Kamp and Joachim Wollasch, 214–30. Berlin, 1982.

———. "Magdeburg und die Ostpolitik der Ottonen," In *Die historische Wirkung der östlichen Regionen des Reiches: Vorträge einer Tagung zum vierzigjährigen Bestehen der Bundesrepublik Deutschland,* 9–29. Cologne, 1989.

Bischoff, Bernhard. "Die Überlieferung der technischen Literature." In *Artigianato et tennica nella societa dell'alto medioevo occidentale, Centro italiano die studi sull'alto medioevo,* 1.267–97. Spoleto, 1971.

———. *Manuscripts and Libraries in the Age of Charlemagne.* Translated and edited by Michael Gorman. Cambridge, 1994.

Bloch, Herman. "Die Sachsengeschichte Widukinds von Korvei." *Neues Archiv* 38 (1913): 97–141.

Bowlus, Charles R. *Battle of Lechfeld and Its Aftermath, August 955: The End of the Age of Migrations in the West.* Aldershot, 2006.

Brömel, Markus. "Widukind von Corvey: Kronzeuge und Herausforderung." In *Auf den Spuren der Ottonen III,* 17–25. Halle, 2002.

Brühl, Carlrichard. *Palatium und Civitas: Studien zur Profantopographie spätantiker Civitates vom 3. bis 13. Jahrhundert.* Vol. 2. Cologne, 1990.

Coupland, Simon. "Carolingian Arms and Armor in the Ninth Century." *Viator* 21 (1990): 29–50.

Dapper, Michael. "Neuinterpretation der Grabungsergebnisse auf der Pfalz Tilleda." In *Deutsche Königspfalzen: Beiträge zu ihrer historischen und archäologischen Erforschung,* vol. 7: *Zentren herrschaftlicher Repräsentation im Hochmittelalter, Geschichte, Architektur und Zeremoniell,* edited by Caspar Ehlers, Jörg Jarnut, and Matthias Wemhoff, 151–69. Göttingen, 2007.

Delbrück, Hans. *Geschichte der Kriegskunst im Rahmen der politischen Geschichte.* 6 vols. Berlin, 1900–1936. Vols. 1–3 in English: *History of the Art of War: Within the Framework of Political,* translated by Walter J. Renfroe. Westport, Conn., 1975–82.

———. *Numbers in History.* London, 1913.

Dette, Christoph. "Kinder und Jugendliche in der Adelsgesellschaft des frühen Mittelalters." *Archiv für Kulturgeschichte* 76 (1994): 1–34.

———. "Schüler im frühen und hohen Mittelalter: Die St. Galler Klosterschule des 9. und 10. Jahrhunderts." *Studien und Mitteilungen zur Geschichte des Benediktinerordens und seiner Zweige* 105 (1994): 7–64.

Die deutsche Königspfalzen: Repertorium der Pfalzen, Königshöfe und übrigen Aufenhaltsorte der Könige im deutschen Reich des Mittelalters. Vols. 1–4. Göttingen, 1982–2000.

Deutschlands Geschichtsquellen im Mittlelalter: Die Zeit der Sachsen und Salier, DasZeitalter des ottonischen Staates (900–1050). Revised by Franz-Josef Schmale. Cologne, 1967.

Donat, Peter. "Berichtigungen und Nachträge: Gebesee." In *Die deutschen Königspfalzen: Repertorium der Pfalzen, Königshöfe und übrigen Aufenthaltsorte der Könige im deutschen Reich des Mittelalters.* Vol. 2 of *Thüringien,* 684–92. Göttingen, 2000.

Ettel, Peter. "Ergebnisse der Ausgrabungen auf der Burg Horsadal, Roßtal bei Nürnberg." In *Frühmittelalterliche Burgenbau in Mittel und Osteuropa,* edited by Joachim Henning and Alexander T. Ruttkay, 127–36. Bonn, 1998.

———. "Der Befestigungsbau im 10. Jahrhundert in Süddeutschland und die Rolle Ottos des Großen am Beispiel der Burg von Roßtal." In *Europa im 10. Jahrhundert: Archäologie einer Aufbruchszeit,* edited by Joachim Henning, 365–79. Mainz, 2002.

Fried, Johannes. "Die Kunst der Aktualisierung in der oralen Gesellschaft: Die Königserhebung Heinrichs I. als Exempel." *Geschichte in Wissenschaft und Unterricht* 44 (1993): 493–503.

———. "Die Königserhebung Heinrichs I. Erinnerung, Mündlichkeit und Traditionsbildung im 10. Jahrhundert." In *Mittelalterforschung nach der Wende 1989*, edited by Michael Borgolte, 267–318. Munich, 1995.

———. "Erinnerung und Vergessen. Die Gegenwart stiftet die Einheit der Vergangenheit." *Historische Zeitschrift* 273 (2001): 561–93.

———. *Die Schleier der Erinnerung: Grundzüge einer historischen Memorik.* Munich, 2004.

Friedrich, Reinhard. "Ottonenzeitliche Befestigungen im Rheinland und im Rhei-Main-Gebiet." *Europa im 10. Jahrhundert: Archäologie einer Aufbruchszeit*, edited by Joachim Henning, 351–63. Mainz, 2002.

Gauer, Adolf. "Das Palatium der Pfalz Werla. Archäologischer Befund und schriftlicheÜberlieferung." In *Deutsche Königspfalzen: Beiträge zu ihrer historischen und archäeologischen Erforschung*, 3.263–77. Göttingen, 1979.

Goldberg, Eric J. *Struggle for Empire: Kingship and Conflict under Louis the German, 817–876.* Ithaca, 2006.

Green, D. H. *Medieval Listening and Reading: The Primary Reception of German Literature, 800–1300.* Cambridge, 1994.

Grewe, Holger. "Die bauliche Entwicklung der Pfalz Ingelheim im Hochmittelalter am Beispiel der Sakralarchitektur." In *Deutsche Königspfalzen: Beiträge zu ihrer historischen und archäologischen Erforschung*, vol. 7: *Zentren herrschaftlicher Repräsentation im Hochmittelalter, Geschichte, Architektur und Zeremoniell*, edited by Caspar Ehlers, Jörg Jarnut, and Matthias Wemhoff, 101–120. Göttingen, 2007.

Grundlach, Wilhelm. *Heldenlieder der deutschen Kaiserzeit.* Vol. 1. Graz, 1896.

Hainer, Carl. "Das epische Element bei den Geschichtsschreibern des früheren Mittelalters." Ph.D. dissertation, Gießen, 1914.

Henning, Joachim. "Der slawische Siedlungsraum und die ottonische Expansion östlich der Elbe: Ereignisgeschichte–Archäologie-Dendrochronlogie." In *Europa im 10. Jahrhundert: Archäologie einer Aufbruchszeit*, edited by Joachim Henning, 131–46. Mainz, 2002.

Hoffmann, Hartmut. *Buchkunst und Königtum im ottonischen und frühsalischen Reich.* MGH Schriften 30. Stuttgart, 1986.

Hofmann, A von. *Das deutsche Land und die deutsche Geschichte.* 3 vols. Stuttgart, 1930.

Jongbloed, Hein H. "Immed 'von Kleve' (um 950). Das erste klevische Grafenhaus (c. 885–c. 1015) als Vorstufe des geldrischen Fürstentums." *Annalen des historischen Vereins für den Niederrhein* 209 (2006): 13–44.

Kaeding, Susanne, Britta Kümmerlen and, Kerstin Seidel. "Heinrich I.–ein 'Freundschaftskönig.'" *Concilium medii aevi* 3 (2000): 265–326.

Köpke, Rudolf. *Widukind von Korvei.* Berlin, 1867.

Koziol, Geoffrey. *Begging Pardon and Favor: Ritual and Political Order in Early Medieval France.* Ithaca, 1992.

Laudage, Johannes. "Widukind von Corvey und die Deutsche Geschichtswissenschaft." In *Von Fakten und Fiktionen: Mittelalterliche Geschichtsdarstellungen und ihre kritische Aufarbeitung*, edited by Johannes Laudage, 193–224. Cologne, 2003.

Leopold, Gerhard. "Archäologische Ausgrabungen an Stätten der ottonischen Herrscher." *Herrschaftsrepräsentation im Ottonischen Sachsen* (1998): 33–76.

Leyser, K. J. "Henry I and the Beginnings of the Saxon Empire." *English Historical Review* 83 (1968): 1–32. Reprinted in *Medieval Germany and Its Neighbours, 900–1250,* by K. J. Leyser, 11–42. London, 1982.

Ludowici, Babette, and Matthias Hardt. "Zwei ottonenzeitliche Kirchen auf dem Magdeburger Domhügel." *Frühmittelalterliche Studien* 38 (2004): 89–99.

Mastandrea, Paolo. *Massimo de Madauros: Agostino, Epistulae 16 e 17.* Padua, 1985.

McCormick, Michael. *Eternal Victory: Triumphal Rulership in Late Antiquity, Byzantium and the Early Medieval West.* Cambridge, 1990.

McKitterick, Rosamond. "Continuity and Innovation in Tenth-Century Ottonian Culture." In *Intellectual Life in the Middle Ages: Essays Presented to Margaret Gibson,* edited by Lesley Smith and Benedicta Ward, 15–24. London, 1992. Reprinted with the same pagination in *The Frankish Kings and Culture in the Early Middle Ages* by Rosamond McKitterick. Aldershot, 1995.

———. "The Written Word and Oral Communication: Rome's Legacy to the Franks." In *Latin Culture and Medieval Germanic Europe: Germania Latina I,* edited by Richard North and Tette Hofstra, 89–112. Gröningen, 1992. Reprinted with the same pagination in *The Frankish Kings and Culture in the Early Middle Ages,* by Rosamond McKitterick. Aldershot, 1995.

———. "Bischöfe und die handschriftlichen Überlieferung des Rechts im 10. Jahrhundert." In *Mönchtum-Kirche-Herrschaft 750–1000. Josef Semmler zum 65. Geburtstag,* edited by Dieter R. Bauer, Rudolf Hiestand, Brigitte Kasten, and Sönke Lorenz, 231–42. Sigmaringen, 1998.

———. "Ottonische Kulture und Bildung." In *Otto der Große. Magdeburg und Europa,* edited by Matthias Puhle, 1.209–24. Mainz, 2001.

Morrison, Karl F. "Widukind's Mirror for a Princess: An Exercise in Self-Knowledge." In *Forchungen zur Reichs—, Papst- und Landesgeschichte. Peter Herde zum 65. Geburtstag von Freunden, Schülern und Kollegen dargebracht,* 2 vols., edited by Karl Borchardt and Enno Bünz, 49–71. Stuttgart, 1998.

Parisot, Gislebert. *Le royaume de Lorraine sous les Carolingiens, 843–923.* Paris, 1899.

Renard, Étienne. "La Politique Militaire de Charlemagne et la Paysannerie Franque." *Francia* 36 (2009): 1–33.

Reuling, Ulrich. "Quedlinburg: Königspfalz-Reichsstift-Markt." In *Deutsche Königspfalzen: Beiträge zu ihrer historischen und archäologischen Erforschung vierter Band: Pfalzen – Reichsgut-Königshöfe,* edited by Lutz Fenske, 184–247. Göttingen, 1996.

Reuter, Timothy. "The Recruitment of Armies in the Early Middle Ages: What Can We Know?' In *Military Aspects of Scandinavian Society in a European Perspective, AD 1000–1300,* edited by A. Norgard Jorgensen and B. L. Clausen, 25–31. Copenhagen, 1997.

Schmidt, Volker. *Drense: Eine Hauptburg der Ukrane.* Berlin, 1989.

Schoenfeld, Edward J. "Anglo-Saxon 'Burhs' and Continental 'Burgen': Early Medieval Fortifications in Constitutional Perspective." *Haskins Society Journal* 6 (1994): 49–66.

Schroller, Hermann. "Die Ausgrabung der Pfalz Werla und ihre Probleme," In

Deutsche Königspfalzen: Beiträge zu ihrer historischen und archäologischen Erforschung, 2.140–49. Göttingen, 1965.

Segers-Glocke, Christiane, and Harald Witthöft, eds. *Aspects of Mining and Smelting in the Upper Harz Mountains (up to the 13th/14th Century) in the Early Times of a Developing European Culture and Economy.* Translated by Claus Wibbelmann. St. Katharinen, 2000.

Shopkow, Leah. *History and Community: Norman Historical Writing in the Eleventh and Twelfth Centuries.* Washington, D.C., 1997.

Szabo, Thomas. "Der Übergang von der Antike zum Mittelalter am Beispiel des Straßennetzes." In *Europäische Technik im Mittelalter 800 bis 1400: Tradition und Innovation, Ein Handbuch,* 4th ed., edited by Uta Lindgren, 25–43. Berlin, 1996.

Ulrich, Jens. "Der Burgwall von Klempenow, Lkr. Demmin." *Archäologische Berichte aus Mecklenburg-Vorpommern* 11 (2004): 28–38.

Wattenbach, Wilhelm, and Robert Holtzmann. *Deutschlands Geschichtsquellen im Mittelalter: Deutsche Kaiserzeit.* Berlin, 1938.

Winterbottom, M. "Curtius Rufus." In *Texts and Transmission: A Survey of the Latin Classics,* edited by L. D. Reynolds and P. K. Marshall, 35–36. Oxford, 1983.

Wood, Susan. *The Proprietary Church in the Medieval West.* Oxford, 2006.

Zielinski, Herbert. "Zur Aachener Königserhebung von 936." *Deutsches Archiv für Erforschung des Mittelalters* 28 (1972): 210–20.

Zotz, Thomas. "Die Goslarer Pfalz im Umfeld der königlichen Herrschaftssistze in Sachsen. Topographie, Architektur und historische Bedeutung." In *Deutsche Königspfalzen: Beiträge zu ihrer historischen und archäologischen Erforschung vierter Band: Pfalzen–Reichsgut-Königshöfe,* edited by Lutz Fenske, 248–87. Göttingen, 1996.

Index

Note: b. = brother of; d. = daughter of; f. = father of; s. = son of; w. = wife of

Also in the MEDIEVAL TEXTS IN TRANSLATION SERIES

GUIDO OF MONTE ROCHEN
Handbook for Curates: A Late Medieval Manual on Pastoral Ministry
Translated by Anne T. Thayer

Anchoress and Abbess in Ninth-Century Saxony: The Lives *of Liutbirga of Wendhausen and Hathumoda of Gandersheim*
Translated by Frederick S. Paxton

COSMAS OF PRAGUE
The Chronicle of the Czechs
Translated by Lisa Wolverton

Preaching in the Age of Chaucer: Selected Sermons in Translation
Translated by Siegfried Wenzel

Letters of Peter Abelard: Beyond the Personal
Translated by Jan M. Ziolkowski

LIUDPRAND OF CREMONA
The Complete Works of Luidprand of Cremona
Translated by Paolo Squatriti

Queenship and Sanctity: The Lives *of Mathilda and the* Epitaph *of Adelheid*
Translated by Sean Gilsdorf

INNOCENT III

Between God and Man: Six Sermons on the Priestly Office

Translated by Corinne Vause and Frank Gardiner

Robert of Arbrissel: A Medieval Religious Life

Translated by Bruce L. Venarde

DHUODA

Handbook for William: A Carolingian Woman's Counsel for Her Son

Translated by Carol Neel

HERMAN OF TOURNAI

The Restoration of the Monastery of St. Martin of Tournai

Translated by Lynn H. Nelson